AF564623

FINANCIAL INCLUSION AND INCLUSIVE GROWTH

FINANCIAL INCLUSION AND INCLUSIVE GROWTH

Edited by

BIJU, S.K.

Assistant Professor, K.N.M. Government College,
Kanjiramkulam, Trivandrum.

and

RANI, L.

Assistant Professor, K.N.M. Government College,
Kanjiramkulam, Trivandrum.

REGAL PUBLICATIONS

New Delhi-110027

FINANCIAL INCLUSION AND INCLUSIVE GROWTH

ISBN 978-81-8484-264-7

Typeset by
S.S. COMPOSERS
3190, Mohindra Park, Shakur Basti, Delhi-110034.

Printed in India at
MAYUR ENTERPRISES
WZ Plot No. 3, Gujjar Market, Tihar Village, New Delhi-110018.

Published by
REGAL PUBLICATIONS
F-159, Rajouri Garden, New Delhi-110027.
Phone: +91-11-45546396
E-mail: regalbookspub@yahoo.com

Contents

Preface

There is a growing concern among the policy-makers and academicians that the fruits of the present economic growth be enjoyed by all Indians, i.e. include all sections of the society rather than the urban/rich-centric. Besides serving the objective of a more equitable society with benefits of prosperity reaching all sections of the society, the growth is enjoying a small group, say a so called middle class. Since financé provides the lubricant for growth, inclusive growth presupposes inclusive finance, the policy-makers of the commercial banks constituted Regional Rural Banks (RRBs) in 1975.

Access to financial services is essential to the poor. Financial services enable the poor to maximize the returns on their surplus, smooth their consumption and reduce their vulnerability to risks that they face on a day-to-day basis. They use various forms of financial services to meet their needs. If we provide facilities of financial services to all, i.e. financial inclusion it will leads to an inclusive growth. So there is a belief that if there is a fast growth it leads to inclusive growth as explained in trickledown theory. But it is clear that the poor borrow not just for productive purposes like businesses and agriculture but for a number of consumption purposes. They make savings both in the form of cash and in the form of assets that they may liquidate at a future date. Small loans and savings provide timely relief to them and help them to cope with sudden income shocks or emergencies. The present initiatives may not increase the income or savings but a name that people holding a bank account. But it is amazing that the government in her 11th plan proposed to achieve inclusive growth and 12th plan also projects that it has a brawny commitment towards a more inclusive growth. Now there is a strong concern that whether it stay in paper only or achieve the goal. So it is the time to make a detailed analysis and critical discussion is necessary to reach in a conclusion that whether the present growth is real and required growth? Whether the fin'ancial inclusion will leads to inclusive growth? What are the real indicators of growth?, etc.

The articles contained in this work are meant to provide a

view of the various areas and issues of financial compre strength and weakness of financial inclusion are listed inclusi ral assessment. The twenty-one essays in this compendium with in nature and content. Attempts have been made to avoid are on and overlapping, as far as possible.

du We are thankful to all colleagues and staff of K.N.M. ernment College, Kanjiralkulam, Trivandrum, who were encouraged to work for this book, based on a seminar financial inclusion for inclusive growth – a myth or reality. We hope that this book will be useful to academics, researchers, policy-makers and others who are interested in inclusive growth.

BIJU, S.K. AND RANI, L.

List of Contributors

1. **Biju, S.K.**
   Assistant Professor, K.N.M. Government College, Kanjiramkulam, Trivandrum.

2. **Dr. Sunil John**
   Associate Professor, K.N.M. Government College, Kanjiramkulam, Trivandrum.

3. **Rani, L.**
   Assistant Professor, K.N.M. Government College, Kanjiramkulam, Trivandrum.

4. **Satheesh Babu**
   Assistant Professor, P.G. Department Commerce, Government College, Nedumangad, Trivandrum.

5. **E. Murali**
   Associate Professor of Commerce, Sri C. Achutha Menon Govt. College, Thrissur,

6. **Dr. P.S. Deva Kumar**
   Asstt. Professor of Commerce, Govt. College for Women, Thiruvananthapuram, Kerala.

7. **V.C. Shanker**
   Assistant Professor of Commerce, The M.D.T. Hindu College, Tirunelveli-627010, Tamil Nadu.

8. **Subash, T.**
   Associate Professor, Department of Commerce, K.N.M. Government College, Kanjiramkulam, Thiruvananthapuram.

9. **Dr. Biju, T.**
   Asst. Professor, Department of Commerce, B.J.M. Government College, Chavara, Kollam, Kerala.

10. **A.D. Rajeev Kumar**
Assistant Professor, Department of Commerce, S.A.R.B.T.M. Government College, Koyilandy.

11. **Mahija, K.**
Assistant Professor, Government Victoria College, Palakkad.

12. **Vineeth Chandra, K.S.**
Research Scholar, University of Kerala, Thiruvanathapuram.

13. **Rajesh, T.**
Assistant Professor, Department of Commerce, Mannaniya College of Arts and Science, Pangode, Thiruvananthapuram.

14. **Dr. Dileep, A.S.**
Assistant Professor, Department of Commerce, N.S.S. College, Pandalam. Pathananmthitta, Kerala

15. **G. Thulaseedharan**
Associate Professor in Commerce, M.M.N.S.S. College, Kottiyam, Kollam.

16. **Vinod, G.**
Assistant Professor, Government College for Women, Trivandrum.

17. **Dr. S. Jayadev**
Assistant Professors, P.G. Department of Commerce, N.S.S. College, Dhanuvachapuram.

18. **Jayakrishnan**
Assistant Professors, P.G. Department of Commerce, N.S.S. College Manjeri.

19. **Siju Sebastian**
Assistant Professor, P.G. Department of Commerce, Government College, Manimalakunnu.

20. **Pramod Gopal**
Assistant Professor, K.V.V.S. College of Science and Technology, Adoor.

21. **Saritha**
Guest Lecturer, Department of Commerce, N.S.S. College, Manjeri.

22. **P. Rincy James**
Guest Lecturer, Department of Commerce, N.S.S. College, Manjeri.

23. **Indhu, L.**
Guest Lecturer in Commerce, M.M.N.S.S. College, Kottiyam.

24. **Jissy, S.G.**
Substitute Lecturer, K.N.M. Government College, Kanjiramkulam, Trivandrum.

25. **Krishnaveni, S.**
Assistant Professor, Government College, Nedumangad.

26. **Arun Kumar, T.T.**
Guest Lecturer in M.G. College of Engineering and Technology, Vandithadam.

27. **Aby, R.L.**
Substitute Lecturer, Government College, Nedumangad.

28. **Shijumon, K.J.**
Substitute Lecturer, Government College, Nedumangad.

29. **Dr. Nimi Dev, R.**
Assistant Professor of Commerce, Government College, Nedumangad.

30. **Kaikasy**
Assistant Professor of English, Univarsity College, Thiruvananthapuram.

31. **Remyakrishnan, G.R.**
M.Phil Scholar, University of Kerala.

32. **Dr. Zajo Joseph**
Associate Professor, Department of Commerce, St. Xavier's College, Thumba.

33. **Mithesh Madhavan**
M.Phil Scholar, University of Kerala, Thiruvananthapuram.

34. **Aswani, S.P.**
M.Phil Scholar, University of Kerala, Thiruvananthapuram.

35. **Suba, Kuriakose**
M.Phil Scholar, University of Kerala.

36. **Priji, R.**
Substitute Lecturer, K.N.M. Government College, Kanjiramkulam.

37. **Sreelekha, R.S.**
Assistant Professor, K.N.M. Government College, Kanjiramkulam.

38. **Vijila, V.**
Assistant Professor of Commerce, Government College, Attingal, T.V.P.M.

39. **Anil Kumar, M.**
Research Scholar, Department of Commerce, University of Kerala, T.V.P.M.

40. **Jenipher Carlos Hosanna**
Assistant Professor, Henry Baker College, Melukavu, Kottayam.

41. **Suresh Kumar, K.S.**
Assistant Professor, Government College, Nedumangad.

42. **Aljo C. Cheriyan**
Training Associate, Kerala Institute of Local Administration (KILA), Thrissur.

43. **Dr. Manoj Pillai**
Assistant Professor, Department of Commerce, Mahatma Gandhi Government College Mahe (Pondicherry Administration), (Affiliated to Pondicherry Central University).

44. **Raja Sree, P.S.**
Research Scholar and Guest Faculty, Government College, Nedumangad.

45. **Dr. J.B. Rajan**
Assistant Professor, Kerala Institute of Local Administration (KILA), Thrissur.

Acronyms

ADB	Area Development Society
AFS	Alternative Financial Services
ATM	Automated Teller Machine
BCs	Business Correspondents
BFs	Business Facilitators
BPR	Business Process Re-engineering
CBS	Core Banking Solutions
CDS	Community Development Society
CRM	Customer Relationship Management
DCC	District Consultative Committee
DNS	Deferred Net Settlement
DPC	District Planning Committee
EBT	Electronic Benefit Transfer
ECS	Electronic Clearing System
EDP	Entrepreneurship Development Programme
FD	Fixed Deposit
GCC	General Purpose Credit Cards
GDP	Gross Domestic Product
GHI	Global Hunger Index
GoI	Government of India
GOT	General Orientation Training
HBA	House Building Advance
HDI	Human Development Index
ICT	Information and Communication Technology
IDBI	Industrial Development Bank of India
ILO	International Labour Organisation
IRDA	Insurance Regulatory Development Association
JLGs	Joint Liability Groups
JNNRUM	Jawaharlal Nehru National Urban Renewal Mission
KSFE	Kerala State Financial Enterprises
KSS	Kisan Credit Cards
KYC	Know Your Customer

LIC	Life Insurance Corporation
LSGs	Local Self-Governments
MFIs	Micro-Finance Institutions
MF-NBFCs	Micro-Finance-Non-Banking Finance Companies
MGNREGS	Mahatma Gandhi National Rural Employment Guarantee Scheme
MIS	Management Information System
MoF	Ministry of Finance
NABARD	National Bank for Rural Development
NAV	Net Asset Value
NEFT	National Electronic Fund Transfer
NGO	Non-Government Organisation
NHG	Neighbourhood Group
NSSO	National Sample Survey Organisation
OECD	Organisation for Economic Cooperation and Development
PACS	Primary Agricultural Cooperative Society
PCO	Public Call Office
PSI	Priority Sector Lending
PURA	Provision for Urban Aminities in Rural Areas
RBI	Reserve Bank of India
RRBs	Regional Rural Banks
RTGS	Real Time Gross Settlement
SHGs	Self-Help Groups
SHPIs	Self-Help Promoting Institutions
SJSRY	Swarna Jayanti Shahari Rozgar Yojana
SLBC	State Level Bankers' Committee
STCCS	Short Term Cooperative Credit System
ULG	Urban Local Government
UNA	United Nurses Association
UNDP	United Nations Development Project
WCP	Women Component Plan

1

Financial Inclusion—Policies should be a Passion and not a Fashion for India's More Inclusive Growth

BIJU, S.K AND DR. SUNIL JOHN

ABSTRACT

It is commonly understood that poverty can be reduced through increasing economic growth, improving income distribution or through a combination of both. Economic growth may be followed by a high income inequality and thus an effort to alleviate poverty through economic growth may be hampered. This paper examines the inter-relationships between economic growth, income inequality and poverty within the framework of the economic, health and education data available in Indian context. The empirical results indicate that economic growth that the leaders project is not the real picture of the state but one should look in to the HDI for depicting the faithful picture of India in connection with the preaches India a fast growing economy. The present growth not only reduces poverty but also increases income inequality. As a result, the effectiveness of economic growth in reducing poverty is imperfect to an extent by rising income inequality. The efforts made by the agencies are not from the bottom of heart because of the fear of loss of power, slanted policies and absence of education. The best need efforts are essential to make preaches to reality.

1. INTRODUCTION

It is widely accepted that poverty reduction can be accomplished by economic growth and/or income distribution. Growth can significantly reduces poverty as it is often followed by more output, more income and consequently more well-being of the people. However, growth may increase income inequality where the benefit of growth goes to a few rich rather than the many poor and poverty reduction through economic growth may be hampered. Therefore, the basic issue in reducing poverty through economic growth is not only how to make an economy grow, but also who make it grow, a few or the many. India is believed to have performed well over the years as far as the indicators are concerned. Economic growth rate crossed the 8 percent mark in recent years from a feeble 4 percent or below in the 1980s and 5 percent plus in the second half of the 1990s. The country is thus moving from low to high economic growth. But how this growth benefits the poor has been a central issue and thus the quality of economic growth, apart from quantity, has recently emerged as an area of attention. The objective of this paper is to examine the interactions between economic growth, income inequality and poverty. The study investigates how economic growth and income inequality affect poverty. The results show that poverty which seemed a never ending problem in India witnessed a significant reduction. But the efficiency of poverty reduction through economic growth has been hampered by a rising income inequality.

2. BACKDROP

India's most defining characteristic is its diversity. Other countries are large and populous; many poorer. But, for example, in the complexity of its social arrangements, the variety of its major languages, and the range of ethnicities and religions, India is surely unmatched. As such, an explicit recognition of India's social and economic diversity is crucial to analyzing its political and economic dynamics. The news form the academic literature is not good; diversity has been found to hurt growth and, more seriously, to challenge the integrity of nation itself. However, the lesson also is that diversity needs to be managed and channeled to productive ends. This challenge has been recognized in India, making inclusive growth the central theme for legitimizing economic and social policies. Ultimately, whether inclusion is used creatively to build a stronger action and a better economy—or is hijacked through populist measures to weaken the state—is the outcome of a political process, which continues to unfold.

On the same time of hijacking is continues and a set of middle class people enjoys the fruits of globalization and government's services.

On the same time our rules celebrating the same. Addressing the UN General Assembly, as the global financial crisis deepens; Prime Minister Manmohan Singh said a fast growing India can help the world economy, around which no protectionist barriers should be erected.

> "A fast growing India can expand the boundaries for the global economy. Despite global headwinds, Indian economy has been expanding close to 8 per cent, the second fastest in the world after China. In the backdrop of protectionist measures taken by several developed countries, our prime minister called upon the international community not to let economic slowdown trigger barriers to movement of people, services and capital."

2.1. Highlights of India's Growth

Here one can argue that why do we claim so? Some highlights are; India has one of the lowest median ages among the major economies. When an economy prospers, first its death rate and then, its birth rate falls. As this trend proceeds, there is a big bulge in the working age population while the non-working population (the young and the old) shrink as a share of the population. Though lowering of the dependent (non-working) population to working age population ratio has twin effects. Increased working population increases the national income. When period passes the independent population become dependent population, creates a great burden to the economy. India—most populous democratic country, more intellectuals, world brain providers, culturally standardized, strong history of cultural purification, fast growing, eminent prime minister, high GDP, list of peoples having 100 crores and above asset in the world 69 are Indians. The list goes on.

Is it right from the point of view of a common man? Is this development benefiting whom? The fast growing India means expanding the gap between rich and poor. Is this the real growth? India is a democratic country and constitution ensures equity, social justice, protection of interest. To whom it ensures........?

Table 1 shows the comparative indices of different indicators of development of India and its neighbours. India's picture is not rosy for many indicators even though we claim that our growth rate is in the right track and the growth will lead to the curtailment of poverty and income inequality

Table 2 shows that the per capita increased and India enhanced her rank from four to three, but see all other ranks falls. But still we consider that India is growing and 12th plan document envisages more inclusive growth after inclusive growth in 11th Fivr Yrar Plan completion. It shows that the inability of central tendency though the more peripherals are ignoring in these calculations. So we need to plan and disclose those indexes which should exhibits the real picture.

Table 1

Comparative Growth Indicators

		India	*Sri lanka*	*Bangla-desh*	*Bhutan*	*Nepal*	*Pakistan*	*China*
GNI per capita	1990	877	1240	543	1280	513	1210	813
	2010	3560	4980	1800	4950	1200	2780	7570
Life expectancy At birth	1990	58	69	54	52	54	61	68
	2010	64	74	67	67	67	67	73
Infant Mortality (per 1000 birth)	1990	81	26	99	96	97	96	38
	2010	48	14	38	44	41	70	16
Under 5 mortality rate	1990	115	32	143	139	141	124	48
	2010	63	17	48	56	50	87	18
Maternity mortality ratio	1990	570	91	870	940	870	490	110
	2008	230	39	340	200	380	260	38
Total fertility rate (Children per woman)	1990	3.9	2.5	4.5	5.7	5.2	6	2.3
	2009	2.7	2.3	2.3	2.5	2.8	3.5	1.6
Access to improved sanitation	1990	18	70	39	-	11	28	41
	2008	31	91	53	65	31	45	55
Infant immunization (DPT) %	1990	59	86	64	88	44	48	95
	2008	66	98	94	96	82	80	96
Infant immunization (Measels) %	1990	47	78	62	87	57	50	95
	2008	71	97	98	97	80	82	94
Mean years of schooling	1990	3	6.9	2.9	-	2	2.3	4.9
	2010	4.4	8.2	4.8	-	3.2	4.9	7.6
Female Literacy (age15-24 years)	1991	49	93	38	-	33	-	91
	2009	74	99	77	68	77	61	99
Proportion of underweight children	1990	59.5	29	61.5	34	-	39	13
	2007	43.5	21.6	41.3	12	38.8	-	4.5

Source: Compiled from different HDI reports.

Table 2

Change in Social Sector Indicators during the Post-liberalization Era

Indicators	*1990*	*2009*
GNI (per capita)	4	3
Life expectancy	3	6
Infant mortality	2	5
Access to improved sanitation	5	6
Child immunization	6	6

Source: Economic Review.

2.2. Real Growth Indicators

Development Index (HDI) is a comparative measure of life expectancy, literacy, education and standards of living for countries worldwide. It is a standard means of measuring well-being, especially child welfare. It is used to distinguish whether the country is a developed, a developing or an under-developed country, and also to measure the impact of economic policies on quality of life. The so called fast growing India's position is 134th during 2011 on the basis of HDI. On the same time Norway stands first (0.943) and India 0.547 (127th position in 2004)

(a) Global Hunger Index (GHI)

In the case of Hunger index 78 countries GHI reduced during the last five years. Only three countries GHI increased and India is one among them. One can see during 1996-2011 India's GHI increased from 22.9 to 23.7 is an eye opening index during our shinning growing history and its is also notable that one third of poor people live in India (World Bank statistics). During the period of Nehru era India has a Hindu growth rate (very slow growth rate). But it is notable that during his realm growth rate attained 6 times increase, i.e. below 0.5 percent to above 3 percent. Very attracting growth rate is that in the short period (5 years) of Sri Rajiv Gandhi it attained 70 percent growth. At present stage of fast growing period of 20 years of globalization it has a 50 percent growth. The above clearly exhibit the fact that present growth's pace is very slow and highly limited.

(b) Hallowed Enjoyers of Globalization

With a fast growth rate, India is one of the fastest growing economies of the world. Globally, India is an important consumer economy. With the growth of the economy, there is an emergence of a class popularly known as the middle class in India. If a family is left with more than one-third of its income for discretionary expenditure after paying for food and shelter, then that family can be called a middle class family (Bihek Debruy, *Indian Express*, March, 2009). The Indian middle class is estimated to be 50 million (http://www. Pbs.org/now/shows/ 425/India-middle class.html) and this class is slowing and yet steadily growing. That amounts to 5 percent of Indian population. "Unlike the older middle class, whose members held jobs in the government, state-owned companies, the new middle class has benefited from privatization or economic reform in the past two decades. They owe nothing to state and are eclipsing the old middle class with different aspiration and dreams.

3. WHY FINANCIAL INCLUSION MATTERS?

Most people take access to financial services for granted. They obtain credit, operate bank accounts and make investment decisions. They make choices in a competitive market. They see the benefits of the trend towards a "cashless society". However, for a significant majority of people in India, such financial services seem inaccessible. Such people face higher charges for loans and other financial services. They face barriers in undertaking even simple transactions. They often do not know who to turn to for advice and support. They suffer from the drawbacks of the trend towards a "cashless society".

Financial exclusion can blight the lives of those affected by it. It can limit opportunities for employment and enterprise, impose a premium on the costs of basic services and reinforce social exclusion. Financial exclusion imposes costs on society and the State, making it harder to tackle unfairness and more expensive to distribute benefits. Financial exclusion also has detrimental effects on the financial services industry itself, limiting the chances for companies and other providers to broaden their customer base.

4. WHAT IS FINANCIAL INCLUSION?

Financial inclusion can be defined as the ability of individuals to access appropriate financial products and services. This definition clearly raises as many questions as it answers. It hinges on an understanding of "appropriate" products and services. As will be seen, financial inclusion has fairly different meanings in the context of banking and in the context of a more diverse market such as the credit market. In seeking to understand the challenge of financial inclusion and the measures needed to promote it, we have sought to concentrate not on finding a final definition of the term, but on understanding what is involved in being financially excluded, what can be done to tackle such exclusion, what forms financial inclusion can take and what benefits flow from financial inclusion.

5. THE NATURE OF FINANCIAL EXCLUSION

The India has one of the most innovative and diverse financial services sectors and nationalized well controlled banking sector in the world. Despite this, many individuals struggle to gain access to basic financial products such as bank accounts, credit, insurance and financial advice. Financial exclusion or lack of access to appropriate financial products and services can arise for a variety of often inter-linked reasons. Witnesses suggested a variety of causes including:

Exclusion due to inappropriate or excessively high charges: interest rates for doorstep lenders and other alternative credit products may be high and lead to a long-term cycle of over-indebtedness. See the nationalized bank charges 12.5% on its HBA

Exclusion due to religious beliefs or other cultural barriers: financial services may not comply with Islamic law, which forbids the charging of interest, for example.

Exclusion due to disability: disabled people might find it difficult to access premises, or find it difficult to read marketing material (majority are in english).

Exclusion due to being on lower incomes (banks are ready to give HBA to govt employees at lower rate of interest and not to labours, then how the house less owns a house or start business or even agriculture. Agriculture Gold Loan (AGL) is allowable to those having gold.

Locational exclusion: lack of access in the person's locality to appropriate financial services. (AGL is available in all cities including metropolitan cities).

Regulatory requirements: regulations imposed by the Government or the Ombudsman play a valuable role in enhancing consumer protection, but, where regulations are excessive or are implemented in a way which does not take account of particular circumstances faced by individuals, they might accentuate financial exclusion.

Self-exclusion: where an individual feels that there is little point in applying for financial products because he/she expects to be refused, or is unwilling to engage with the financial services industry as a result of previous experiences.

Information problems: an individual may have difficulty obtaining the information he or she needs, either due to the requirements of the providers (who may be unwilling to lend to people without a credit history), or to the challenge to the individual as consumer, who may not be able to access marketing information or may have particular difficulty choosing between complex products. (Even banks are not ready to share the data base between themselves about their customers and thus reducing the unwanted time delay even though they share ATM)

Some witnesses believed that financial exclusion would become a bigger challenge in the future. One reason why such a development seemed likely was the increasing responsibility placed on individuals to plan for their retirement. Another factor cited was that delivery of the Government's welfare strategy will increasingly involve the direct payment of benefits, like MGNREGs remuneration, welfare pensions and benefits, into bank accounts, with increasing moves to "individualised budgets"—leaving people to manage larger amounts of money and make payments for the provision of public and private services. This trend could serve as an opportunity to introduce people to financial services, increasing the importance of claimants being able to access and operate appropriate accounts. However, where people have difficulty in managing accounts, benefits and tax credits could go unclaimed. Technological change may lead to greater market segmentation by financial institutions, allowing them to exclude groups of customers whom they perceive to be less likely to be a source of profit. On the other hand, technological progress can work to promote inclusion if it can allow financial service providers to better identify and reduce the risks of lending to low-income consumers or to use automated processes to reduce costs.

6. REASONS FOR UNREALIZED EFFORTS

Indian efforts for financial inclusion are in no way last part in inclusive growth because:

Politicians may be feared because they feel that the power and influence among the poor may be limited and their importance may be lost in the future, if the poverty reduced.

Fear of rich people that their position may be lost in the future because of the reduction in disparity between rich and poor

Lack of education: Nehru and Mahalonobis era believed that heavy industries leads to employment and growth (Mr. Dom Mories, an English poet who secured his great poets award at the age of 19, in his travelogue "gone away" describes his talk with Nehru on 1958-59 and his question about primary education, Nehru replied that "it comes").

Inability of policy-makers and planning commission for proposing and preparing area specific projects considering the vast and diverse culture of Indian society

Reluctance of Financial Institutions especially banks in giving savings bank accounts to the poor because of over workload and less profit, it is very evident in MGNREGS accounts

Absence of interest/reluctance of media especially in reporting development activities of rural India. They are unenthusiastic to report the farmer suicides as it is 2.25 lakhs in a year on the other hand report the delivery of a celebrity, accidental death, politicians' immature and disrespectful statement against opponents, etc.

Growth is slow: During the Nehru era the growth attained from below one to 3.4 percent and tremendous growth during eighties, and post liberalization period the growth rate is stable but very slow in pace as compared with the eighties, because the present growth attained during the last 20 years.

7. CONCLUSION

Early studies on the relationship between growth and poverty believed that benefits of economic growth automatically trickle down to the poor. The recent studies view that income distribution largely determines how much the poor benefit from economic growth. The present study confirms that economic growth significantly reduces poverty. However, income inequality tends to rise with economic growth which affects the poverty reduction capacity of growth. As a result, the objective of poverty reduction through economic growth is partially cancelled out by the corresponding increase of income inequality. The study also discovers that the tremendous growth of service sector, as compared with agriculture and industry reduces poverty considerably while the slow growth of infrastructure sector has insignificant effect on poverty reduction. The study finds that economic growth and income inequality are intrinsically linked and they matter for poverty reduction. There is no doubt that growth is good for poverty reduction. But it must be considered how much benefit the poor get out of growth in their existing share of income because growth effect on poverty reduction may sometimes be dominated by income inequality effect. For India, growth effect on poverty reduction dominates income inequality effect. Yet income inequality matters as long as poverty reduction is concerned. Thus, any policy for poverty reduction should be directed toward achieving an economic growth which reduces poverty fast and at the same time produces less income inequality.

REFERENCES

Chavan, Pallavi (2007), "Access to Bank Credit Implications for Dalit Rural Households", *Economic and Political Weekly*, August.

Government of India (2001), Final Population Totals – Census of India, 2001, New Delhi.

Jayaraman, R. (2005), "Performance Analysis of Fisherwomen Self-Help Groups in Tamil Nadu", Report submitted to National Bank for Agriculture and Rural Development, Mumbai.

Kalpana, K. (2005), "Shifting Trajectories in Micro-finance Discourse", *Economic and Political Weekly*, December.

"Faster, Sustainable and more Iinclusive Growth", An approach to the 12th Five Year Plan Document.

Reserve Bank of India (2006a), "Financial Inclusion and Millennium Development Goals", Address by Usha Thorat, Deputy Governor of the Reserve Bank of India, January 16, available at http://www.rbi.org.in.

Reserve Bank of India (2006a), "Financial Inclusion and Millennium Development Goals", Address by Usha Thorat, Deputy Governor of the Reserve Bank of India, January 16, available at http://www.rbi.org.in.

2

Role of Financial Inclusion for Inclusive Growth in India—Issues and Challenges

SATHEESH BABU, A.T. AND RANI, L.

ABSTRACT

Financial inclusion provides formal identity, access to payments system and deposit insurance. The objective of financial inclusion is to extend the scope of activities of the organized financial system to include within its ambit people with low incomes. Through credit, the attempt must be to lift the poor from one level to another so that they come out of poverty. There is a need for coordinated action between the banks, the Government and others to facilitate access to bank accounts amongst the financially excluded. It is universally opined that the poor need financial assistance at reasonable costs and that too with uninterrupted pace. However, the economic liberalization policies have always tempted the financial institutions to look for more and more greener pastures of business ignoring the weaker sections of the society. It is essential for any economy to aim at inclusive growth involving each and every citizen in the economic development progression. It is in this context that financial inclusion should be aimed at inclusive growth in the Indian context. Financial inclusion is integral to the inclusive growth process and sustainable development of the country.

INTRODUCTION

Financial inclusion is about ensuring every person has the chance to access the financial services products needed to participate fully in fast growing modern-day society and the economy. Financial exclusion affects some of the most vulnerable members of society – extensive research has shown that those living on low incomes, and experiencing multiple forms of disadvantage, are most likely to be affected by financial exclusion. Financial inclusion or inclusive financing is the delivery of financial services at affordable costs to sections of disadvantaged and low income segments of society. Unrestrained access to public goods and services is the *sine qua non* of an open and efficient society. It is argued that as banking services are in the nature of public good; the availability of banking and payment services to the entire population without discrimination is the prime objective of this public policy. The term "financial inclusion" has gained importance since the early 2000s, and is a result of findings about financial exclusion and its direct correlation to poverty. Financial inclusion is now a common objective for many central banks among the developing nations.

The review of literature suggests that financial inclusions are context-specific, originating from country-specific problems of financial exclusion and socio-economic conditions. Thus, the context-specific dimensions of financial exclusion assume importance from the public policy perspective. The operational definitions of financial inclusion, have also evolved from the underlying public policy concerns that many people, particularly those living on low income, cannot access mainstream financial products such as bank accounts and low cost loans, which, in turn, imposes real costs on them—often the most vulnerable people. Importance of financial inclusion arises from the problem of financial exclusion of nearly 3 billion people from the formal financial services across the world.

FINANCIAL INCLUSION AND INCLUSIVE GROWTH IN INDIA

The 'inclusive growth' as a strategy of economic development received attention owing to a rising concern that the benefits of economic growth have not been equitably shared. Growth is inclusive when it creates economic opportunities along with ensuring equal access to them. Apart from addressing the issue of inequality, the inclusive growth may also make the poverty reduction efforts more effective by explicitly creating productive economic opportunities for the poor and vulnerable sections of the society. The inclusive growth by encompassing the hitherto excluded population can bring in several other benefits as well to the economy. The concept "Inclusion" should be seen as a process of including the excluded as agents whose participation is essential in the very design of the development process, and not simply as welfare targets of development programmes (Planning Commission, 2007). Thus, financial inclusion is no longer a policy choice today but a policy compulsion. And as agents entrusted with the task of achieving financial inclusion, the role of the mainstream financial sector in achieving inclusive growth becomes central.

From an annual average growth rate of 3.5 per cent during 1950 to 1980, the growth rate of the Indian economy accelerated to around 6.0 per cent in the 1980s and 1990s. In the last four years (2003-04 to 2006-07), the Indian economy grew by 8.8 per cent. In 2005-06 and 2006-07, the Indian economy grew at a higher rate of 9.4 and 9.6 per cent, respectively. (Planning Commission of India). Reflecting the high economic growth and a moderation in population growth rate, the per capita income of the country also increased substantially in the recent years. Despite the impressive numbers, growth has failed to be sufficiently inclusive, particularly after the mid-1990s. Agricultural sector which provides employment to around 60 per cent of the population lost its growth momentum from that point, though there has been a reversal of this trend since 2005-06. The percentage of India's population below the poverty line has declined from 36 per cent in 1993-94 to 26 per cent in 1999-2000. While India has witnessed unprecedented economic growth in recent past, its development has been lopsided with the country trailing on essential social and environmental parameters of development. The approach paper to the Eleventh Plan indicated that the absolute number of poor is estimated to be approximately 300 million in 2004-05. Accordingly, the 11th Five Year Plan has adopted "faster and more Inclusive growth" as the key development paradigm The importance of this study lies in the fact that India being a socialist, democratic republic, it is imperative on the policies of the government to ensure equitable growth of all sections of the economy. With only 34% of population engaged in formal banking, India has, 135 million financially excluded households, the second highest number after China. Further, the real rate of financial inclusion in India is also very low and about 40% of the bank account holders use their accounts not even once a month (Report of the Central Government). It is universally opined that the resource poor need financial assistance at reasonable costs and that too with uninterrupted pace. However, the economic liberalization policies have always tempted the financial institutions to look for more and more greener pastures of business ignoring the weaker sections of the society. In India, the financially excluded sections comprise largely rural masses comprising marginal farmers, landless labourers, oral lessees, self-employed and unorganized sector enterprises, urban slum dwellers, migrants, ethnic minorities and socially excluded groups, senior citizens and women. Some of the important causes of relatively low extension of institutional credit in the rural areas are risk perception, cost of its assessment and management, lack of rural infrastructure, and vast geographical spread of the rural areas with more than half a million villages, some sparsely populated (Mohan, 2006). It is essential for any economy to aim at inclusive growth involving each and every citizen in the economic development progression. It is in this context that financial inclusion should be aimed at inclusive growth in the Indian context.

The broad strategy for financial inclusion in India in recent years comprises the following elements: (i) encouraging penetration into unbanked and backward areas and encouraging agents and intermediaries such as NGOs, MFIs, CSOs and Business Correspondents (BCs); (ii) focusing on a decentralised strategy by using existing arrangements such as State Level Bankers' Committee (SLBC) and District Consultative Committee (DCC) and strengthening local institutions such as cooperatives and RRBs; (iii) using technology for furthering financial inclusion; (iv) advising banks to open a basic banking 'no frills' account; (vi) emphasis on financial literacy and credit counseling; and (vii) creating synergies between the formal and informal segments

INCLUSIVE GROWTH: ROLE OF FINANCIAL SECTOR

There are supply side and demand side factors driving Inclusive Growth. Banks and other financial services players largely are expected to mitigate the supply side processes that prevent poor and disadvantaged social groups from gaining access to the financial system. Access to financial products is constrained by several factors which include: lack of awareness about the financial products, unaffordable products, high transaction costs, and products which are not convenient, inflexible, not customized and of low quality. Financial Inclusion promotes thrift and develops culture of saving and also enables efficient payment mechanism strengthening the resource base of the financial institution which benefits the economy as resources become available for efficient payment mechanism and allocation. The empirical evidence shows that countries with large proportion of population excluded from the formal financial system also show higher poverty ratios and higher inequality. If we are talking of financial stability, economic stability and inclusive growth with stability, it is not possible without achieving Financial Inclusion. Thus, financial inclusion is no longer a policy choice but is a policy compulsion today. And banking is a key driver for inclusive growth. However, we must bear in mind that apart from the supply side factors, demand side factors, such as lower income and/or asset holdings also have a significant bearing on inclusive growth. Owing to difficulties in accessing formal sources of credit, poor individuals and small and macro-enterprises usually rely on their personal savings or internal sources to invest in health, education, housing, and entrepreneurial activities to make use of growth opportunities

INCLUSIVE GROWTH: THE APPARITION OF RBI

The key driver of our country's vision of inclusive growth is financial inclusion. RBI has adopted a 'Blank-led' model for ensuring financial inclusion to provide low cost, efficient, ICT-based banking services utilizing multiple delivery channels including intermediary low cost brick and mortar structures, branchless banking through Business Correspondents (BCs) and other modes like mobile vans, rural ATMs, etc., so as to cover all the villages in due course. RBI, as a part of financial inclusion, initiates Governments to disburse social security payments through the banking channel leveraging Electronic Benefit Transfers for financial intermediation. For the purpose of financial inclusion it is highly required to ensure that the initiatives taken by the RBI are following by the banking sector:

1. **To Avoid Income Barrier** *(to accommodate the low income group)*

   - RBI directed banks to offer a basic banking '**no frills'** account with low or zero minimum balances and minimum charges to expand the outreach of such accounts to the low income groups.

2. **To Avoid Norms Barrier** *(banks follow strict norms for even small advances)*

   - Banks were directed to introduce a General Purpose Credit Card (GCC) facility up to Rs. 25,000;, i.e. Easier Credit Facility.

3. **To Avoid Identity Barrier** *(many Indians have no address proof like election ID, ration card and the like)*

   - In order to ensure that the people belonging to the low income groups both in rural and urban areas, do not encounter difficulties in opening bank accounts 'Know Your Customer' (KYC) procedure is simplified for those accounts with balances not exceeding Rs. 50,000 and credits thereto not exceeding Rs. 1,00,000 in a year;, i.e. Simplification of KYC Norms

4. To Improve Efficiency in Service Delivery

- Banks have been urged to scale up information technology initiatives for financial inclusion speedily while ensuring that solutions are highly secure, amenable to audit, and follow widely accepted open standards to ensure eventual inter-operability among the different systems; and
- To encourage banks to adopt Information and Communication Technology (ICT) solutions for enhancing their outreach RBI formulated a scheme to quicken the pace of adoption of the smart card-based Electronic Benefit Transfer (EBT) mechanism by banks and rolled out the EBT system in the States that are ready to adopt the scheme. Banks are advised to work in co-ordination with the respective government departments at the Central and State levels to ensure that all State benefits are delivered to individuals only through bank accounts within a specific time frame.

5. To Avoid Distance Barrier *(i.e. distance to service point)*

- *Business-Correspondent (BC) Model*—This model ensures a closure relationship between the poor people and the organized financial system. The RBI permits the banks to use the following as BCs—
  - o Non-government organizations;
  - o Micro-finance Institutions;
  - o Retired bank employees;
  - o Ex-service men;
  - o Retired Government employees;
  - o Section 25 companies;
  - o Individual/medical/fair shop owners;
    Individual Public Call Office (PCO) operators;
  - o Agents of small savings schemes of Government of India/Insurance companies;
  - o Individuals who own petrol pumps;
  - o Retired teachers;
  - o Authorized functionaries of well run Self-Help Groups (SHGs) to linked banks; and
  - o Other civil society organizations.
- *Bank Branch and ATM Expansion Liberalized*—RBI has permitted domestic scheduled Commercial Banks, other than regional rural banks, to open branches in tier 3 to tier

6 centers (with population up to 49,999 as on 2001 census) without having the need to take permission of RBI in each case. RBI also totally freed the location of ATMs from prior authorization.

6. To Avoid the Knowledge Barrier

- *Project Financial Literacy*—RBI has initiated a 'Project Financial Literacy' with the objective of disseminating information regarding the Central Bank and general banking concepts to various target groups. RBI's financial website line offers basics of banking, finance and central banking for children of all ages. In a comic book format, RBI simplifies the complexities of banking, finance and central banking with the goal of making the learning fun and interesting;
- *Financial Literacy and Credit Counseling*—RBI has advised to set-up a financial literacy-*cum*-counseling centre in any one district on pilot basis to provide free financial education to people in rural and urban areas on the various financial products and services while maintaining arm's length relationship with the parent bank and based on that experience to extend the facility to other districts in due course.

ISSUES AND CHALLENGES

The bottlenecks and difficulties in achieving complete financial inclusion in our country are fairly well known. The major obstacles are:

(i) The gigantic nature of the task, keeping in view the number of financially excluded people.
- In India, almost half the country is unbanked.
- Of the 6 lakh villages in India, only approximately 50,000 have access to finance.
- India has the highest number of households (145 million) excluded from Banking.
- Only 10% of the population has any kind of life insurance and 9.6% of the population has non-life insurance coverage.
- 2.5 billion adult, just over half of world's adult population, do not use formal financial services to save or borrow *(Source: 'Half the World is Unbanked'', 2009, Financial Access Initiative).*

(ii) Non-availability of appropriate banking technology till a few years ago. Lack of proper physical infrastructure, digital connectivity, etc. in some parts of the country. If Financial Inclusion is to take place, it can only be through Information and Communication Technology (ICT) based models.

(iii) *Lack of proper Business Models*: Banks still perceive this as a burden and an imposition and not as a viable Business Model.

(iv) *Lack of cost effective scalable Delivery Models*: There is no facilitating and effective Delivery Model especially when problems are encountered. Business Correspondent (BC) based Delivery Model is still in the evolutionary stage.

(v) The costs of administering low value transactions and of financial intermediation are perceived to be on the higher side by the bank (the banks are not ready to provide interest on MGNREG accounts emphasis the fact).

(vi) Planned, strategic and concerted efforts were lacking. It requires massive efforts from all stakeholders.

(viii) Bank Branches are required to be increased as it has a direct impact on the progress of financial inclusion. It is clearly established that as the bank branches increase number of bank accounts also increase significantly.

(ix) *Spatial Distribution of Banking Services*: Even though after often emphasized policy intervention by the government and the concerted efforts of Reserve Bank of India and the public sector banks there has been a significant increase in the number of bank offices in the rural areas; but it is7not in tune with the large population living in the rural areas. For a population of 70% only 45% of bank offices provide the financial services.

However, some of the critical indicators for access to finance in India along with benchmark indicators for selected high-income Organisation for Economic Cooperation and Development (OECD) member countries reveal that(see Table 1) while there have been improvements during 2001-08 but it is still very adverse as compared to OECD economies.

WAY FORWARD?

The literature shows that there are many gray areas need more clarity and initiatives, some of them are:

TABLE I

Getting Finance Indicators for India, 2001-08

Indicator	*2001*	*2002*	*2003*	*2004*	*2005*	*2006*	*2007*	*2008*	*Bench-mark (OECD)*
Branches per 1,00,000 people	6.42	6.33	6.25	6.26	6.33	6.37	6.35	6.6	10-69
ATMs per 1,00,000 people					1.63	1.93	2.4	3.28	47-167
Deposit accounts per 1000 people	416.77	421	418.7	426.1	432.1	443	459.5	467.4	976-1671
Loan accounts per 1000 people	50.99	53.9	55.84	61.88	71.42	78	83.59	89.03	248-513
Branches per 1000 km^2	22.18	22.3	22.41	22.57	22.99	23.5	24.13	25.49	1-159
ATMs per 1000 km^2					5.93	7.11	9.11	12.68	1-437

Note: The Benchmark Indicator ranges are for selected high-income OECD member-countries (Australia, Canada, France, Germany, Italy, Japan, the republic of Korea, New Zealand and the United States).

Source: Reserve Bank of India.

Formation of National Financial Inclusion Mission

Many proponents of financial inclusion recommend formation of National Financial Inclusion Mission on the lines of National Literacy Mission to carry out systematic and coordinated drive for financial inclusion.

Involvement of Education Sector for Furthering Financial Inclusion

Involving educational institutions, particularly college students for financial inclusion drive would not only be cost effective but also would create wide public awareness.

Financial Inclusion as a Part of Course Curriculum in High Schools

Financial Inclusion should be imbibed into the course curriculum in high schools so that the students would understand the importance of financial inclusion for inclusive growth in the economy which in turn would motivate them to automatically participate in the financial system.

Exclusive Focus on the Socially Excluded and the Poor

It is imminent to encompass the socially excluded sections and the poor like, tenant farmers, oral lessees and share croppers, marginal farmers with small un-economical landholdings, agricultural labourers, rural artisans and people involved in making handicrafts and also majority of weavers in handloom Sector.

Extensive use of Co-operatives

PACS (Primary Agricultural Cooperative Societies) could provide valuable services to their members with a sense of belongingness. Accordingly, there is a need to revitalize these cooperatives as per the Vaidyanathan Committee recommendations and use them extensively for financial inclusion in the rural areas.

Role of RBI

Reserve Bank needs to take a pro-active role in the accelerating financial inclusion by involving all the stakeholders in the financial system by using its power of moral suasion as well as regulatory powers

Proactive Role of Government

State Governments should be asked by the Central Government to play a proactive role in facilitating Financial Inclusion. Issuing official identity documents for opening accounts, creating awareness and involving district and block level functionaries in the entire process, meeting cost of cards and other devices for pilots, undertaking financial literacy drives are some of the ways in which the State and district administration have involved themselves. Post Offices in rural areas can be asked to provide their services in accelerating the financial inclusion activity. In view of the postman's intimate knowledge of the local population and the enormous trust reposed in him post offices can be good use in the process of financial inclusion

Effective Use of Information Technology Solutions

The use of IT enables banks to handle the enormous increase in the volume of transactions for millions of households for processing, credit scoring, credit record and follow-up. The use of IT solutions for providing banking facilities at doorstep holds the potential for scalability of the Financial Inclusion initiatives.

Financial Inclusion as a Corporate Social Responsibility of all the Banks and Financial Institutions

It should be the endeavour of all the financial institutions to adopt financial inclusion as a corporate social responsibility and chalk out strategies in tune with the national policy on financial inclusion.

Targets fixed for each Branch of Commercial Bank/Regional Rural Bank to:

- Open 250 accounts every year.
- Issue 100 Farmers' Credit Cards.

- Issue 100 General Credit Card.
- Distribute 100 micro-insurance policies.

Micro-Finance Sector (Development and Regulation) Bill, 2007 under consideration.

Setting up of Rural Credit Information Bureau.

Ensuring effectiveness of Business Facilitator(BF)/Business Correspondent (BC).

Micro-Finance Development and Equity Fund.

Micro-Finance Ombudsman.

Regulatory and developmental power to NABARD.

CONCLUSION

Importance of financial inclusion arises from the problem of financial exclusion of nearly 3 billion people from the formal financial services across the world. With only 34% of population engaged in formal banking, India has 135 million financially excluded households, the second highest number after China. Further, the real rate of financial inclusion in India is also very low and about 40% of the bank account holders use their accounts not even once a month. Financial inclusion provides formal identity, access to payments system and deposit insurance. The objective of financial inclusion is to extend the scope of activities of the organized financial system to include within its ambit people with low incomes. The agencies can provide small credit for self-employment, when the repayment completed gives another. If the borrower pay the second she/he should be self-sufficient to generate own capital for his activity. Through *small repeating credit*, the attempt must be to lift the poor from one level to another so that they come out of poverty. There is a need for coordinated action between the banks, the Government and others to facilitate access to bank accounts amongst the financially excluded. The vision and initiative RBI need whole-hearted support from banks as a social responsibility and not compulsion to achieve the millennium development goal achievement.

REFERENCES

Government of India (2006): Report of the Working Group on Savings Eleventh Five Year Plan, Planning Commission, December

Government of India (2007), Eleventh Five Year Plan Document, Planning Commission.

Mohan, R. (2006): 'Agricultural Credit in India: Status, Issues and Future Agenda'.

Report of the Committee on Financial Inclusion in India (Chairman: C. Rangarajan) (2008), Government of India

Reserve Bank of India (2008), Report on Currency and Finance, 2006-08.

Reserve Bank of India (2009), "100 per cent Financial Inclusion – Evaluation by External Agencies Broad Findings", Circular dated January 22.

Progress of Financial Inclusion Process in India

E. MURALI

ABSTRACT

The number of office house of banks increased considerably and the population per house was reduced to one third in between the period of nationalization and financial liberalization. But further reduction was not happened during the liberalized era. The share of both deposit mobilization and the share of credit provision in rural and semi rural areas in their respective totals for the entire nation are found decreased. A poor farmer in rural area or a micro-entrepreneur such as cobbler, or rickshaw driver in urban area may not approach a bank for opening a saving account. To include such groups in the net work of formal banking the best way is to collect their savings and provide small credit preferably on weekly or monthly basis by offering banking services at his/her door step. The SHGs, Extension of RRB services, no frill accounts etc are playing a great role in the financial inclusion process in India. The BC model ensures a closer relationship between poor people and the organized financial system. RBI considers financial literacy as a stepping-stone toward financial inclusion. To further financial inclusion, the Reserve Bank also chose several outreach events across the country. An important aspect of the outreach activities was making the Banking Ombudsman an integral part of the activities so that there could be spot redressal of some of the grievances.The present progress is not sufficient and the governments, regulative authorities and non government institutions should play a great role in this regard.

1. INTRODUCTION

A well-functioning financial system is a crucial part of development of a nation. A financial system becomes more efficient and functions better when it is more inclusive. When the financial system becomes more inclusive, it provides more growth opportunities to more individuals and entrepreneurs. However, when the financial system serves only limited segment of the population, the society is likely to lose opportunities to grow. Therefore, a country to achieve a sustainable and inclusive growth has necessarily to connect the banked and unbanked sectors and to enable the unbanked to become vibrant and productive participants in the economic growth process. It is in this philosophy the concept of financial inclusion has been emerged.

Financial inclusion denotes delivery of financial services at an affordable cost to the vast sections of the disadvantaged and low-income groups. The various financial services include credit, savings, insurance and payments and remittance facilities. "Financial inclusion may be defined as the process of ensuring access to financial services and timely and adequate credit where needed by vulnerable groups such as weaker sections and low income groups at an affordable cost." (Report of Committee on Financial inclusion Jan. 2008.) Thus, the objective of financial inclusion is to extend the scope of activities of the organized financial system to include within its ambit people with low incomes.

Statistics show that though the incidence of poverty has declined from 36 per cent in 1993-94 to 27.5 per cent in 2004-05 (as per the NSS data), the absolute level of poverty remains daunting. Employment growth in the organised sector during 1994-2007 had also declined (Govt. of India, *Economic Survey*, 2009-10). One of the avenues through which the welfare of the poor and unemployed could be improved is better access to credit and financial services. But figures show that only 5.2% of India's 650,000 villages have bank branches and just about 40 per cent of the population across our country has bank accounts. With regard to adult population in India only 59% has bank accounts and there is a large gap between the coverage of banking services in urban and rural pockets. In rural India, the coverage among the adult population is 39% against 60% in urban India (http://toostep.com/insight/financial-inclusion-in-india-some-key-statistics). Further, a very few people in the low-income bracket have access to formal banking channels in India. Only 34% of people with annual earnings less than Rs. 50,000 in urban India had a bank account in 2007. The comparative figure in rural India is even lower, 26.8%. (http://toostep.com/insight/financial-inclusion-in-india-some-key-statistics). Similarly in India people having debit cards comprise only 13 per cent and those having credit cards only a marginal 2 per cent. Though agriculture contributes only just above 20 percent of India's GDP, it is considered as the backbone of our nation as it provides employment to nearly two third of our population (*RBI Bulletin*, September 2009). Statistics also reveal that of the 119 million Indian farmers, 97.7 million(82.1%) are small and marginal (*RBI Bulletin*, September 2009). As per the National Sample Survey, in 2003 45.9 million farmer households in the country (51.4%), out of a total of 89.3 million households do not access credit, either from institutional or non-institutional sources. Further, despite the vast network of bank branches, only 27% of total farm households are indebted to formal sources (of which one-third also borrow from informal sources). Farm households not accessing credit from formal sources as a proportion to total farm households is especially high at 95.91%, 81.26% and 77.59% in the North Eastern, Eastern and Central Regions respectively (Report of Committee on Financial inclusion Jan. 2008).

2. OBJECTIVE

In the backdrop of the above, the present paper is aimed to evaluate the progress of the financial inclusion process in India.

3. METHODOLOGY

To study the extent of the financial inclusion process in India the progress of some selected measures in Indian banking sector namely, spread of branches in rural and semi-urban areas, provision of credit, generation of deposit, Self-Help Group (SHG) linkage, Regional Rural Bank Expansion, No Frill Accounts, Financial Education Literacy Activities, Electronic Benefit Transfer (EBT), and Business Correspondent Model (BCM) are analysed. Secondary data collected from Annual Reports of RBI, and various websites, including RBI are used in the study.

4. ANALYSIS AND DISCUSSION

It is a fact that the efforts at financial inclusion in India, both the Union Government and the Reserve Bank of India have been pursuing this goal over the last several decades through building the rural cooperative structure in the 1950s, the social contract with banks in the 1960s and the expansion of bank branch networks in the 1970s and 1980s. These initiatives have paid off in terms of a network of branches across the country. (http://www.rbi.org.in/scripts/BS_SpeechesView.aspx?Id=452). However, giving a thrust to inclusive growth,the concept of "financial inclusion" was first mooted by the Reserve Bank of India in its annual policy statement of 2005-06. As a result in the recent years both the Union Government and the Reserve Bank have made some innovative interventions in banking sector to widen the net of financial inclusion. The analysis on the progress and trends of some of the traditional and innovative measures initiated by the Government and RBI is made as follows.

4.1. Credit and Deposit of Commercial Banks

During the last several decades commercial banks came a long way with a substantial spread of branches in rural and semi-urban areas. As per the October 2009 Policy Review of the RBI, domestic scheduled commercial banks (other than RRBs) are now free to open branches in towns and villages with less than 50,000 population by ensuring that at least one-third of such branch expansion happens in the under banked districts of under banked states.

While analyzing the data on the progress and trends of commercial banking, on the one hand, the total number of offices of commercial banks across the country increased considerably from 8262 to 59752 from 1969 to 1990 and further to 82408 in 2009. Similar is the case of per capita deposit and credit in absolute terms. But on the other hand it is very relevant to note that though the population per office had decreased from 61000 to 21000 from 1969 to 1980 and further decreased to 14000 in 1990, the figure has however, gone up to 14490 in 2009. This shows that though the population per office was reduced to one-third during the period from 1969 to 1990. But further reduction was not achieved even after two decade. While an analysis of location of bank office/branch is made, the percentage of offices in rural and semi urban area put together in the total bank offices/branches was 63 percent in 1969 this figure was improved to 76 percent in 1990 but the same was again decreased to 63 percent, which is the level of 1969. When we move to the deposit and credit of commercial banks, these figures stood at Rs. 4665.19 and 3608.86 crore respectively at the end of June 1969. Though, these figures in absolute terms increased to Rs. 3937335 and 2857525 crore in March 2009,with regard to rural urban disparity, the share of deposit from rural plus semi urban areas in the total bank deposit in the country in 1969 was 25 percent. This figure reached to the level of 35 percent in 1980 and again increased to 46 percent in 1990.But when the data for the year 2005 and 2009 are considered the share of rural plus semi urban areas in total deposit was decreased to the level of 29 percent and 23 percent respectively. A similar trend is visible in credit distribution also. The share of credit to rural plus semi urban areas in the total bank credit in the country in 1969 was 13 percent. This figure reached to the level of 26 percent in 1980 and again increased to 33 percent in 1990. But the share of these areas together in total credit was decreased to the level of 22 percent and 17 percent respectively for the year 2005 and 2009. It is again relevant note that the Credit Deposit ratio at all India level in 2009 (73%) was less than that of 1969 (77%).These relevant data are exhibited in Tables 1, 2, 3 and 4.

TABLE I

Select Indicators of Commercial Banking Services in India

Items	*1969*	*1980*	*1990*	*2009 (Provisional)*
Bank offices (nos.)	8262	32419	59752	82408
Population per office	64000	21000	14000	14490
Per capita deposit (Rs.)	88	494	2098	34372
Per capita credit (Rs)	68	327	1275	24945
Credit-deposit ratio (%)	77	66	61	73

Source: RBI.

TABLE 2

Distribution of Credit of Commercial Banks in India on the Basis of Population Group

(Rs. Crore)

	1969 June	*1980 June*	*1990 March*	*2005 March*	*2009 March*
Rural	54.29 (1.5)	2165.34 (9.7)	16067.85 (15.5)	106497 (9.20)	208694 (7.30)
Semi-Urban	406.57 (11.3)	3615.17 (16.1)	17875.51 (17.1)	130596 (11.3)	266736 (9.30)
Urban	722.00 (20)	5049.13 (22.6)	23594.42 (22.6)	189593 (16.4)	461870 (16.20)
Metropolitan	2426.00 (67.2)	11551.62 (51.6)	46774.15 (44.8)	731121 (63.1)	1920225 (67.20)
Total	3608.86 (100)	22381.26 (100)	104311.93 (100)	1157807 (100)	2857525 (100)

Note: Figures in parentheses are percentages.
Source: RBI.

TABLE 3

Distribution of Deposits of Commercial Banks in India on the Basis of Population Group

(Rs. Crore)

	1969 June	*1980 June*	*1990 March*	*2005 March*	*2009 March*
Metro	2287.00 (49.0)	13276.22 (39.8)	66892.00 (38.9)	867201 (49.5)	2215437 (56.30)
Rural	144.96 (3.1)	3975.27 (11.9)	26233.64 (15.2)	213536 (12.2)	365491 (9.30)
Semi-Urban	1024.06 (22)	7653.01 (23.0)	36369.64 (21.2)	296303 (16.8)	531944 (13.50)
Total	4665.19 (100)	33321.39 (100)	171911.39 (100)	1753173 (100)	3937335 (100)
Urban	1209.17 (25.9)	8416.89 (25.3)	42416.11 (24.7)	376133 (21.5)	824463 (20.90)

Note: Figures in parentheses are percentages.

Source: RBI.

TABLE 4

Select Indicators of Commercial Banking Services in India

Year	*No. of Banks*				*Total*
	Rural	*Semi Urban*	*Urban*	*Metropolitan*	
1969	1833	3342	1584	1503	8262
1980	15105	8122	5178	4014	32419
1990	31114	11132	7322	5842	55410
2009	31684	18892	15428	13731	79735

Note: The figures for 1969, 1980 and 1990 show the Number of Bank offices while same for 2009 represent number of branches which does not include Administrative offices.

Source: RBI.

4.2. SHG-Bank Linkage Programme

Self-Help Groups play a great role in the process of financial inclusion. SHGs are usually groups of women who get together and pool money from their savings and lend money among them. Usually they work with the support of an NGO. Banks give loans to SHGs against the group members' guarantee. Peer pressure within the group helps in improving recoveries. The SHG-Bank Linkage Programme can be regarded as the most potent initiative since Independence for delivering financial services to the poor in a sustainable manner. The SHG-Bank Linkage Programme was started as a pilot project by NABARD in 1992. It led to the evolution of a set of RBI approved guidelines to banks to enable SHGs to transact with banks. Initially there was slow progress in the programme up to 1999 as only 32,995 groups were credit linked during the period 1992 to 1999. Since then the programme has been growing rapidly (Table 5). Through SHGs nearly 40 million households are linked with the banks at present. (http://www.chllibreeze.com/articles various/Indian-Finance.asp) However, the spread of the SHG - Bank Linkage Programme in different regions has been uneven with Southern States accounting for the major chunk of credit linkage (Report of Committee on Financial inclusion Jan.2008).

TABLE 5

Number of SHG Group Linked to Bank

Year	*Cumulative number of group linked*
From 1992 to 1999	32995
31-3 2002	461000
31-3-2004	1073000
31-3-2007	2925000

Source: Report of Committee on Financial Inclusion, Jan. 2008.

4.3. Extension of Regional Rural Bank (RRB) Services

Regional Rural Banks were established under the provisions of an Ordinance promulgated on the 26th September 1975 and the RRB Act, 1976 with an objective to ensure sufficient institutional credit for agriculture and other rural sectors. The RRBs mobilize financial resources from rural/semi-urban areas and grant loans and advances mostly to small and marginal farmers, agricultural labourers and rural artisans. The number of branches of RRBs was only 13,920 on 31 March 1989. GoI initiated the process of structural consolidation of RRBs by amalgamating RRBs sponsored by the same bank within a State as per the recommendations of the Vyas Committee (2004). As a result of the amalgamation, the number of RRBs was reduced from 196 to 133 as on 31 March, 2006 and to 96 as on 30 April 2007.RRBs post-merger represent a powerful instrument for financial inclusion. As on 31 March 2006, there was a network of 14,494 branches. As on March 2009 this figure increased to 15127 which consists of 11626, 2746, 667, and 88 branches in rural,semi urban,urban and metropolitan areas http//www.rbi.org.in). RRBs account for 37% of total rural,15% of total semi urban, 4% of total urban and 0.64% of total metropolitan branches of all scheduled commercial banks in 2009 March (http//www.rbi.org.) They account for 31% of deposit accounts and 37% of loan accounts in rural areas. RRB's have a large presence in regions marked by financial exclusion of a high order. They account for 34% of all branches in North-Eastern, 30% in Eastern and 32% in Central regions. Out of the total 22.38 lakh SHGs credit linked by the banking industry as on 31st March 2006, 33% of the linkages were by RRBs (Report of Committee on Financial Inclusion, Jan. 2008).

TABLE 6

Branch Expansion of Regional Rural Banks

Year (March)	*Number of Branches*
1989	13920
2004	14446
2005	14484
2006	14494
2009	15127

Source: http//www.rbi.org.in

4.4. No Frill Accounts

The Reserve Bank of India in its annual policy statement of 2005-06 made clear to banks that they are obliged to provide banking services to all segments of the population on an equitable basis. In that Annual Policy Statement, the RBI also called upon Indian banks to design a 'no frills account' a no precondition, low 'minimum balance maintenance' account. All banks were also advised to give wide publicity to the facility of such 'no-frills' account, including on their web sites, indicating the facilities and charges in a transparent manner. In order to ensure that people having low income in urban and rural areas, do not encounter difficulties in opening bank accounts; the RBI has simplified the KYC (Know your customer) norms for opening an account. With this measure an individual can open an account without identity proof and address proof. In such cases banks can take the individual's introduction from an existing customer whose full KYC norm procedure has been completed. And the introducer must have a satisfactory transaction with the bank for at least 6 months. This simplified procedure is available to those who intend to keep a balance not exceeding Rs. 50,000 in all accounts taken together and credits thereto not exceeding Rs. 100,000 in a year.

While analyzing the progress in number of No Frill accounts it is revealed that the number has increased from merely 0.49 million to 50.6 million from 2006 to 2010 (Table 7). Data also show that by March 2010, No Frill accounts had an outstanding balance of 5,386 crore. In 2009-10, RBI advised banks to provide small overdrafts on such accounts. By March 2010, banks had provided 0.18 million overdrafts amounting to 28 crore. (RBI, Annual Report, 2009-10). However, a report by Skotch Development Foundation revealed that though 25 million no-frill accounts were opened between April 2007 and May 2009, only 11% of them are operational.

TABLE 7

Number of No Frill Accounts in Banking Sector in India by the end of March

(in Million)

2006	*2007*	*2009*	*2010*
0.49	6.73	43.02	50.6

Source: RBI Annual Reports, 2008-09, 2009-10 and *RBI Bulletin*, September 2009.

4.5. Electronic Benefit Transfer (EBT)

Many government schemes involving large amounts of money often do not reach the targeted group of people in the absence of adequate penetration of banks. Financial inclusion could enhance the benefits of government programmes through direct transfer of the amounts to the bank accounts of the beneficiaries. Therefore, Reserve Bank introduced a scheme in 2008 to quicken the pace of adoption of electronic benefit transfer (EBT) mechanism by banks and roll out the EBT system in the states that were ready to adopt the scheme. As per the scheme, the Reserve Bank partially reimbursed the banks the cost of opening accounts with bio-metric access (through which payment of social security benefits, payments under NREGA and other government benefit programmes would be routed) at the rate of 50 per account. The incentive package was dependent on the state governments agreeing to pay to the transacting banks a mutually agreed transaction fee. The scheme closed on June 30, 2010 (RBI, Annual Report, 2009-10).

4.6. Business Correspondent Model

Business Correspondent (BC) model is an important initiative of the Reserve Bank for widening financial inclusion. The BC model ensures a closer relationship between poor people and the organized financial system. Recognizing this, in 2006, RBI permitted banks to use the services of non-governmental organizations, micro-finance institutions, retired bank employees, ex-servicemen, retired government employees, Section 25 companies, and other civil society organisations as Business Correspondents in providing financial and banking services. RBI further enlarged the scope of the BC model by permitting banks to appoint individual kirana/medical/fair price shop owners, individual Public Call Office (PCO) operators, agents of Small Savings schemes and insurance companies, individuals who own petrol pumps, retired teachers and self-help groups linked to banks as BCs. With a view to ensuring the viability of the BC model, banks have also been permitted to collect reasonable service charges from the customer in a transparent manner. In April 2010, the BC ambit was further widened by permitting banks to engage any individual as BC, subject to their comfort level and their carrying out due diligence, as also instituting additional safeguards considered appropriate to minimise agency risks.

4.7. Financial Education and Literacy Activities

RBI considers financial literacy as a stepping-stone toward financial inclusion. Recognising this fact, the Reserve Bank has initiated a "Project Financial Literacy" with the objective of disseminating information regarding the central bank and general banking concepts to various target groups. Website of RBI is now available in 13 languages. 'Financial Education' web site link of RBI offers basics of banking, finance and central banking.

RBI advised the convener-bank of each State Level Bankers' Committee to set-up a financial literacy-*cum*-counseling centre in any one district on a pilot basis, and based on that experience, to extend the facility to other districts in due course. So far, 154 credit counseling centers have been set-up in various states of the country. These centres are expected to provide free financial education to people in rural and urban areas on the various financial products and services, while maintaining an arm's-length relationship with the parent bank.

The Reserve Bank commenced its financial literacy drive by collaborating with state governments across the country to include financial literacy curriculum in the school syllabus. It launched a pilot in Karnataka. RBI gave material on banking, personal finance as well as on the Reserve Bank to the State Government. The Karnataka Government has adapted, translated and included much of this material in the curriculum for high school classes from the academic year 2010. Considering the experience, RBI wants to mainstream this initiative across the country.

To further financial inclusion, the Reserve Bank also chose several outreach events across the country. An important aspect of the outreach activities was making the Banking Ombudsman an integral part of the activities so that there could be spot redressal of some of the grievances. In its outreach programme information was disseminated through lectures, demonstrations, interactions, skits, posters, short films, pamphlets, comic books, displays and computers. Quiz and essay competitions, exchange of notes and coins were also organised. The target groups included students, SHG members, villagers, farmers, NGOs, bankers, government employees, senior citizens, housewives, panchayat members, rag pickers, daily wage earners and defense personnel. The top management of the Reserve Bank participated in 40 outreach programmes organised in remote unbanked villages across the country during 2009-10. Out of the 167 villages identified for transformation into 'model villages', 160 are unbanked (RBI,Annual Report 2009-10)

SUGGESTIONS AND CONCLUSION

From the above discussions it is imperative that the number of brick and mortar banks in urban and rural areas of our country has been steadily increasing since nationalization of banks in 1969. Now the Reserve Bank of India has significantly scaled up its efforts aimed at increasing the level of penetration of bank services in the economy by using fancy models. However, the analysis show that scales of extension required to meet the needs of our huge population, especially rural and semi urban is still to achieve. Some suggestions to increase banking footprint and penetration across different sections of the population are as follows.

The share of both deposit mobilization and the share of credit provision in rural and semi rural areas in their respective totals for the entire nation are found decreased as analysed above. Each day Indian farmers altogether receive an estimated amount of Rs. 800 crore which is taken home (Business line 11-9-10). Similarly, a poor farmer in rural area or a micro-entrepreneur such as cobbler, or rickshaw driver in urban area may not approach a bank for opening a saving account. To include such groups in the net work of formal banking the best way is to collect their savings and provide small credit preferably on weekly or monthly basis by offering banking services at his/her door step. In this direction commercial banks can follow the path of India Post that mobilizes deposits from rural areas through licensed agents (Mahila pradhan). Similarly, banks can enter into a marketing a tie up with India Post to promote their products through postman, as proposed by Godrej and Boyce manufacturing Company to market its low cost cooling appliance for storing milk and vegetables . They can also use mobile vans with core banking connectivity to provide deposit and credit transitions for the needy villagers at their door steps. In order to increase the number of Savings accounts and to make them more operational all the banks should allow the students, pensioners, low income groups to open their account without minimum balance and waive off completely or at least minimise the charges for the services (eg.issue of demand draft) other than those pertaining to bounced cheques. The attempt of IDBI bank in this direction is commendable.

It seems to be an impressive growth in linkage of households with banks through SHG model .However, as the Southern States accounting for the major chunk of credit linkage as reports reveal, all banks, especially RRBs should give more concentration in under served States or regions to remove this unevenness.

When we think of the adoption of Electronic Benefit Transfer (EBT) for making payment of social security benefits, payments under NREGA and other government benefit programmes, it is also high time to have certain compulsions to root some other monetary transactions through the formal system of banking. Fees collections from the students who seek their higher education in all government and private institutions and payment of various benefits to them under various government schemes should be routed through the banks. Similarly, salary or wage payments to the employees of organisations who come in the net of GPF or EPF or ESI should also be disbursed through bank only.

Today, the ambit of Business Correspondent Model (BC) is so wide, where in a situation has aroused that everybody in the society is seemed to be eligible to become a bank agent. Can a banker outsource its bread and butter functions effectively to satisfy the needs of millions of rural customers in transparently? This million dollar question will get an answer only in future. Therefore, Business Correspondent Model of banking services should not be treated as an alternate for brick and mortar banks. Banks should establish more branches with their own staff in un-banked rural and semi urban areas. The top management of the banks should be more liberal in establishing its extension counters in higher educational institutions. Similar extension counters should also be established in the building of every village office with the financial assistance from local governments or the concerned Member of Parliament or Member of Legislative Assembly. Each bank must be given specific quota for establishing such centers.

The RBI with support of State government should take initiative for formation of farmers' club and, Small entrepreneurs' in rural and semi urban areas. The bank officials can convene the meeting of the members of these clubs in regular intervals to promote their products with customer orientation.

The top management of the banks should recruit adequate number of qualified staff and post them in their own State as far as possible, so that they can communicate with people in the mother tongue. Bank staff will have to get out of the comfort zone and play a pro-active approach in serving weaker sections of the society for which they need behavioural training. Branch manager of every bank should be developed as relationship manager and he should spare some time to deliver invited talks in seminar and other similar meetings organised by local authorities, educational institutions, farmers' and entrepreneurs' clubs.

Last but not the least; it is relevant to note that proliferation of ATMs and mobile banking has started to fossilize the brick and mortar banking system in western world. But the traditional style of banking is essential in a country like India to serve its vast un-banked areas. We should not allow technology to replace man at this juncture at least in rural areas .At the same time; we should apply technology for the benefits of customer rather than to keep the customer away from the direct contact of service employees.

While concluding it is relevant to consider the estimations of two agencies.

According to Economist Intelligence Unit (EIU), a leading research and advisory firm, India is all set to overtake the giant China in growth by 2018. Similarly, Credit Suisse Research Institute in its Global Wealth Report said that India's wealth would double to 6.4 trillion USD from the present level of 3.5 trillion USD by 2015 when the global wealth would increase to 315 trillion USD from the present level of 195 trillion USD, an increase of 61% by the same time (*Business Line*, 8-10-10). All these estimations are not found exaggerations, when we consider the immense potentials of India. However, the Union and State Governments, and regulators should shoulder the responsibility to ensure that when India grows like this, individuals and entrepreneurs belonging to different segments in the society such as people living below poverty line, which comes around 300 million and the expanding middle class of 250 to 300 million obtain more growth opportunities . If they fail do to so, our economic growth will only be shallow one and the same will not be socially and ethically acceptable.

REFERENCES

Business Line, 11-9-10.

Business Line, 8-10-10.

FICCI, Indian Banking System: The Current State and Road Ahead, Annual Survey,Feb 2010, New Delhi.

Govt. of India, *Economic Survey*, 2009-10.

RBI Bulletin, September 2009.

RBI, Annual Report, 2008-09.

RBI, Annual Report, 2009-10.

Report of Committee on Financial Inclusion, Jan. 2008.

http:/track.in/tags/business/2010/03/20/asia-economic-clout-post-recession

http://indiacurrentaffairs.org/financial-inclusion-of-rural-and-urban-poor-shri-pranab-mukherjee-finance-mini

http://www.micro-financefocus.com/news/2009/07/28/only-11-out-of-25-million-no-frills-accounts-in-india-operational-skotch-report/.

http://toostep.com/insight/financial-inclusion-in-india-some-key-statistics

http://www.rbi.org.in/scripts/BS_SpeechesView.aspx?Id=452

http://www.rbi.org.in/scripts/statistics_.asp

http//www.rbi.org.in

Financial Inclusion—Challenges in Evolving a Cost Effective Delivery Model

DR. P.S. DEVA KUMAR

ABSTRACT

India's economic growth failed to craft an inclusive one and the inclusion made are just opening a bank account. The intensity of exclusion among the lower strata of the income distributed is at highest level, means that the banks and financial institutions are interested in focusing the elite group only because of cost equations involved. The cost of financial service can be changed through the adoption of stable ICT models. Technology brings in broader reach for consumer banking and financial services, enhanced capacity for continued and inclusive growth, effective risk management and strategic decision-making, reduces the cost of financial transactions and improves the allocation of financial resources, reduces the interest rate float and thereby addressing the NPA accounts and reduces the cost of intermediation. Banks will have to adopt a system of Business Process Re-engineering (BPR) to change their business processes, delivery models, as also information processing systems The RBI should play a major role in developing a unique software and cost reduction strategies for all-encompassing financial inclusion.

Keywords: Financial Inclusion, Business Process Re-engineering, Customer Relations Managerial, Business Correspondent Model, No-frill Account, Real Time Gross Settlement.

INTRODUCTION

It takes more than $700 to open a bank account in Cameroon—more than the country's GDP per capita. Fees to maintain a saving account exceed 25 percent of GDP per capita in Sierra Leone. More than four types of documents are required to open a deposit account in Bangladesh. It takes more than 20 days to process a consumer loan application in Pakistan. It costs $50 to transfer $250 internationally in the Dominican Republic.

In India, the picture is not different altogether. 45.9 Million farmer households out of a total of 89.3 million households do not have access to credit either from the institutional or non-institutional sources. One branch is catering to the banking needs of 16,000 population. Only 17 credit accounts and 54 saving accounts are there per 100 persons with all the institutions. Only 13 per cent are availing loans from the banks in the income bracket of less than Rs. 50,000. 53 Per cent people are still taking loans from the institutional and non-institutional sources only for emergency purposes. Minimum amount to open a saving a/c is 8.85% of GDP. (Report, National Statistical Organisation, 2008).

The economic growth has failed to be sufficiently inclusive particularly after the mid-1990s. Majority of the population is elusive of basic health and education facilities even during high growth phases. Mis-match in growth rate of employment and acceleration in the rate of growth of labour force. Poverty ratio declining during the recent period, but continues to remain at a very high level of 27.5 per cent. Percentage of persons having annual income less than Rs. 50,000 show that 28.3 per cent had bank accounts and only 13 per cent had availed of bank finance. Most disturbing fact—income inequality as commonly measured by consumption expenditure has increased.

Our country has marched forward to greater extent as can be seen from the statistics reported below:

Number of No-Frill Accounts—3,30,24,761 at end-March 2011
Number of rural bank branches—31,727 constituting 39.7% of total bank branches (as on June, 31, 2011)
Number of ATMs—54,897 (as on May 31, 2011)
Number of POS—4,70,237 (as on May 31, 2011)
Number of Credit Cards—167.09 million (as on May 31, 2011)
Number of Kisan Credit Cards—76 million
Number of Mobile phones—403 million (as on April 30, 2011), out of which 187 million (46%) do not have a bank account

However, inclusion is not just opening a bank account alone. The proportion of people having any kind of life insurance cover is as low as 10 per cent. The proportion having non-life insurance is an abysmally low 0.6 per cent. People having debit cards comprise only 13 per cent and those having credit cards a marginal 2 per cent. Even where bank accounts have been opened, a significant portion of them are dormant. (Report, National Statistical Organisation, 2008).

Now the big questions come into the fray, whether the bottom of the pyramid is bankable? When they have no or few assets, nothing to offer as collateral, no business experiences, cannot be trained for availing financial services, no credit history and cannot understand the nuances of banking due to illiteracy or less education.

We have to explore the ways to bring the poor under the banking net through State-driven intervention by way of statutory enactments, through voluntary effort by the banking community and by creating a demand by the people themselves to pull the banks to offer banking and financial services at a competitive and affordable rate. Banking sector depth and growth can addressed by tapping GDP per capita, productivity growth, poverty reduction, firm growth and entry of new players into the markets.

However, there exist a number of barriers in access to financial services. Maintenance of minimum balances for saving bank accounts, annual fees, number of document required, number of delivery channels for lending products, ceiling for consumer loans relative to GDP per capita (28.79%) and the number of days to process consumer loans are some of the major impediments to list out.

Here comes the role of technology, the game changer for the future. Scaleable financial inclusion is impossible without stable ICT (Information and Communication Technology) models. Technology brings in broader reach for consumer banking and financial services, enhanced capacity for continued and inclusive growth, effective risk management and strategic decision-making, reduces the cost of financial transactions and improves the allocation of financial resources, reduces the interest rate float and thereby addressing the NPA (Non-performing Assets) accounts and reduces the cost of intermediation.

TABLE I

Cost of Various IT enabled Services

Services	*Minimum Cost (Rs.)*	*Maximum Cost (Rs)*
Cash Withdrawal	10/Trsn.	20/Trsn.
Balance Enquiry	5/Trsn.	8/Trsn.
Switching Charges	1/Trsn.	3/Trsn.

So far Scheduled Commercial banks have already gone for 100% automation with still untapped technology leverages to be achieved. On the other hand co-operative banks including Regional Rural Banks were not fully gone for ICT model delivery channels with tremendous potential for scalability of the financial inclusion initiatives left in the anvil. However, IT solutions are not that cheap as one would imagine.

The automation achieved by State Co-operative Banks (SCBs) can be rated as a success story. The volume of ECS (Electronic Clearing System) transactions handled has increased from 69,019 thousand in 2006-07 to 88,394 thousand in 2009-10 in the case of SCBs. The volume of ECS (Debit) transactions increased from 75,202 thousand to 1,60,055 thousand during this period. The number of CBS (Core Banking Solutions) enabled bank branches offering National Electronic Fund Transfer (NEFT) service has increased from 42,900 to 54,200 in 2008-09 and to 60,839 as on September 30, 2010. The volume of transactions in EFT/NEFT (Electronic Fund Transfer) increased from 4,776 thousand in 2006-07 to 32,161 thousand in 2009-10. The aggregate value of transactions increased from Rs. 77,446 crore to Rs. 2,51,956 crore during this period. The number of bank branches offering Real Time Gross Settlement service has increased from 43,512 to 55,000 in 2009-10 and to 60,144 as on September 30, 2010. The daily average volume of transactions is 90,000 for about Rs. 1,200 billion of which 82,000 transactions for about Rs. 980 billion pertained to customer transactions as at end of September 2010.

But, then it is right time to go beyond Core Banking Systems. The banking sector was bogged down by some of the hitches thrown open by the much hyped system of the like:

Poor strategic alignment between business and IT strategy
Absence of appropriate and re-engineered business processes and delivery models,
Lack of project ownership,
Poor risk management, and
Ineffective resource management.

This has warranted a bit of fine tuning of SCB strategies for ICT Model. Customer centric platforms, more well-governed technological solutions, improving MIS (Management Information System) capability in terms of quality, speed and integrity, harnessing IT for effective CRM (Customer Relationship Management), thereby increasing business and profitability, robust IT security and better IT governance for achieving better risk management are some of the focus areas to be attended to. Need is felt to look into areas like Business Process Re-engineering, Customer Relationship Management, Management Information System and Information Technology governance. This can be enabled by adopting a system of Business Process Re-engineering, by having a unified and integrated approach for technology up-gradation in the banks and by developing new process manuals and train personnel.

But here one is required to tackle the strategy shift imbroglio that is being created. Customer-centric growth is going to be the key to combating competitive market forces. There should be focus on growth in customer base through acquisition and retention of existing customers. Targeting on operational CRM and Business Intelligence CRM also needs to be done on a war footing. In addition to these measures banks need to leverage on IT to develop comprehensive Customer Relationship Management techniques to increase the volume, quality and profitability of business.

The status of non access to credit by farm households in the various regions across India has shown much variation as is self-explanatory from the table given below:

TABLE 2

Status of Non-access to Credit by Farm Households across Regions

Region	Farmer from formal (No. Lakhs)	Household borrowing and informal sources (% of total HH)	Farmer from formal (No. Lakhs)	Household not borrowing and informal sources (% of total HH)
Northern	56.26	51.40	53.20	48.60
North Eastern	7.04	19.90	28.36	80.10
Eastern	84.22	40.00	126.39	60.00
Central	113.04	41.66	158.29	58.34
Western	55.74	53.77	47.92	46.23
Southern	117.45	72.70	44.11	27.30
Group of UTs	0.49	33.10	0.99	66.90
All India	434.20	48.60	459.26	51.40

Similarly, the intensity of exclusion among the lower strata of the income distributed is at the highest level. This means that the banks and financial institutions are interested in focusing the elite group only as can be seen from Table 3.

Financial Inclusion Plan for RRBs (Regional Rural Banks)

Regional Rural Banks need to evolve a unique technology that will

TABLE 3

Categories-wise Status of Non-access to Credit by the Farm

Category of farmer household	*Size class of land owned (Ha)*	*Total Farmer Households (No. lakh)*	*Non-indebted farmer House-holds (No. lakh)*	*Incidence of exclusion by both formal and non formal sources (%)*
Marginal	<1.00	589.06	324.04	55.0
Small	1.01 –2.00	160.60	78.68	49.0
SF/MF Total	<1.0 to 2.0	749.66	402.72	53.7
Semi-medium	2.01– 4.00	93.50	39.10	41.8
Medium	4.01 –10.0	42.58	14.84	34.9
Large	10.00 +	7.76	2.60	33.6
All sizes		893.50	459.26	51.4

cater their specific requirements. The technology so evolved should be scalable technology solutions. The RRBs should also be core-banking enabled. Business correspondent (BC) model coupled with biometric technology needs to be deployed. Performance criteria of staff should include achievement of financial inclusion targets. Connectivity issues need to be sorted out by service providers.

Businesses Expansion and the Risk of Failure in IT Systems

Some banks could not participate for more than a day in the NEFT/RTGS (Real Time Gross Settlement) product offerings. Problems in the internet channel interface going unnoticed. Data clean-up in the database is not getting adequate attention. Ignoring hardware sizing aspects has turned out to be a major impediment. Poor quality control of data and its use for improving banking efficiency has not materialised. Lack of protection of information and customer confidentiality also brought in further lethargy into the technology space. Absence of IT models to improve the efficiency of banking and unfriendly technology interface has made the situation further worse blocking an immediate revival.

Software and Hardware Glitches

Any automated system, if it has to deliver quality and timely output should be free from software and hardware glitches. Advance Fee frauds, Database and Server Hacking, Network attacks, Denial of Service attack, Web Defacing, Cross Site scripting and IP Spoofing are some of the major glitches.

Potential of IT in the Near Future

With all the limitations inherent in the IT format, it opens up a wide variety of areas for innovation. It helps in enabling differentiation in customer service, facilitating Customer Relationship Management, improving asset-liability management for banks, enhancing compliance with anti-money laundering regulations and complying with Basel II Basel III norms.

Implementation Challenges

IT is not yet a very comfortable choice for millions. Creating consumer awareness is a major challenge. Banks must pass on the benefits of lower costs from technology. Alignment of IT and business, alignment of IT and HR and alignment of IT and organizational structure are the solutions. Security in an IT-based transaction processing environment needs to be ensured. Capacity building and talent retention needs to be addressed on a war footing. In this context the recommendations of the Rangarajan Committee on Repositioning the Institute for Development and Research in Banking Technology (IDRBT) are worth noting. It has identified the need for giving thrust on research and development be taken up in the next 3 to 5 years, revamping education and training activities with the aim to develop in-house expertise. Becoming a member of global technology standard setting bodies active in the area of banking and developing a cadre of faculty focusing on technology requirements of the banking industry.

CONCLUSION

The banks are faced with high operating cost in extending the financial services to the remote areas. High maintenance cost of these accounts as well as small ticket size of the transactions is also adding to the problem. Absence of a single window facility for customers needs to be addressed urgently. Reaching out to the illiterate people or people who can handle only the regional languages warrants also attention. Offering a single loan product not linked to the purpose of the loan, the collateral or assets held or income earned by the household but is purely based on cash flow and credit record of the household. The banking technology initiatives meant for financial inclusion should be collaborative and innovative with an objective to reduce the transaction costs. Customer-centric growth is the key to combating competitive market forces and staying ahead of the curve. Banks will have to adopt a system of

Business Process Re-engineering (BPR) to change their business processes, delivery models, as also information processing systems. An associated area which needs improvement is the integrity and reliability of the data. With the high rate of technological obsolescence for CRM to succeed, the need for proper IT governance, particularly in the case of co-operative banks, is gaining prominence. It is essential to create shared interests and proactive involvement of all the players including the regulator. With the meager operating spreads available and mounting NPAs, the co-operative institutions will find the going tough in adopting a technology and maintain the same for the enhanced customer base.

We need to transform in to mission mode with deliverable targets, bring the customer focus, bring more people to the banking fold and evolve product as per customer requirement and map it. Establishing technology and Business Correspondent based delivery model which is simple and cost effective is the only way out. Information and Technology must be integrated to ensure MIS streamlining and centralised processing. This will help in achieving proper IT governance structure.

SUGGESTIONS

The only solution seems to be an earliest and major intervention from the part of the Regulator, Reserve Bank of India by investing in a unique software solution that can address the requirement of RRBs and SCBs. The maintenance cost burden can be passed on to the beneficiary banks on a traffic bearing capacity basis in order to avoid a possible disequilibrium in cost equations.

5

Financial Inclusion for Selected Service Sector in Kerala

V.C. SHANKER

ABSTRACT

Financial inclusion a global perspective—Financial inclusion in India—Explaining Financial Inclusion concept—the supply side and demand side of financial inclusion—implementation of Financial Inclusion in India—steps taken for its success.

Service sector in India and Kerala—Paramedical services, a leading service in Kerala—United Nurse Association (Case Study in light of financial inclusion).

FINANCIAL INCLUSION—GLOBAL SCENARIO

Financial Inclusion enjoys global policy priority. It has become one of the most critical aspects in the context of inclusive growth and development. Many countries look at it as a means of comprehensive growth. It enables each citizen of a nation to use their earnings as a financial resource that they can put to work to improve their future financial status, adding to the nation's progress. Legislative measures have been initiated to promote financial inclusion as follows:

Name of Legislation/Facility	*Year*	*Purpose*
Community Reinvestment Act (U.S.A.)	1997	Banks to offer credit to their entire area of operation and prohibits them from targeting only rich neighbourhood.
Law of Exclusion (France)	1998	Emphasises an individual's right to have a bank account.
Voluntary code of German Bankers' Association	1996	Provide everyman with banking account which facilitates basic banking transactions
'Mzansi'-launched by South African Banking Association	2004	Low cost bank account
Financial Inclusion Task Force—United Kingdom	2005	Monitor the Financial Inclusion system in U.K.

Financial Inclusion—Indian Scenario

India has presence of 260 million poor forming around 26% of the total population. Countries like India which have large population reveal with empirical evidence that, with a large proportion of population excluded from the formal financial system, show higher poverty ratios and higher inequality. This makes financial inclusion not as a policy choice but as a policy compulsion. At the policy level organisations like FICCI (Financial Inclusion Committee), UNDP and RBI are involved in India. At the implementation level, all scheduled commercial banks play vital roles which are supported by Non-Banking Financial Companies, NGOs and Mutual Fund Institutions. These institutions drive the supply side of financial inclusion concept. The Financial Stability and Development Council headed by the finance minister is mandated to focus on financial inclusion and financial literacy.

The demand side factors are lower income and/or asset holding of excluded ones. India has to go a long way in addressing concerns of absolute poverty. Low-income Indian households in the informal or subsistence economy often have to borrow from friends, family or usurious moneylenders. Access to financial products is constrained by several factors which include lack of awareness about the financial products, unaffordable products, high transaction costs, products which are not convenient, not customized and of low quality. The proportion of rural residents who lack access to bank accounts is nearly 40% and that of East/North Eastern region is 60%. Expectation of poor people from the financial system is security and safety of deposits, low transaction costs, convenient operating time, minimum paper work, frequent deposits, quick and easy access to credit and other products like remittances suitable to their income and consumption.

Owing to difficulties in accessing formal sources of credit, poor individuals and small/micro-enterprises rely on their personal savings or internal sources or take recourse to these informal sources to invest in health, education, housing and entrepreneurial activities to make use of growth opportunities. They have little or no awareness about insurance products that could protect their financial resources in unexpected circumstances like illness, property damage or death of the primary breadwinner. For inclusion, the design and implementation of pro-poor and inclusive livelihood promotion strategies with focus on excluded groups such as women, minorities, below-the-poverty line/migrant households and involuntarily displaced people is required.

> "Financial inclusion is the process of ensuring access to appropriate financial products and services needed by all sections of the society in general and vulnerable groups such as weaker sections and low income groups in particular, at an affordable cost in a fair and transparent manner by regulated mainstream institutional players."

Financial inclusion promotes thrift and develops culture of savings, improves access to credit—both entrepreneurial and emergency. It also promotes efficient payment mechanism thereby strengthening the resource-base of financial institutions.

Implementation of Financial Inclusion

The provision of uncomplicated, small, affordable products can help bring low-income families into the formal financial sector. Taking into account their seasonal inflow of income from agricultural operations, migration from one place to another seasonal and irregular work availability and income, the existing financial system needs to be designed to suit their requirements.

The following model is used for effective implementation of financial inclusion:

Bank led model for promoting financial inclusion.

Information Communication Technology (ICT)-based agent bank model through Business Correspondents (BC) for ensuring door-step delivery of financial products and services.

Four Basic products and services are available at present:

Savings Account with overdraft facility,

A remittance product,

A pure savings product (preferably variable recurring deposit),

An entrepreneurial credit with Kisan Credit Card (KCC) or General purpose Credit Card (GCC).

Steps taken for Success

1. Relaxation of Know Your Customer norms—The following procedures are accepted for new account opening:
   Introduction by a KYC compliant customer,
   Job card issued under National Rural Employment Guarantee Act duly signed by a state government official
   Letters issued by Unique Identification Authority of India containing details of name, address and Aadhar number.
2. Simplified Branch Authorisation:
   Banks are permitted to open at Tier 3 to Tier 6 centers with population less than 50,000 under general permission.
   In North eastern states scheduled commercial banks can open branches in rural, semi-urban and urban centers without the permission of Reserve Bank of India but reporting is essential.
3. Pricing of advances are at the liberty of the respective lending agency.
4. Liberalisation of BC model.
5. Opening branches at un-banked rural centres by allocating at least 25% of the total number of branches at these places.

The committee on Financial Inclusion headed by Dr.Rangarajan and the committee on Financial Sector reforms headed by Dr.Raghuram Rajan are functional to achieve greater financial inclusion. The recommendations made in these reports will go a long way in modifying the credit delivery system of the banks and other related institutions to meet the credit requirements of marginal and sub-marginal farmers in the rural areas.

Service Sector in India and Kerala

Service sector contributes to 57.2% of the National Income of India. It makes 34% of employment in India. The country is ranked 13th in terms of services rendered. Kerala contributes 60% of its state income from service sector. The employment generation in the state due to service sector is 67%. Tourism, Information technology, para-medical services are most common breadwinning in this state.

Case Study (United Nurse Association—UNA)

Paramedical Services (Nurses) are one of the largest work forces in the state, across the country and beyond. Nurses working in private hospitals, one of the most disorganised groups in the services sector and have been the most exploited group have found new strength through this venture. The starting point was at Kottayam when a few nurses came together to help one of their friends who had fallen into debt and wanted to commit suicide.

With the death of Beena Baby, a nurse who served in a Mumbai hospital, more than 30 nurses met at Thrissur and began a campaign demanding welfare measures and this message was posted in the eminent social networking site 'facebook'. Meeting the bank manager to find out a solution for the debt of the nurse was the first step. The manager pointed out that there were many cases like this and something has to be done about it.

The group posted a scheduled meeting to discuss the need to help each other in an organised group. Around 130 nurses turned up for the meeting in mid November – 2011, which made Mr.Jasmin Sha the group leader to realize the vulnerability of the group. Within four days about 3000 members joined the group and now it has around 14,750 members. That also brought the first agitation of nurses when the group spoke on behalf of their counterparts in a private hospital at Thrissur. In order to improve its organisational strength the association was registered. The registration number was R 751/11. There are innumerable hospitals where nurses are working for Rs. 1,000 to Rs. 3,000—which is much below the minimum wages set by the government for the private sector hospitals. The founder has resigned from his lucrative post as a nurse from abroad and got himself involved in the group.

The objectives of the group are:

- To bring all the Nurses of our country under one roof
- To work for the progress and Welfare of all nurses and to solve all the problems among them.
- The financial support at present available to them is for higher education (even at foreign countries)—more like an educational loan.

Suggestions

The following areas need to be focussed to make them financially independent:

- Engage nurses for a better salary above the minimum prescribed by the government. This increases the supply of income which may reduce poverty related suicides.
- Access to financial inclusions through the existing three products out of the four offered for the financially excluded viz. No frills account or a savings account with overdraft facility, a pure savings product (a variable recurring deposit) and General Purpose credit cards (GCC).

Salary payments to nurses should be urged to be made through banks. This will make banks come forward for business entanglements with the work group.

Relaxation from KYC norms can be extended to such vulnerable work groups.

Compulsory enrolment of staffs in any hospital under group insurance schemes as well as pure life schemes individually for financial protection in case of life loss.

CONCLUSION

The above remedial measures suggested are an attempt to establish social security among paramedical work forces which constitute a major chunk of service sector in Kerala state. Financial inclusion can thus be implemented in a phased manner engulfing different professions in the service sector.

REFERENCES

Reserve Bank of India Bulletin (Nov. 2011)—www.bulletin.rbi.org.in

The Hindu dated 7th January, 2011.

www.facebook.com (United Nurse Association).

6

Financial Inclusion: Role of Banking Industry

T. SUBASH

ABSTRACT

Access to finance by the poor and vulnerable groups is a prerequisite for poverty reduction and social cohesion. This has to become an integral part to promote inclusive growth. Financial Inclusion denotes delivery of financial services at an affordable cost to the vast sections of the disadvantaged and low-income groups. The various financial services include credit, savings, insurance and payments and remittance facilities. The objective of financial inclusion is to extend the scope of activities of the organized financial system to include within its ambit people with low incomes. Financial inclusion is necessary for the nation. For banks, Financial Inclusion initiatives offer a great opportunity. Though India is prospering and the GDP growth is encouraging, the prosperity is not equitably distributed among the population. The gap between the rich and the poor is ever-widening and more than 35 crores of the population still live below the poverty-line wherever line is. Hence, there is a need for inclusive growth, a growth that will include and embrace all sections of the society. It is imperative that nobody should be financially excluded.

INTRODUCTION

Financial inclusion is the process of ensuring access to

appropriate financial products and services needed by vulnerable groups such as weaker sections and low-income groups at an affordable cost in a fair and transparent manner by mainstream institutional players. Financial inclusion has become one of the most critical aspects in the context of inclusive growth and development. The importance of an inclusive financial system is widely recognized in policy circles and has become a policy priority in many countries. Several countries across the globe now look at financial inclusion as the means to more comprehensive growth, wherein each citizen of the country is able to use earnings as a financial resource that can be put to work to improve future financial status and adding to the nation's progress. Initiatives for financial inclusion have come from financial regulators, governments and the banking industry. The banking sector has taken a lead role in promoting financial inclusion. Legislative measures have been initiated in some countries.

The German Bankers' Association introduced a voluntary code in 1996 providing for a so-called "everyman" current banking account that facilitates basic banking transactions. In South Africa, a low-cost bank account, called Mzansi, was launched for financially excluded people in 2004 by the South African Banking Association. In the UK, a Financial Inclusion Task Force was constituted by the government in 2005 in order to monitor the development of the process. Several African countries have harnessed the unique aspects of mobile banking to drive financial inclusion. A G-20 (Group of Twenty) Financial Inclusion Experts Group has been launched. The Principles for Innovative Financial Inclusion serve as a guide for policy and regulatory approaches with the objectives of fostering safe and sound adoption of innovative, adequate, low-cost financial delivery models, helping provide conditions for fair competition and a framework of incentives for the various banking, insurance, and non-banking entities involved and delivery of the full range of affordable and quality financial services.

India has, for a long time, recognized the social and economic imperatives for broader financial inclusion and has made an enormous contribution to economic development by finding innovative ways to empower the poor. Starting with the nationalization of banks, priority sector lending requirements for banks, lead bank scheme, establishment of regional rural banks (RRBs), service area approach, self-help group-bank linkage programme, etc. multiple steps have been taken by the Reserve Bank of India over the years to increase access to the poorer segments of society.

ASPECTS OF FINANCIAL INCLUSION

Three major aspects of financial inclusion are:

Make people to access financial markets
Make people to access credit markets
Make people to learn financial matters

Thus financial inclusion includes accessing of financial products and services like: Savings facility, credit and debit cards access, electronic fund transfer, all kinds of commercial loans, overdraft facility, cheque facility, payment and remittance services, low cost financial services, insurance, financial advice, pension for old-age and investment schemes, access to financial markets, micro-credit during emergency, entrepreneurial credit, etc.

SCOPE OF FINANCIAL INCLUSION

There is huge scope of business at the bottom of the pyramid, where almost half the population of the county is unbanked. 45% population has no deposit account and only 9% have credit accounts with bank. There are only 33,495 rural branches in more than 6 lakhs villages. There is one bank branch per 14,000 people. Only 20% population has any kind of insurance and 9.6% of the population has non-life insurance coverage.

INITIATIVES TAKEN BY GOVERNMENT FOR FINANCIAL INCLUSION

1. Concept of No-frills Accounts

Basic banking no-frills accounts with nil or very low minimum balance as well as charges that make such accounts accessible to vast sections of the population. Banks have been advised to provide small overdrafts in such accounts.

2. Relaxation on Know-Your-Customer (KYC) Norms for Opening of No-frill Accounts

KYC requirements for opening bank accounts were relaxed for small accounts in August 2005, thereby simplifying procedures by stipulating that introduction by an account holder who has been subjected to the full KYC drill would suffice for opening such accounts. The banks were also permitted to take any evidence as to the identity and address of the customer to their satisfaction. It has now been further relaxed to include the letters issued by the Unique Identification Authority of India containing details of name, address, and Aadhaar number.

3. Introduction of General Credit Cards

With a view to helping the poor and the disadvantaged with access to easy credit, banks have been asked to consider introduction of a general purpose credit card facility up to Rs. 25,000 at their rural and semi-urban branches. The objective of the scheme is to provide hassle-free credit to banks. customers based on the assessment of cash flow without insistence on security, purpose or end-use of the credit. This is in the nature of revolving credit entitling the holder to withdraw up to the limit sanctioned.

4. Business Correspondents (BCs) and Business Facilitators (BFs) Model

The Reserve Bank permitted banks to engage BCs and BFs as intermediaries for providing financial and banking services. The BC model allows banks to provide doorstep delivery of services, especially cash-in-cash-out transactions, thus addressing the last-mile problem. The list of eligible individuals and entities that can be engaged as BCs is being widened from time to time. With effect from September 2010, for-profit companies have also been allowed to be engaged as BCs.

5. Use of Technology and Micro-Credit

Recognising that technology has the potential to address the issues of outreach and credit delivery in rural and remote areas in a viable manner, banks have been advised to make effective use of information and communications technology (ICT), to provide doorstep banking services through the BC model where the accounts can be operated by even illiterate customers by using biometrics, thus ensuring the security of transactions and enhancing confidence in the banking system.

6. Creation of Funds for Financial Inclusion

Financial Inclusion Fund and Financial Inclusion Technology Development Fund were created by Central Government for meeting the costs of development, and promotional and technology interventions. A fund of Rs. 5,000 crores in NABARD was also created to enhance its re-finance operations to short term co-operative credit institutions.

7. Branch Authorization in Tier III to Tier VI Centres

To address the issue of uneven spread of bank branches, domestic scheduled commercial banks were permitted to freely open branches in Tier III to Tier VI centres with a population of less than 50,000 under general permission, subject to reporting. In the north-eastern states and Sikkim, domestic scheduled commercial banks can now open branches in rural, semi-urban and urban centres without the need to take permission from the Reserve Bank in each case, subject to reporting.

8. New Branches in Unbanked Rural Centres

To further step up the opening of branches in rural areas so as to improve banking penetration and financial inclusion rapidly, the need for the opening of more bricks-and-mortar branches, besides the use of BCs, was felt. Accordingly, banks have been mandated to allocate at least 25% of the total number of branches to be opened during a year to unbanked rural centres.

9. Banking Services in Unbanked Villages with a Population of more than 2000

Banks were advised to draw up a road-map to provide banking services in every unbanked village having a population of over 2000 by March 2012. The Reserve Bank advised banks that such banking services need not necessarily be extended through a brick-and mortar branch, but could also be provided through any of the various forms of ICT-based models. About 73,000 such unbanked villages were identified and allotted to various banks through state-level bankers 'committees.

10. Plan of Banks for Financial Inclusion

The Reserve Bank advised all public and private sector banks to submit a board-approved, three-year Financial Inclusion Plan (FIP) starting April 2010. These plans broadly include self-set targets in respect of rural brick-and-mortar branches opened; BCs employed; coverage of unbanked villages with a population above 2000, as also other unbanked villages with population below 2000 through branches; BCs and other modes; no-frills accounts opened, including through BC-ICT; Kisan Credit Cards (KCCs) and General Credit Cards (GCCs) issued; and other specific products designed by them to cater to the financially excluded segments.

11. Consolidation of Regional Rural Banks

The Central Government has kicked-off a major consolidation exercise among RRBs which will play an important role in the country's scheme of financial inclusion. The number of banks will be cut to 46 from 82 after the merger process. A consolidation of existing rural banks will make them more viable.

12. Parameter for Performance Appraisal of Bank Staff

Banks were advised by RBI to integrate board approved FIPs with their business plans and to include the criteria on financial inclusion as a parameter in the performance evaluation of their staff.

PERFORMANCE OF COMMERCIAL BANKS

The performance of commercial banks during the year 2010-11 clearly indicates that banks are on the right path towards deploying BCs, villages covered, opening of no-frills accounts, and grant of credit through KCCs and GCCs.

1. Coverage of Villages

Banks have, up to June 2011, opened banking outlets in 1.07 lakhs villages up from just 54,258 as on March 2010. Out of these, 22,870 villages have been covered through brick-and-mortar branches, 84,274 through BC outlets and 460 through other modes like mobile vans, etc.

2. Opening of No-frills Accounts

Basic banking No-frills account, with nil or very low minimum balance requirement as well as no charges for not maintaining such minimum balance, were introduced as per RBI directive in 2005. As on June 2011, 7.91 crores No-frills accounts have been opened by banks with outstanding balance of Rs. 5,944.73 crores. These figures, respectively, were 4.93 crores and Rs. 4,257.07 crores in March 2010.

3. General Credit Cards

Banks have been asked to consider introduction of a General Purpose Credit Card (GCC) facility up to Rs. 25,000 at their rural and semi-urban braches. The credit facility is in the nature of revolving credit entitling the holder to withdraw up to the limit sanctioned. Based on assessment of household cash flows, the limits are sanctioned without insistence on security or purpose. Interest rate on the facility is completely deregulated. As on June 2011, banks had provided credit aggregating Rs. 2,356.25 crores in 10.70 lakh General Credit Card (GCC) accounts.

4. Kisan Credit Cards

Kisan Credit Cards to small farmers have been issued by banks. As on June 30, 2011, the total number of KCCs issued has been reported as 202.89 lakhs with a total amount outstanding to the tune of 1,36,122.32 crores.

CONCLUSION

Economic development, in a country, is not possible without people's active participation. People of a developed country should not only enjoy the benefits but they generally generate those benefits as well. If growth benefits only the rich and higher income earner segment of the society, it is not sustainable and cannot be termed as development. This development and sustainable economic growth is not possible without the participation of around more than half the population. Thus, financial inclusion is a great step to alleviate poverty in India. But to achieve this, the government should provide a less perspective environment in which banks are free to pursue the innovations necessary to reach low income consumers and still make a profit. Financial service providers should learn more about the consumers and new business models to them.

References

Arindam Banerjee and Pranav Saraswat Financial Inclusion in India : An Overview, *The Management Accountant*, January 2012.

Balbir Singh, Financial Inclusion—Role of Banking Industry, *The Management Accountant*, January 2012.

Jana, Madan Mohan (2011), Corporate Financial Inclusion Plan in India: An inclusive growth approach—An Empirical Study, *The Management Account*, October, p. 897.

Report of the Committee on Financial Inclusion, Chairman C. Rangarajan, January 2008.

Report of the Committee on Financial Inclusion, January 2008.

Research report on Financial Inclusion, Ernst and Young, 2010.

www.rbi.org.in

7

Financial Inclusion—An Indian Perspective

DR. BIJU T.

ABSTRACT

"Financial inclusion is a quasi-public good—increasingly, in developing countries access to finance is positioned as a public good, which is as important and basic as access to safe water or primary education".
(Dr. Vijay Kelkar, Chairman, Finance Commission, in NP Sen Memorial Lecture at Hyderabad (Date: 13/1/08))

The recent developments in banking technology have transformed banking from the traditional brick-and-mortar infrastructure like staffed branches to a system supplemented by alternative delivery channels like automated teller machines (ATM), credit/debit cards, internet banking, online money transfers, etc. The moot point, however, is that access to such technology is restricted only to certain segments of the society. Indeed, some trends, such as increasingly sophisticated customer segmentation technology—allowing, for example, more accurate targeting of sections of the market—have led to restricted access to financial services for some groups. There is a growing divide, with an increased range of personal finance options for a segment of high and upper middle income population and a significantly large section of the population who lack access to even the most basic banking services. This is termed "financial exclusion". These people, particularly, those living on low incomes, cannot access mainstream financial products such as bank accounts, credit, remittances and payment services, financial advisory services, insurance facilities, etc.

EXTENT OF FINANCIAL EXCLUSION AND ITS REASONS

Based on the latest UN Report almost 2.5 billion adults do not use formal financial services to save or borrow, of which approx. 2.2 billion live in Africa, Asia, Latin America, and the Middle East. Of the 1.2 billion adults whose formal financial services in Africa, Asia, and the Middle East, at least two-thirds (a little more than 800 million) live on less than USD 5 per day. In India, almost half the country is unbanked. Only 55 per cent of the population have deposit accounts and 9 per cent have credit accounts with banks. India has the highest number of households (145 million) excluded from Banking. There was only one bank branch per 14,000 people. Also, less than 20% of the population has any kind of life insurance and 9.6% of the population has non-life insurance coverage. Just 18 per cent had debit cards and less than 2 per cent had credit cards. *Inter alia,* NSSO data reveals that 45.9 million farmer households in the country (51.4%), out of a total of 89.3 million households do not access credit, either from institutional or non-institutional sources. Further, despite the vast network of bank branches, only 27% of total farm households are indebted to formal sources (of which one-third also borrow from informal sources). Farm households not accessing credit from formal sources as a proportion to total farm households is especially high at 95.91%, 81.26% and 77.59% in the North Eastern, Eastern and Central Regions respectively. Thus, apart from the fact that exclusion in general is large, it also varies widely across regions, social groups and asset holdings. The poorer the group, the greater is the exclusion.

The policy-makers, in most of the countries, have set-up their task force/committees to understand how to overcome financial exclusion and how can financial inclusion be achieved. The main question that comes to the mind of policy-makers is that why can't financial inclusion happen on its own? Like any other product or service, why can't it find a market of its own? The reasons are:

High Cost

It has also been seen that poor living in urban areas don't utilize the financial services as they find financial services are costly and thus are unaffordable. Hence, even if financial services are available, the high costs deter the poor from accessing them. For example, to open a checking account in Cameroon, the minimum deposit requirement is over 700 dollars, an amount higher than the average GDP per capita of that country, while no minimum amounts are required in South Africa or Swaziland. Annual fees to maintain a checking account exceed 25 percent of GDP per capita in Sierra Leone, while there are no such fees in the Philippines. In Bangladesh, Pakistan, Philippines, to get a small business loan processed requires more than a month, while the wait is only a day in Denmark. The fees for transferring 250 dollars internationally are 50 dollars in the Dominican Republic, but only 30 cents in Belgium.

Non-price Barriers

Access to formal financial services also requires documents of proof regarding a persons' identity, income, etc. The poor people do not have these documents and thus are excluded from these services. They may also subscribe to the services initially but may not use them as actively as others because of high distance between the bank and residence, poor infrastructure, etc.

Behavioural Aspects

Research in behavioural economics has shown that many people are not comfortable using formal financial services. The reasons are difficulty in understanding language, various documents and conditions that come with financial services, etc.

CONCEPT OF FINANCIAL INCLUSION

Financial inclusion is the process of ensuring access to financial services and timely and adequate credit needed by vulnerable groups such as weaker sections and low income groups at an affordable cost. Financial Inclusion has become a buzzword now but in India it has been practiced for quite sometime now. Deliberations on the subject of Financial Inclusion contributed to a consensus that merely having a bank account may not be a good indicator of financial inclusion. Apart from the regular form of financial intermediation, it may include a basic no frills banking account for making and receiving payments, a savings product suited to the pattern of cash flows of a poor household, money transfer facilities, small loans and overdrafts for productive, personal and other purposes, insurance (life and non-life), etc. Further, indebtedness as quantified in the NSSO 59th round (2003) may not also be a reflective indicator. This would require re-engineering of existing financial products or delivery systems and making them more in tune with the expectations and absorptive capacity of the intended clientele. India set-up a committee under the chairmanship of Mr. C. Rangarajan to suggest measures to increase financial inclusion (hence called the Rangarajan Committee on Financial Inclusion). The World Bank had organized a conference in March 2007 and has released a report titled "Finance for All" in November 2007.

FINANCIAL INCLUSION IN INDIA—POLICY INITIATIVES OF RBI

RBI has taken various measures to inculcate the concept of Financial Inclusion in India. Priority sector lending was instituted to provide loans to small and medium enterprises and agricultural sector. Further special banks were set-up for rural areas like Rural Cooperative Banks, Regional Rural Banks, etc. Also, in association with Government of India, set-up national level institutions like NABARD, SIDBI to empower credit to rural areas and small and medium enterprises. The efforts were further intensified by RBI, and Banks are urged to review their existing practices to align them with the objective of financial inclusion. This RBI focus led to a few key developments, as mentioned below:

No-Frill Accounts

In November 2005, RBI asked banks to offer no-frills savings account which enables excluded people to open a savings account. Normally, the savings account requires people to maintain a minimum balance and most banks now even offer various facilities with the same. No-frills account requires no (or negligible) balance and is without any other facilities leading to lower costs both for the bank and the individual. The number of no-frills account has increased mainly in public sector banks against private sector banks/foreign banks. This is understandably so as majority of rural and sub-urban bank offices are in public sector banks.

Usage of Regional Language

The Banks were required to provide all the material related to opening accounts, disclosures etc in the regional languages.

Simple KYC Norms

In order to ensure that persons belonging to low income group both in urban and rural areas do not face difficulty in opening the bank accounts due to the procedural hassles, the KYC procedure for opening accounts has been simplified for those persons who intend to keep balances not exceeding rupees fifty thousand (Rs. 50,000) in all their accounts taken together and the total credit in all the accounts taken together is not expected to exceed rupees one lakh (Rs. 1,00,000) in a year.

Easier Credit facilities: Banks have been asked to consider introducing General purpose Credit Card (GCC) facility up to Rs. 25,000 at their rural and semi urban branches. GCC is in the nature of revolving credit entitling the holder to withdraw upto the limit sanctioned. The limit for the purpose can be set based on assessment of household cash flows, the limits are sanctioned without insistence on security or purpose. The Interest rate on the facility is completely deregulated. A simplified mechanism for one-time settlement of overdue loans up to Rs. 25,000 has been suggested for adoption. Banks have been specifically advised that borrowers with loans settled under the one time settlement scheme will be eligible to re-access the formal financial system for fresh credit.

Other Rural Intermediaries

Banks were permitted in January 2006, to use other rural organisations like Non-Governmental Organizations, Self-Help Groups, Micro-Finance Institutions, etc. for furthering the cause of financial inclusion.

Using Information Technology

A few Pilot projects have been initiated to test how technology can be used to increase financial inclusion. Usha Thorat in her speech (June 19, 2007) pointed to a few measures:

Smart cards for opening bank accounts with biometric identification.

Link to mobile or hand held connectivity devices ensure that the transactions are recorded in the bank's books on real time basis.

Some State Governments are routing social security payments as also payments under the National Rural Employment Guarantee Scheme (NREGS) through such smart cards. The same delivery channel can be used to provide other financial services like low cost remittances and insurance.

The use of IT also enables banks to handle the enormous increase in the volume of transactions for millions of households for processing, credit scoring, credit record and follow up.

Financial Education

RBI has taken number of measures to increase financial literacy in the country. It has set-up a multilingual website in 13 languages explaining about banking, money, etc. It has started putting up comic strips to explain various difficult subjects like importance of saving, RBI's functions, etc. These comics explain myriad and complex concepts in an entertaining manner. The website states: The Reserve Bank of India has undertaken a project titled "Project Financial Literacy". The Objective of the project is to disseminate information regarding the central bank and general banking concepts to various target groups, including, school and college going children, women, rural and urban poor, defence personnel and senior citizens.

STEPS TO IMPROVE FINANCIAL INCLUSION

While financial inclusion, in the narrow sense, may be achieved to some extent by offering the services mentioned, the objective of "Comprehensive Financial Inclusion", to provide a holistic set of services encompassing all of the above, request for proper improvement and consensus in financial system coupled with co-ordinated efforts of various governmental agencies, etc. as mentioned below:

(a) *Strengthening Demand Side Factors*: While financial inclusion can be substantially enhanced by improving the supply side or the delivery systems, it is also important to note that many regions, segments of the population and sub-sectors of the economy have a limited or weak demand for financial services. In order to improve their level of inclusion, demand side efforts need to be undertaken including improving human and physical resource endowments, enhancing productivity, mitigating risk and strengthening market linkages.

(b) *Establishment of a National Mission on Financial Inclusion*: The task of financial inclusion must be taken up in a mission mode as a financial inclusion plan at the national level. A National Mission on Financial Inclusion (NaMFI) comprising representatives from all stakeholders may be constituted to aim at achieving universal financial inclusion within a specific time frame. The Mission should be responsible for suggesting the overall policy changes required for achieving the desired level of financial inclusion, and for supporting a range of stakeholders—in the domain of public, private and NGO sectors—in undertaking promotional initiatives. A National Rural Financial Inclusion Plan (NRFIP) may be launched with a clear target to provide access to comprehensive financial services, including credit, to atleast 50% of financially excluded households, say 55.77 million by 2012 through rural/semi-urban branches of Commercial Banks and Regional Rural Banks. The remaining households, with such shifts as may occur in the rural/urban population, have to be covered by 2015. Semi-urban and rural branches of commercial banks and RRBs may set for themselves a minimum target of covering 250 new cultivator and non-cultivator households per branch per annum, with an emphasis on financing marginal farmers and poor non-cultivator households.

(c) *Development and Technology Funds*: There is a cost involved in this massive exercise of extending financial services to hitherto excluded segments of population. Such costs may come down over a period of time with the resultant business expansion. However, in the initial stages some funding support is required for promotional and developmental initiatives that will lead to better credit absorption capacity among the poor and vulnerable sections and for application of technology for facilitating the mandated levels of inclusion. The Committee has, therefore, proposed the constitution of a core fund jointly by GoI, RBI and other related authorities.

(d) *Business Correspondent Model*: This concept envisages leveraging technology to open up channels beyond branch network. Adoption of appropriate technology would enable the branches to go where the customer is present instead of the other way round. This, however, is in addition to extending traditional mode of banking by targeted branch expansion in identified districts. The Business Facilitator/ Business Correspondent (BF/BC) models riding on appropriate technology can deliver this outreach and should form the core of the strategy for extending financial inclusion. Ultimately, banks should endeavour to have a BC touch point in each of the 6,00,000 villages in the country.

(e) *Procedural Changes*: Procedural Changes like simplifying mortgage requirements, exemption from Stamp Duty for loans to small and marginal farmers and providing agricultural/business development services in the farm and non-farm sectors respectively, will help in extending financial inclusion.

(f) *Role of RRBs*: RRBs represent a powerful instrument for financial inclusion. Their outreach *vis-à-vis* other scheduled commercial banks particularly in regions and across population groups facing the brunt of financial exclusion is impressive. RRBs account for 37% of total rural offices of all scheduled commercial banks and 91% of their workforce is posted in rural and semi-urban areas. They account for 31% of deposit accounts and 37% of loan accounts in rural areas. RRB's have a large presence in regions marked by financial exclusion of a high order. They account for 34% of all branches in North-Eastern, 30% in Eastern and 32% in Central regions. Significantly the more backward the region the greater is the share of RRBs which is amply demonstrated by their 56% share in the North-Eastern, 48% in Central and 40% in Eastern region. RRBs are, thus, one of the the best suited vehicles to widen and deepen the process of financial inclusion.

(g) *SHG-Bank Linkage Scheme*: The SHG-Bank Linkage Programme can be regarded as the most potent initiative since Independence for delivering financial services to the poor in a sustainable manner. The programme has been growing rapidly and the number of SHGs financed has been substantially increasing every year. The spread of the SHG-Bank Linkage Programme in different regions has been uneven with Southern States accounting for the major chunk of credit linkage. Many States with high incidence of poverty have shown poor performance under the programme. NABARD has identified 13 States with large population of the poor, but exhibiting low performance in implementation of the programme. NABARD may open dedicated project offices in these 13 States for upscaling the SHG-Bank Linkage Programme. The State Govternments and NABARD may set aside specific funds, out of the budgetary support, for the purpose of promoting SHGs in regions with high levels of exclusion. For the North-Eastern Region, there is a need to evolve SHG models suited to the local context of such areas. NGOs have played a commendable role in promoting SHGs and linking them with banks.

(h) *Promoting Formation of Joint Liability Groups*: SHG-bank linkage has emerged as an effective credit delivery channel to the poor clients. However, there are segments within the poor such as share croppers/oral lessees/tenant farmers, whose loan requirements are much larger but who have no collaterals to fit into the traditional financing approaches of the banking system. To service such clients, Joint Liability Groups (JLGs), an upgradation of SHG model, could be an effective way. NABARD had piloted a project for formation and linking of JLGs during 2004-05 in 8 States of the country through 13 RRBs. Based on the encouraging response from the project, a scheme for financing JLGs of tenant farmers and oral lessees has also been evolved. The JLGs concept could be another effective method for purveying credit to mid-segment clients such as small farmers, marginal farmers, tenant farmers, etc. and thereby reduce their dependence on informal sources of credit.

(i) *Micro-Finance Institutions: NBFCs*: Micro-Finance Institutions (MFIs) could play a significant role in facilitating inclusion, as they are uniquely positioned in reaching out to the rural poor. Except a few, many of them operate in a limited geographical area, have a greater understanding of the issues specific to the rural poor, enjoy greater acceptability amongst the rural poor and have flexibility in operations providing a level of comfort to their clientele. Greater legitimacy, accountability and transparency will not only enable MFIs to source adequate debt and equity funds, but also eventually enable them to take and use savings as a low cost source for on-lending. There is a need to recognize a separate category of Micro-finance—Non-Banking Finance Companies (MF-NBFCs), without any relaxation on start-up capital and subject to the regulatory prescriptions applicable for NBFCs. Such MF-NBFCs could provide thrift, credit, micro-insurance, remittances and other financial services up to a specified amount to the poor in rural, semi-urban and urban areas. Such MF-NBFCs may also be recognized as Business Correspondents of banks for providing only savings and remittance services and also act as micro-insurance agents.

(j) *Revitalising the Cooperative System*: Though the network of commercial banks and RRBs has increased substantially in rural/semi-urban areas, their reach in the countryside both in terms of the number of clients and accessibility to the small and marginal farmers and other poorer segments is far less than that of cooperatives. In terms of number of agricultural credit accounts, the Short Term Cooperative Credit System (STCCS) has 50% more accounts than the commercial banks and RRBs put together. On an average, there is one PACS for every 6 villages; these societies have a total membership of more than 120 million rural people making it one of the largest rural financial systems in the world. However, the health of a very large proportion of these rural credit cooperatives has deteriorated significantly and needs proper revival and rejuvenation. A financially sound cooperative structure can do wonders for financial inclusion given its extensive outreach.

(k) *Micro-Insurance*: Micro-insurance is a key element in the financial services for people at the bottom of the pyramid. The poor face more risks than the well off. It is becoming increasingly clear that micro-insurance needs a further push and guidance from the Regulator as well as the Government. There is, therefore, a need to emphasise linking of micro-credit with micro-insurance.

CONCLUSION

The financial system in India has grown rapidly in the last three decades. The functional and geographical coverage of the system is truly impressive. Nevertheless, data do show that there is exclusion and that poorer sections of the society have not been able to access adequately financial services from the organized financial system. There is an imperative need to modify the credit and financial services delivery system to achieve greater inclusion. The credit delivery system of the banks and other related institutions to meet the credit requirements of marginal and sub-marginal farmers in the rural areas in a fuller measure needs proper review and improvement. This needs to be supplemented by efforts to improve the productivity of small and marginal farmers and other entrepreneurs so that the credit made available can be productively employed. While banks and other financial institutions can also take some efforts on their own to improve the absorptive capacity of the clients, it is equally important for Government at various levels to initiate actions to enhance the earnings capacity of the poorer sections of the society. The two together can bring about the desired change of greater inclusion in the near future.

Bank Linkage Model and Financial Inclusion: A Demand and Supply Perspective

A.D. RAJEEV KUMAR AND MAHIJA, K.

ABSTRACT

Financial inclusion means bringing the disadvantaged people who are so far believed to be unbankable within the ambit of formal financial system. In India, a sizable portion of the population, particularly the poor, continue to remain excluded from the basic banking services. As part of financial inclusion drive, NABARD launched SHG bank linkage model in 1992 as a pilot project by linking 500 SHGs with banks. Through this, the poor are provided with hassle free timely finance and it is considered to be the best way to provide credit to the people who need it most. As per this scheme, the SHG is linked to a bank, where it can maintain an account to deposit the contributions of its members and avail loan to disburse among them. It has proved to be the most successful micro-finance model in the world in terms of outreach. In this context, this paper analyses the benefits of SHG-Bank Linkage model from a demand and supply perspective. The analysis shows that this model is highly beneficial for both sides and clearly works against the various aspects of financial exclusion and thus facilitates financial inclusion

INTRODUCTION

Financial inclusion means bringing the disadvantaged people who are so far believed to be unbankable within the ambit of formal financial system. Financial inclusion may be defined as "the process of ensuring access to financial services and timely and adequate credit where needed by vulnerable groups such as weaker sections and low income groups at an affordable cost."[1] The various financial services include savings, credit, insurance and payments and remittance facilities. Growing global recognition of financial inclusion as a means to achieve sustainable inclusive growth led to the development of various concepts, models and schemes across the world. Among these, the concept of micro-finance stands apart as a widely accepted tool for financial inclusion. Self-Help Group-Bank Linkage Scheme, the Indian edition of micro-finance is one of the largest and successful models of its kind in the world. Given the context, the study attempts to highlight the relevance of SHG-Bank Linkage model by bringing out its benefits from both supply and demand side perspectives.

Self-Help Group (SHG)

SHGs are association of small groups of poor people who share some common socio- economic characteristics formed to fulfil the individual and collective goals through mutual help and joint responsibility. Members of SHG make regular contributions to the common fund and from which small loans are given to the needy members as per the decisions of the group. Considering the socio-economic state of women, this concept is more appropriate and functional for them. It helps to empower the women socially and economically.

SHG-Bank Linkage Model

As part of financial inclusion drive, NABARD-launched SHG bank linkage model in 1992 as a pilot project by linking 500 SHGs with banks. The main aim of this scheme was to enhance rural poor's access to formal financial system in a cost effective and sustainable manner by making use of SHGs. Through this, the poor are provided with hassle free timely finance and it is considered to be the best way to provide the credit to the people who need it the most. As per this scheme, the SHG is linked to a bank, where it can maintain an account to deposit the savings of its members and avail loan to disburse among them. The bank will sanction the loan on the basis of assessment of 15 point criteria prescribed by NABARD and normally the amount is arrived at 4 to 5 times of the total saving amount deposited with the bank. It has proved to be the most successful micro-finance model in the world in terms of outreach. For instance, by the end of March 2010, total number of SHGs linked to banks went up to 69.53 lakh, thus more than 97 million poor households in India were associated with this programme. As on 31st march, 2010, the total savings amount of SHGs with banks were Rs. 6198.71 crore and total amount of loans outstanding was Rs. 28038.28 crore.[2] There are three following models of linking SHGs with banks.

Model 1: Bank-SHG-Members	: The bank itself acts as a self-help group promoting institution (SHPI).
Model 2: Bank-Facilitating Agency-SHG-Members	: Facilitating NGOs, government agencies or other community-based organisations form groups.
Model 3: Bank-NGO-MFI-SHG-Members	: NGOs act as both facilitators and micro-finance intermediaries. First, they promote groups, nurture them, and train them, and then they approach banks for bulk loans for lending to the SHGs.

Dimensions of Financial Exclusion

Financial exclusion is a state where poorer members of society are excluded from formal financial services by not having access to basic products like deposit account, credit, insurance, payment and remittance facilities. In addition to the difficulty in having physical and geographical access to banking services, the various other dimensions of financial exclusion are:

Access Exclusion

The restriction of access through the processes of risk assessment.

Condition Exclusion

Where the conditions attached to financial products make them not suitable for the needs of poor people.

Price Exclusion

Where poor people can gain access to financial products only at affordable prices.

Marketing Exclusion

Whereby poor people are effectively excluded through targeted marketing and sales.

Self-exclusion

People may decide that there is little point in applying for a financial product because they believe that it will be refused.

SHG-Bank Linkage Model—Positive Aspects

Given the context, the study attempts to highlight the relevance of SHG-Bank Linkage model by bringing out its benefits from both supply and demand side perspectives.

Demand Side Perspectives

Demand side includes the members of SHGs and from their perspective, this scheme brings them following benefits.

1. *Access to financial services*: The members of SHGs get access to various financial services like savings, credit, etc. even without an account in their individual names.
2. *No physical collateral security*: The members can avail loan from banks through SHGs without any physical collateral security, a major hurdle faced by the poor in obtaining credit.
3. *Save cost*: As there is a single joint account for the group, the transaction cost will be less. Individual members can also save the traveling and other costs related with depositing their contributions as it is collected and deposited with the bank for the group as whole.
4. *Becomes a target group*: Becoming groups they proved themselves to be a profitable market segment for banks.
5. *Avoids self-exclusion*: Easy access to banking services and increased self-worth helps to avoid the case of self-exclusion resulting from the feeling that these services are not meant for them.
6. *Encourages thrift*: Instill the habit of thrift among members through regular and continuous savings.
7. *Affordable price*: Rate of interest charged for internal lending and external borrowings are much less in comparison to the private moneylenders, the alternatives available for them.

Supply Side Perspectives

Supply side includes the formal financial institutions, i.e. banks to which the SHGs are linked. From the perspective of banks, this scheme offers following benefits:

1. *Better coverage*: It gives the banks an opportunity to extend its financial services to the poor, who are not covered so far.

2. *Market at the BOP*: Banks can enjoy the market at the 'bottom of the pyramid' through serving the needs of poor profitably.[3]
3. *Improves liquidity*: The regular and collective contributions of many helps to improve the liquidity of banks.
4. *Cost effective*: A single account is kept in the name of SHG for the whole members; hence the transaction and maintenance costs will be less.
5. *High recovery rate*: The recovery rate of loans given to SHGs will be high as there is joint liability and peer group pressure among members for repayment. For example, in India, out of 302 banks which have reported the recovery data, 203 banks (67.2%) had more than 80% recovery of SHG loans as on 31 March 2010.[4]
6. *Re-finance and promotional support*: NABARD provides refinance support to banks to the extent of 100 per cent of the bank loans disbursed to SHGs. They are also given the grant assistance for promoting SHGs.
7. *CSR*: It gives an opportunity to perform the corporate social responsibility through banking functions itself.

CONCLUSION

Analysis of the positive aspects of SHG bank linkage programme from both supply and demand perspective shows that this model is highly beneficial for both sides. A close examination of individual benefits of this scheme from both sides clearly shows how it works against the various aspects of financial exclusion. In short, this model facilitates financial inclusion through lifting the hurdles, which in turn results in inclusive growth and development.

NOTES AND REFERENCES

1. Report of the Committee on Financial Inclusion, 2008, p. 1.
2. NABARD, Status of Micro-Finance in India, 2009-10, p. vi.
3. Financial Services Authority, "In or out? Financial Exclusion: a literature and research review", FSA, 2000, p. 9.
4. NABARD, *op. cit.*, p. ix.

Empowerment through Savings—Role of KSFE

VINEETH CHANDRA, K.S. AND RAJESH, T.

ABSTRACT

Non-banking companies also play a pivotal role in sphere of savings mobilization in rural areas. KSFE which was established in the year 1969 plays a vital role in the matter of savings mobilizations especially from rural areas. Its various chitty funds and deposit mobilization schemes helps the rural mass to enjoy the banking services. KSFE offer so many innovative schemes to attract the rural population. Through these schemes the banking habits among the rural community has been developed and it also helps them to provide funds for future needs. The present study is an attempt to evaluate the various policies adopted by KSFE in providing financial services to the rural population.

Indian economy in general and banking services in particular have made rapid strides in the recent past. However, a sizeable section of the population, especially the rural population and weaker sections continue to remain excluded from even the most basic opportunities and services provided by financial sector. A lack of savings facilities in rural areas creates problems at three levels: (i) the level of the individual; (ii) the level of the financial institution; and (iii) the level of the national economy.

At the level of the individual, the lack of appropriate institutional savings facilities forces the individual to rely upon in-kind savings such as savings in the form of gold, animals or raw materials, or upon informal financial money-keepers. These informal savings options, however, do not offer a combination of security of funds, ready access or liquidity, positive real return and convenience in order to meet the various needs of the particular saver.

At the institutional level, micro-finance institutions (MFIs) have microproducts service windows on both sides of the balance sheet, serving micro-and small savers and borrowers with an average savings balance or loan amount below the average per capita annual income in the respective countries. Yet the number of MFIs that exclusively offer credit is much larger than MFIs with both savings and credit facilities. Empirical studies have demonstrated that the performance records of credit-only MFIs in outreach and sustainability have not been widely successful. Those MFIs lacking effective savings mobilization strategies are unable to increase their outreach to a significant number of clients on a regional or national scale. In addition, few MFIs that do not mobilize savings have attained full financial self-sufficiency, independently covering their expenses for operations, loan loss, cost of funds and inflation with their revenues. Throughout the world, MFIs have often experienced that exclusively offering credit services can lead to undue dependency on external sources of financing. This dependency can cause the MFIs to concentrate on the demands of the donors rather than on the demands of potential clients, especially potential savings clients.

At the level of the national economy, high levels of savings increase the amount of national resources and decrease the need to resort to foreign indebtedness in order to cover domestic investment and consumption demand. Numerous countries with low internal savings rates must borrow from abroad, which results in a debt service burden. This clearly underlines the importance of savings mobilization to sustain economic growth with national financial resources.

OBJECTIVES OF THE STUDY

The study mainly concerned with analyzing and evaluating various saving mobilization scheme of KSFE in rural areas. In pursuance for this objectives the following sub-objectives have been set.

- To analyse various innovative savings mobilization schemes of KSFE.
- To evaluate how far these schemes are help in mobilizing savings and its effect on aggregate business on KSFE

ROLE OF KSFE IN SAVINGS MOBILISATION IN RURAL AREA

The Kerala State Financial Enterprises Limited (KSFE) was incorporated in November 1969 as a Government Company with a view to socializing Chitty business in the State, so as to ensure safety, security and better service to the public thereby protecting them from exploitation by private financial institution. The company also provides other facilities such as Chitty Loan. Gold Loan, Fixed Deposit Loan, Reliable Consumer Loan, Trade Loan, Hire purchase loan, Loans under new housing finance scheme and house modernizing scheme, special car loan, sugama savings deposit, akshaya deposit, Kerala Golden Jubilee Chitty (KGJC) scheme, etc to the public especially in rural areas. The company with an authorized capital of Rs. 25 crore and paid up capital of Rs. 10 crore earned and operational profit of Rs. 44.12 crore based on an annual turnover of Rs. 268.32 crore during 2005-06 as per the certified annual accounts.

Vision of KSFE

KSFE was established as government owned company in the year 1969 with the aim of establishing chit fund business inorder to inculcate the habit of thrift and mobilize savings from rural population. This establishment also envisaged to provide banking facility to the rural mass which were not met by ordinary commercial banks and other financial institutions. The vision of KSFE from its inception was focused on middle and low income rural people. Its vision statement is the following.

The vision of KSFE from its inception was focused on middle and low income rural people. Its vision statement is the following:

- Providing a whole range of quality services and products to the people especially in rural areas.
- Adopting technology and benchmark standards in customer service and performance.
- Spreading our wings beyond the borders of Kerala, on a global level.
- Retaining the pre-eminent role in Chitty business.
- Continuing focus on extending resources to the Govt. of Kerala.
- Sustaining commitment to the weaker sections of society especially rural people, as the neighbourhood institution for support, trust and security.

SCHEMES OF KSFE IN SAVINGS MOBILISATION FROM RURAL AREAS

Chitty Funds

The word 'Chit', suggests the origin of Chit Funds. 'Chit ' means a written note on a small piece of paper. In the Malayalam language, it is known as 'Kuri', which has been derived from 'Kurippu' (which means a piece of writing or script). The 'Chitty' or 'Kuri' is a derivative, the root being the 'lot'. The foreman writes the name of each subscriber on a small piece of paper and folds it several times with the name inside for the purpose of deciding the prize-winner. He calls it the 'Kuri' or 'Chit' or 'Narukku' and in the transaction, one 'Narukku' also means one member.

Unique Features of Chit Funds

Creating savings habits
A boom for the borrowers
Familiarity
Transparency and Accessibility

TABLE 1

Chitty Turnover

Year	*Urban*	*% of Change*	*Rural*	*% of Change*	*Total*	*% of Change*
2001-02	1152.6	100	298.55	100	1451.15	100
2002-03	1195.8	103	399.41	133	1595.21	109
2003-04	1287.4	111	359.58	120	1646.98	113
2004-05	1296.5	112	394.57	132	1691.07	135
2005-06	1348.7	117	438.1.	146	1786.8	123
2006-07	1487.4	129	505.57	169	1992.97	137
2007-08	1947.6	169	622.89	208	2570.49	177
2008-09	2267.6	196	1374.27	461	3641.87	251

The chitty turn for the last eight years have been depicted in Table 1. From the table it is clear that the total chitty over has increased 151% from the year 2001-02 to 2008-09. While analyzing the table we can found that the urban chitty turnover was increased 96% from the year 2001-02 but chitty turnover from rural areas shows a tremendous increase of 361%. Thus KSFE's various chitty schemes have helped the rural mass to inculcate the habit of savings

Deposit Mobilization

KSFE offer so many innovative schemes to attract the rural population. Through these schemes the banking habits among the rural community has been developed and it also helps them to provide funds for future needs.

Sugama Deposit Scheme

This scheme is quite comparable to the Savings bank deposits in banks, but of course, with marked difference in interest rates. Whereas the maximum interest offered by banks for this scheme is 3.5%, KSFE is offering 5.5%. This is undoubtedly the best offer in the financial service sector, among the deposit schemes belonging to the SB a/c category.

Fixed Deposit

This scheme has many features of the FDs in banks. But the returns are comparatively higher and the effective returns are really higher than the published interest rates, because of monthly payment of interest (in the case of all other institutions, the interest is paid quarterly). The annual interest rate in case of deposits from the public is 7% per annum. Interest for chitty prize money deposits is 8% per annum. Due to the monthly payment of interest, the effective rate will be higher than this rate. Senior citizen will get 7.25% for fresh deposits and 8% for prize money deposits.

Deposit-in-Trust Scheme

Deposit-in-Trust means the prize money, in full/part entrusted to the Company (depending on the future liability) by the prized subscriber of a chitty as security against future liability intending to withdraw the same on furnishing adequate alternate security or repayable on termination of the chitty. However, amount deposited under this scheme should not exceed the future liability in the chitty.

Sugama Security Scheme

The Sugama Security Scheme is intended for accepting amount outstanding in Sugama Deposits as security towards future liability in chitty and other schemes. The advantage under this scheme is that the advance will be secured and the monthly instalments can be adjusted from the account and at the same time the customers can enjoy interest income on the Sugama Deposit.

The total deposit mobilization of KSFE has been depicted in Table 2. In the table it is evidenced that total deposit mobilization from urban and rural areas taking together has increased 83%. While analyzing table it is clear that the deposit mobilsation from urban areas show an

TABLE 2

Total Deposit Mobilisation

Year	*Urban*	*% of Change*	*Rural*	*% of Change*	*Total*	*% of Change*
2001-02	1100.2	100	117.44	100	1217.64	100
2002-03	1287.3	117	142.38	121	1429.68	117
2003-04	1289.5	118	142.74	121	1432.24	118
2004-05	1188.6	108	117.41	100	1304.01	107
2005-06	1287.6	117	278.52	238	1566.12	128
2006-07	1327.5	120	369.33	315	1696.83	139
2007-08	1456.6	132	409.67	350	1866.27	153
2008-09	1567.8	142	668.95	570	2239.75	183

increase of 42% over the last eight years. But deposit mobilization from rural areas show a tremendous increase of 470%. It is through its various attractive schemes and innovative marketing strategies; KSFE is enabling to acquire this large amount of deposit from rural areas.

TABLE 3

Aggregate Business

Year	*Urban*	*% of Change*	*Rural*	*% of Change*	*Total*	*% of Change*
2001-02	2856.7	100	352.08	100	3208.78	100
2002-03	2967.3	103	567.76	161	3535.06	110
2003-04	2987.3	104	571.46	162	3558.76	111
2004-05	2985.2	104	567.56	161	3552.76	110.5
2005-06	3200.6	112	800.32	227	4000.92	124
2006-07	3576.9	125	963.46	273	4540.36	141
2007-08	4124.5	144	1338.13	380	5462.36	170
2008-09	5476.7	191	1689.02	479	7165.72	223

The aggregate business generated by KSFE for the last eight years has been depicted in Table 3. From the table it evidenced that the aggregate business of KSFE shows an increase of 123% over the last eight years. On analyzing the table it is known that the urban business shows an increases of 91% over the base year, but the rural business shows a bombastic increase of 379%. Thus KSFE conduct most of the business among rural people.

FINDINGS

KSFE has a large way of innovative schemes for attracting savings from rural areas.

KSFE through its various chitty programmes helps the rural mass in inculcating the habit of thrift and the rural mass are attracted to the various chitty fund schemes of KSFE.

Through the various innovative products and marketing strategies KSFE is able to attract a large amount deposit from rural areas.

KSFE conducts majority of the business among the rural population it generates most of their fund from the rural mass.

REFERENCES

Annual Report of KSFE 2001 to 2008.

Panikar, P.G.K., 1987, Rural household savings and investment, Trivandrum, Eds.

Pandit, B.L., The growth and structure of savings in India: An economic analysis; Bombay, Oxford University Press.

10

Financial Inclusion—Role of Primary Agricultural Societies

DR. DILEEP, A.S. AND G. THULASEEDHARAN

ABSTRACT

The banking sector in general, and the commercial banks and cooperative banks in particular, have achieved tremendous progress over years in terms of various parameters, such as growth of branches, deposits, asset creation and credit deployment. Their performance was highly admirable. Co-operative banks have been in existence for many decades. They play a crucial role in mobilising the savings of the rural households and also support the agricultural sector by meeting the credit needs of the farmers. The growth of rural-based activities is very much linked with the operations of these prestigious institutions of our country. Co-operative banks also extended their field of operation from rural to urban and semi-urban areas, marking a remarkable development in the field. The main intent of this study is to evaluate the role of primary agriculture credit societies in financial inclusion.

The banking industry has shown tremendous growth in volume and complexity during the last few decades. Despite making significant improvements in all the areas relating to financial viability, profitability and competitiveness, there are concerns that banks have not been able to include vast segment of the population, especially the underprivileged sections of the society, into the fold of basic banking services.

Internationally also efforts are being made to study the causes of financial exclusion and designing strategies to ensure financial inclusion of the poor and disadvantaged. The reasons may vary from country to country and hence the strategy could also vary but all out efforts are being made as financial inclusion can truly lift the financial condition and standards of life of the poor and the disadvantaged.

Financial Inclusion is the process of ensuring access to appropriate financial products and services needed by all sections of the society in general and vulnerable groups such as weaker sections and low income groups in particular at an affordable cost in a fair and transparent manner by mainstream institutional players.

In India the focus of the financial inclusion at present is confined to ensuring a bare minimum access to a savings bank account without frills, to all. Internationally, the financial exclusion has been viewed in a much wider perspective. Having a current account/savings account on its own, is not regarded as an accurate indicator of financial inclusion. There could be multiple levels of financial inclusion and exclusion. At one extreme, it is possible to identify the 'super-included', i.e., those customers who are actively and persistently courted by the financial services industry, and who have at their disposal a wide range of financial services and products. At the other extreme, we may have the financially excluded, who are denied access to even the most basic of financial products. In between are those who use the banking services only for deposits and withdrawals of money. But these persons may have only restricted access to the financial system, and may not enjoy the flexibility of access offered to more affluent customers.

CONSEQUENCES OF FINANCIAL EXCLUSION

It has been found that financial services are used only by a section of the population. There is demand for these services but it has not been provided. The excluded regions are rural, poor regions and also those living in harsh climatic conditions where it is difficult to provide these financial services. The excluded population then has to rely on informal sector (moneylenders, etc.) for availing finance that is usually at exorbitant rates. This leads to a vicious cycle. First, high cost of finance implies that first poor person has to earn much more than someone who has access to lower cost finance. Second, the major portion of the earnings is paid to the moneylender and the person can never come out of the poverty.

Consequences of financial exclusion will vary depending on the nature and extent of services denied. It may lead to increased travel requirements, higher incidence of crime, general decline in investment, difficulties in gaining access to credit or getting credit from informal sources at exorbitant rates, and increased unemployment, etc. The small business may suffer due to loss of access to middle class and higher-income consumers, higher cash handling costs, delays in remittances of money. According to certain researches, financial exclusion can lead to social exclusion

The banking sector in general, and the commercial banks and cooperative banks in particular, have achieved tremendous progress over years in terms of various parameters, such as growth of branches, deposits, asset creation and credit deployment. Their performance was highly admirable. Co-operative banks have been in existence for many decades. They play a crucial role in mobilising the savings of the rural households and also support the agricultural sector by meeting the credit needs of the farmers. The growth of rural-based activities is very much linked with the operations of these prestigious institutions of our country. Co-operative banks also extended their field of operation from rural to urban and semi-urban areas, marking a remarkable development in the field.

Generally, we associate the term Financial Inclusion with our initiatives of bringing poor people in the rural areas into the banking fold; however, we have to realize that there are still a large number of people in the urban area who are financially excluded. They have the need for availing the various types of banking services, especially the savings and money remittance services. This section of financially excluded people in the rural areas provides a good opportunity for the PACS to step in and fill this void.

OBJECTIVES OF THE STUDY

The main intent of this study is to evaluate the role of primary agriculture credit societies (PAC) in financial inclusion in financial inclusion.

Methodology

In pursuance of the above mentioned objective, the following methodology was adopted for conducting the study. The present study is of empirical nature and is based on secondary data. The secondary data for the present study have been collected from various publications of NABARD, NAFSCOB, National Co-operative Union, RBI, etc.

Glimpses of Performance of PACS

In order to assess the role of primary agricultural credit societies in financial inclusion the following variables are selected for an in-depth analysis. The variables thus selected for the analysis are:

Number of Branches
Amount of Deposits
Amount of Loans/Advances
Number of Branches

The co-operative banks carry out their operations through a wide net work of branches. They open branches in every nook and corner of the country in order to fulfil their obligation towards the targeted customers. The branch expansion of a business is an indicator of two important aspects-one is the efficiency in the operation and the other is the intensity of the coverage of the operation. Hence, the branch-wise expansion is a real indicator to assess the progress of primary agricultural credit societies in India.

TABLE I

Branch-wise Expansions of PACS

Year	*PACS*	
	Number of branches	*Annual percentage growth rate*
1999-00	91110	
2000-01	92300	1.31
2001-02	91588	-0.77
2002-03	93278	1.85
2003-04	93600	0.35
2004-05	93816	0.23
2005-06	100604	7.24
2006-07	95670	-4.90
2007-08	99000	3.48
2008-09	112309	13.44
Average annual growth rate	2.47	

Source: NAFCOB.

In a hurry to capture business and to fulfil the avowed objectives, it is the tendency of the co-operative banks to open more number of branches in different places of the country. Table 1 indicates these phenomena clearly. It also shows that the annual growth rate of PACS is upward, though fluctuating. It is true that during certain years a negative etrend is also visible. The re-organisation of many unviable units is the major contributing factor for this disturbing state of affair.

Amount of Deposits

Accepting deposits is the core function of a banking institution. Mobilising the scattered savings and channelising of the funds for various purposes, particularly for the organisation's growth agenda as well as for the overall development of the nation, constitute the basic objective of banking organisations. The amount of deposit makes the

TABLE 2

Total and Per Branch Deposit of PACS

Year	*PACS*			
	Total Deposits (Rs. In lakhs)	*Annual percentage of growth rate*	*Per Branch Deposit (Rs. In lakhs)*	*Annual percentage of growth rate*
1999-00	296177		3.25	
2000-01	385770	30.25	4.18	28.545
2001-02	611357	58.48	6.68	59.727
2002-03	672997	10.08	7.24	8.090
2003-04	703532	4.54	7.52	4.179
2004-05	720497	2.41	7.68	2.182
2005-06	1099616	52.62	10.93	42.321
2006-07	1313531	19.45	13.73	25.617
2007-08	1595522	22.47	16.12	17.382
2008-09	1943527	21.82	17.30	7.32
Average annual growth rate	22.48		19.87	

Source: NAFCOB.

balance-sheet of a banking organisation impressive and it is also a matter of attraction to those who monitor the functioning and progress of the bank and to those who have dealings with the bank. If deposits are on hike year after year, it is an indication that the bank is on the path of progress rather than on the way to failure or disaster.

Table 2 clearly discloses that the PACS play a significant role in mobilising deposits. During the period under study the total and per branch deposit mobilisation of PACS were remarkable and increasing.

Amount of Loans/Advances

Lending is one of the major activities of banking institutions. Advances constitute an important asset of the bank. Lending of money mobilised by way of deposits provides rhythm in the functioning and a better scope in the survival of banking institutions. Lending of money by banks also helps many needy borrowers to tackle their financial crisis. Through lending banks earn income for their survival and good reputation which are the bases of their growth. A banks progress can be well gauged by measuring the amount of advances made by it. A sizeable amount of advances naturally means the bank is better in its business and there is a hope for further expansion and growth. Table 3 gives a picture of total and per branch loan issued by PACS

TABLE 3

Total and Per Branch Loan Advances of PACS

Year	PACS			
	Total Loans (Rs. In lakhs)	*Annual percentage of growth rate*	*Per Branch Loan (Rs. In lakhs)*	*Annual percentage of growth rate*
1999-00	1079470		11.848	
2000-01	1204684	11.60	13.052	10.16
2001-02	1625279	34.91	17.746	35.96
2002-03	1793994	10.38	19.233	8.38
2003-04	1668626	-6.99	17.827	-7.31
2004-05	1902378	14.01	20.278	13.75
2005-06	2473857	30.04	24.590	21.27
2006-07	2932644	18.55	30.654	24.66
2007-08	3461077	18.02	34.960	14.05
2008-09	4480115	29.44	39.89	14.10
Average annual growth rate	15.82		13.28	

Source: NAFCOB.

The analysis, clearly points out that PACS play a significant role in performing the lending function effectively and efficiently. The overall lending performance of PACS is commendable. It is also observed that in certain years during the period of study there was progressing even though fluctuating, in the lending function of these three institutions.

FINDINGS

The number of branches of PACS was 91110 in 1999-2000. In 2008-09, it was 112309. During the period the number of branches of PACS grew at an average annual growth rate of 2.47 per cent.

There has been a continuous and steady increase in the amount of deposits of the PACS during the period under review. The average annual growth rate of deposit for the period indicates that the amount of deposit has been growing at an average annual growth rate of 22.48 per cent. The per branch growth rate of deposits of PACS is 19.87 per cent.

In respect of loan advancements, the performance of PACS is commendable. The average annual growth rate with respect to the amount of loan advancement during the study period was 15.82 per cent. The per branch growth for the same is 13.28 per cent. This indicated

PACS's strength as a good provider of finance and their role as mediators in disbursing huge amounts entrusted by the apex institutions to the needy borrowers.

CONCLUSION

The following are the major conclusion arrived at on the basis of findings of the study.

The number-wise growth of PACS is satisfactory. PACS spreading there branches considerably at higher pace.

In the midst of competition also PACS are able to mobilise sizeable amount of deposit from their customers. In the deposit mobilisation front PACS effort are commendable.

The involvement of PACS in providing loan to rural customers is very high and PACS is the major provider of loan to rural customers.

REFERENCES

Agarwal, B.P., 1981, Commercial Banking in India after Nationalisation, New Delhi: Classical Publishing Company.

Basu, K., 1971, Review of Current Banking: Theory and Practice, Calcutta: MacMillan.

Chopra, Kiran, Dr., 1997, Managing Profits, Profitability and Productivity in Public Sector Banking, Jalandhar: ABS Publications.

Mohapatra, G.P., 1997, Rural Bank for Rural Development, New Delhi: Discovery Publishing House.

Shekhar, K.C. and Shekhar, Lekshmi, 2005, Banking: Theory and Practice, New Delhi: Vikas Publishing House Private Limited.

Swabhiman Banking—A Leap to Financial Inclusion

VINOD, G. AND BIJU, S.K.

ABSTRACT

Even after the great effort and campaign from the Government, RBI and Banks, the real dream to make everyone the part of banking and financial dealing through banks that will further in turn accelerate the matter of development of economy and the individual concerned, could'nt achieve. It is a reality that more than 50% of the population is still outside the purview of banking. In this context the government launched a new nationwide campaign for financial inclusion, **Swabhiman**, aimed at bringing unbanked areas in to banking fold. *Swabhiman banking is a movement started by the Ministry of Finance, Government of India and the Indian Banks Association to bring banking within the reach of the masses of the Indian population. This movement helps the rural poor in banking activities like depositing, withdrawals, loan and small overdraft.* It is possible through any of the various forms of ICT-based models with the help of hand held machines, smart card and Business Correspondents. Though it has so many bottlenecks in the form of connectivity problem, illiteracy, etc. but the firm intention to achieve complete financial inclusion of the government can overcome.

Financial inclusion is a broad term but in simple words it means, credit for the poor, bank accounts for them and the discounted rate of interest.

Around 38% of banks have branches in rural India while a mere 40% of the country's population has bank accounts. The number of bank branches has risen from 8,700, at the time of bank nationalization in 1969, to around 85,300 presently. However, only 32,000 of these are in rural areas. The average population per bank branch is 13,900. That means 60% of the population is still away from banks, banking products and services and from the wide concept of financial inclusion.(RBI, 2010).

There are a number of reasons for keeping away the poor and illiterate rural folk from across the country from the meaning and the real spirit of financial inclusion campaign of the Nation. Even today there a large number in our country who are incapable to comply with the Know Your Customer (KYC) norm for opening an account. As per RBI norm while opening a new account the banker is required to observe the recent KYC guidelines.

The main purpose of introducing KYC norms in the late 1990s in the United States was to restrict money laundering and terrorist financing. The U.S. Government turned very strict after 9/11 and all regulations were finalised before 2002 for KYC.

In India inorder to prevent identity theft, identity fraud, money laundering, terrorist financing, etc., the RBI had directed all banks and financial institutions to put into practice a policy frame work to know their customers before opening any account. In 2004 RBI has issued the KYC guidelines under Section 35(A) of the Banking Regulation Act, 1949. The guidelines are divided into—

1. Customer acceptance policy
2. Customer identification procedures
3. Monitoring of transactions
4. Risk management

Customer Acceptance Policy

Before commencing a business relationship with a prospective customer, the bank has to ensure that no account is opened in anonymous or fictitious/benami names and customers are categorised based on risk perceptions in terms of the nature of business activity, location of customer, mode of payments, volume of turnover, social and financial status, etc.

Customer Identification

Customer identification means identifying the customer and verifying his or her or its identity by using reliable source documents, data or information. Customer identification is carried out at the time of:

1. Establishing banking relationship
2. Carrying out a financial transaction
3. When the banker has a doubt about the authority or adequacy of the previously obtained customer identification data.

   The following identification documents are to be submitted by the customers for opening a new savings or current account in the bank:

   1. The identity of the customer, his or her address, location
   2. Two copies of his or her recent photograph
   3. PAN (Permanent Account Number)

      Documents to be submitted for name proof photo identification—

      - Passport
      - Voters identity card
      - PAN card
      - Driving license
      - Government or defense identity card
      - ID cards of reputed employers
      - Letter from a recognised public authority or public servant.

The originals should be submitted for verification and attested copy should be kept along with the account opening form.

Documents to be submitted for address proof:

- Telephone bill
- Bank account statement
- Income or wealth tax assessment order
- Credit card statement
- Electricity bill
- Ration card
- Letter from employer

So if this is the case it would be simply impossible to bring everyone to the meaning of financial inclusion and even at to open a bank account. As we know in our country a large number are not having a house of their own, an Id proof, address proof, photo Id and so on to satisfy the KYC norm. In one side there are norms and on the other side we are talking about financial inclusion. More over poor and illiterate rural folk is always reluctant to visit and deal with the bank and its services. Their financial transactions end with the moneylenders of their locality. Once they reluctant to visit the bank, the bank should visit and reach to them and if they are incapable to satisfy the KYC norm and without violating the same, how they can be brought to the purview of bank and its products and services. It was the thinking of both administrators and academicians in this respect. Swabhiman banking is one of the solutions in the way to bring those who reluctant and incapable to satisfy the banking norm towards banking and the campaign of financial inclusion.

SWABHIMAN BANKING

Swabhiman banking is a movement on track by the Ministry of Finance, Government of India and the Indian Banks Association to bring banking within the reach of the masses of the Indian population. "Swabhiman"—Swabhiman (pronounced as swaa-bhi-maan) meaning self-respect comes from Swa-(meaning Self) and—abhiman (meaning Respect or Pride) in Sanskrit language, a nationwide programme on financial inclusion, estimated to cover approximately 5 crore households, is now ready for roll out. The BANK SAATHI (the business correspondent) visits the customers at their door steps or at a common meeting place where the banking transactions take place. He collects deposits, gives small overdraft, loans and facilitates withdrawals. He keeps a small machine with him for customer identification feeded with the bio-metric finger identity of all the ten fingers. As most of them are working in the field they can use any finger for identification. The machine also facilitate for effecting the transaction as well. The business correspondent called bank saathi remits the collection to his bank on the next day morning.

The government has planned financial 'Swabhiman'—a program to ensure banking facilities in habitation with a population in excess of 2000, by March 2012. The program will use various models and technologies, including branchless banking through business correspondents. The government launched a new nationwide campaign for financial inclusion, Swabhiman, aimed at bringing unbanked areas in to banking fold. The idea is to transform the programme into a broad-based political movement. Through the financial inclusion programme, the government seeks to enlarge banking services spread into the selected 73,000 villages having population up to 2000, by March, 2012. The idea behind the campaign is not only to create awareness among the nearly 4 crore beneficiaries of the programme, but also to spread financial literacy. Swabhiman is path-breaking initiative by Government of India (GoI) and banks in state to cover the economic distance between rural and urban India. It promises to bring basic banking services to all unbanked villages in the country with population above 2000. The swabhiman movement facilitate opening of bank accounts, provide need based credit, remittance facilities and help to promote financial literacy in rural India using various models and technologies including branchless banking models through Business correspondents.

Through the Swabhiman programme, Government is not only concerned about opening of nearly 4 crore no-frills accounts in the country. The Government also want that there must be transactions through those accounts to make it a huge success. Through Swabhiman, the banks can look at launching their services like small overdraft facility, remittance, small loans and small deposits to increase their current account and savings bank account. Finally, the Government expects the banks to adopt the route to popularise the electronic benefit transfer (EBT) scheme too, through which the government makes payments to the workers involved in various government-run schemes by way of smart cards.

Swabhiman—Our Account Our Pride was launched by Smt. Sonia Gandhi, the Chairperson of the UPA in the presence of Shri Pranab Mukherjee, the Union Finance Minister on February 10, 2011. It is the campaign started by the Ministry of Finance, GoI and the Indian Banks Association (IBA) to bring banking within the reach of the masses of the Indian population. This campaign or the movement is started to promote banking facilities and basic banking services to 73,000 villages in the country which are not served by any bank so far.

Mr. Pranab Mukherjee (the Finance Minister of GoI) says that the finance ministry expects to cover at least 73,000 new habitations, with a population of 2000 and above, and we will open at least 5 crores new accounts. "The business correspondents will help reach banking facilities to these interior areas, through technologies that reduce cost and have the ability to record banking transactions and to communicate the record of such transactions, to the bank using the internet facilities and GPRS," he states.

The aim of the government is to bring a bank within the reach of every village with a population of over 2000 by the end of March, 2012. The bank in the village will facilitate the opening of an account by a villager. It will provide a need-based credit to the villagers. Remittance facilities to transfer funds from one place to another will also be the part of the banking services to these villagers. The main objective of the government is to promote and bring about a financial literacy in rural parts of India. New computer based technology connecting all the banks with one another in the country, is going to play a very important role in this campaign. The other partners in promoting this gigantic programme will be our newspapers and the electronic media carrying the news of this programme to even the remote corners of the country.

The business correspondents and writers will play a great role in this mammoth campaign launched for promoting the banking sector with a social outlook. This great initiative of the government of India and the Indian Banks Association to cover up the gap between the rural and urban India is going to complete the banking revolution which started in our country in the sixties by nationalising the banks and giving them a social outlook. This will be a path-breaking achievement of the government to help the rural masses of India.

Swabhiman Banking—Targets and Strategies

Under the programme, it is proposed to open five crores new rural bank accounts. Opening accounts for so many illiterate and semi literate people of rural India is apparently going to test the mettle and perseverance of the banking officials. The banking sector has also to ensure that banking transactions are safe and secure. The linking of the rural population with the urban markets will be a great achievement of this revolutionary campaign. It is reported that the banking will be taken door to door through business correspondents who will be called **'Bank Saathi (Friend)'.**

Taking into account of the illiterate nature of the rural people, the procedures for opening the bank accounts will be simplified. Facilities of easy access to credit and saving products will be provided under this scheme. There will be a speedy transfer of funds and payment of government subsidies and other developmental funds allotted by the government from time to time for the rural sector. The social security benefits can be directly transferred to the beneficiary accounts removing the operations of middlemen who loot the illiterate rural population before the benefits finally reach them. The scheme will also promote the micro-insurance and micro-pension plans for the villagers. Financial Inclusion is an important priority of the Government as only about 38 per cent of the 85,292 bank branches of Scheduled Commercial Banks are in rural areas and only 40 per cent of the country's population has bank accounts. To address this need, the GoI has directed all banks to provide appropriate banking facilities to habitations having population in excess of 2000 by March, 2012 using various models and technologies including branchless banking through Business Correspondents (BCs). The banks have formulated their road maps for Financial Inclusion and have identified about 73,000 habitations having a population of over 2000 for providing banking in India.

SWABHIMAN—Maharashtra Experience

RBI on the basis of recommendations of High Level Committee on Lead Bank Scheme directed lead banks to draw a road map by March 2010 to provide banking services through a banking outlet in every village having a population of over 2000, by March 2012 and further stated that such banking services may not necessarily be through a brick and mortar branch but can be provided through any of the various forms of ICT-based models with the help of hand held machines, smart card and Business Correspondents.

In view of the above, SLBC (include the full form first then use it) has taken various steps/initiatives for preparation of Financial Inclusion Plan (FIP) for providing banking services in every village having a population of over 2000 as below:

All Lead District Managers (LDMs) were advised to constitute a Sub-Committee of the District Consultative Committee to draw a roadmap for Financial Inclusion for each district. All LDMs have been provided list of villages having population over 2000 in the state as per census 2001 and finalise the allocation of villages to bank branches in each district by sub-committee of DLCC. The allocation of unbanked villages is to be done on lines erstwhile service area guidelines, proximity to bank branches and contiguity of villages, etc. and submit the final list of unbanked villages and their allocation to bank branches to SLBC for approval. As per census 2001, there are 7312 villages in the state having population above 2000, of which 4292 villages have been identified as unbanked in the state. The same was allocated to various banks in state and approved by SLBC.

The Bank-wise summary of number of identified villages having population above 2000 for providing banking services, targets of public sector, private sector and RRBs are given at end of this paper.

FINANCIAL INCLUSION—ROLE OF STATE GOVERNMENT

High Level Committee on Lead Banks in its final recommendations has also emphasized the importance of role of State Governments to be played in FI process as below:

- In extending necessary support to achieve the objective of FI ranging from ensuring conducive law and order situation, water supply and irrigation facilities, road and digital connectivity, developing proper land records, to assisting in the identification process, publicity drives, recovery, etc.
- In centers where bank branches are required as per public policy for general banking, currency, forex and government business, but banks are constrained to open the branches due to lack of infrastructure, absence of viability and security concerns, State Governments will need to extend support by providing premises, security, etc.
- Since State Governments are also keen to disburse MGNREGA and social security funds through bank

accounts, banks should explore partnership with them and State Governments should also be able to leverage on the benefits of undertaking government business accruing to banks to incentivize their involvement in Government sponsored schemes and Programmes.

Swabhiman, though is in planning stage, has some assured benefits for the common man. A common man can now be included in the organized financial sector without the tedious paperwork. It will not only ensure availing of a variety of financial services at doorstep but also easy enrolment to all public welfare schemes. Reaching out at such a grand scale can face a number of challenges that are meticulous in nature. Ranging from connectivity of handheld devices, geographical connectivity to literacy rate of the population can raise issues in smooth implementation of the program. But, tackling these challenges and bottlenecks is now expected from Indian Government.

A. Public Sector Banks

Sr. No.	*Name of the Bank*	*No. of unbanked villages*	*Sr. No.*	*Name of the Bank*	*No. of unbanked villages*
1.	Allahabad Bank	33	11.	Indian Overseas BK	21
2.	Andhra Bank	01	12.	Oriental Bank of Commerce	06
3.	Bank of Baroda	176	13.	Punjab National Bank	26
4.	Bank of India	506	14.	State Bank of Hyderabad	215
5.	Bank of Maharashtra	853	15.	State Bank of India	855
6.	Canara Bank	40	16.	Syndicate Bank	50
7.	Central Bank of India	436	17.	Union Bank of India	189
8.	Corporation Bank	03	18.	UCO Bank	23
9.	Dena Bank	158	19.	Vijaya Bank	03
10.	Indian Bank	11	20	IDBI	82
Total (1 to 10)		2217	Total (11 to 20)		1470
Total villages for Public Sector Banks			3687		

B. Regional Rural Banks

Sr. No.	*Name of the Bank*	*No. of unbanked villages*
1.	Maharashtra Gramin Bank	355
2.	Vidarbh Kshetriya Gramin Bank	63
3.	Wainganga Krishna Gramin Bank	92
Total villages for RRBs		510

C. Private Sector Banks

Sr. No.	*Name of the Bank*	*No. of unbanked villages*	*Sr. No.*	*Name of the Bank*	*No. of unbanked villages*
1.	HDFC	01	4.	Ratnakar Bank	21
2.	ICICI Bank	72	5.	Karnataka Bank Ltd.	01
Total (1 to 2)		73	Total (4 to 5)		22
Total villages for Private Sector Banks			95		

D. The District-wise Summary of Number of Identified Unbanked Villages is given as below:

Sr. No.	*Name of the District*	*No. of villages having population above 2000*	*No. of unbanked villages*	*Sr. No.*	*Name of the District*	*No. of villages having population above 2000*	*No. of unbanked villages*
1.	Ahmednagar	540	296	17.	Nagpur	127	62
2.	Akola	109	59	18.	Nanded	345	206
3.	Amravati	164	103	19.	Nandurbar	128	104
4.	Aurangabad	234	127	20.	Nasik	424	273
5.	Bhandara	129	94	21.	Osmanabad	181	132
6.	Beed	211	129	22.	Parbhani	129	76
7.	Buldhana	232	148	23.	Pune	424	276
8.	Chandrapur	138	66	24.	Raigad	142	103
9.	Dhule	198	130	25.	Ratnagiri	133	101
10.	Gadchiroli	72	44	26.	Sangli	316	135
11.	Gondia	132	96	27.	Satara	360	186
12.	Hingoli	86	52	28.	Sindhudurg	70	47
13.	Jalgaon	377	135	29.	Solapur	467	261
14.	Jalna	144	92	30.	Thane	288	209
15.	Kolhapur	378	212	31.	Wardha	90	37
16.	Latur	240	154	32. 33.	Washim Yavatmal	94 210	54 93
Grand Total of villages			7312			4292	

Summary of Allocation to Banks

Sr. No.	*Particulars*	*No. of unbanked villages*		*% to total villages*
1.	Public Sector Banks	3687		85.90
2.	Regional Rural Banks	510		11.88
3.	Private Sector Banks	95		02.22
Total:		4292	100.00	

References

Banking and Financc Theory, Law and Practice—Clifford Gomez.
Banking Theory, Law and Practice—Gordan Natarajan.
Swabhiman Our Account Our Pride—G.S. Oinam.
The Financial Express 5th and 8th May 2012.
www.bankofmaharashtra.in
www.sify.com
www.moneycontrol.com

12

Signifinance of Financial Inclusion in Enriching Downtrodden Section of the People

DR. S. JAYADEV, JAYAKRISHNAN, AND SIJU SEBASTIAN

ABSTRACT

Globally, over one billion poor people are still without access to formal financial service and 200 million of them are living in India. In spite of the phenomenal outreach of formal credit institutions, the rural poor still depend upon the informal sources of credit. Two major causes for this are the large number of small borrowers with small and frequent needs. In addition, the ability of these borrowers to provide collateral is very limited. Besides, a considerable number of them live in the rural area and are very poor. A considerable gap is exists between demand and supply for all financial services in our state too. The present formal financial sector is unable to bridge this gap because of its long and cumbersome formalities coupled with rules and regulations and their risk perception have been limiting factors.

INTRODUCTION

Finance is the art and science of managing money. The word finance comes from the Latin word 'Finis'. It is the management of money. In the modern sense, using economy, finance may be defined as the provision of money at the time it is wanted. Financial inclusion, banking to all, is a recent global phenomenon suggested by Nobel Prize winnèr Dr. Mohammad Yunus of Bangladesh in the 1980's. Before Dr. Mohammad Yunus, the poor were not allowed to access to credit and loans due to the pervasive belief that the poor could not repay the loan. Dr. Yunus' project, Grameen Bank, began with loans of less than $50 to poor basket weavers in Bangladesh. In past 30 years Grameen Bank has grown over to 3.7 million borrowers worldwide with a 98% repayment rate, higher than any commercial bank. Dr. Yunus has proven that the poor are indeed responsible enough to manage credit and repay loans.

WOMEN AND FINANCIAL INCLUSION

"When women move forward, the family moves, the village moves and the nation moves" words of Jawaharlal Nehru about the status of women that is closely associated with their economic position, which in turn depends upon their access to productive resources of the country and the opportunities for participation in economic activities. Women's participation in work force in India is only 25.68% of the female population. So many problems of women are due to lack of financial independence.

However, the governmental and non-governmental Institutions in India began to play an important role in mobilizing women, brought in rural and urban areas to become economically strong by providing income-generating programmes, training and employment. A woman should have a vision for herself, her children, her home, rather than just being course and concerned about the meals and pleasing her husband. Thus, availability of finance to women ensures that the resources and profits generated are ploughed back into the development of the immediate household and family. Protection of family values, health and safety of household members and a more even distribution of income can be seen as a result. In addition to this, under privileged sections in rural and urban areas like farmers, small vendors, agriculture and industrial labourers, people engaged in unorganised sectors, unemployed children, old people and physically challenged people are the beneficiary of financial inclusion.

NEED AND SIGNIFICANCE OF THE STUDY

Globally, over one billion poor people are still without access to formal financial service and 200 million of them are living in India. In spite of the phenomenal outreach of formal credit institutions, the rural poor still depend upon the informal sources of credit. Two major causes for this are the large number of small borrowers with small and frequent needs. In addition, the ability of these borrowers to provide collateral is very limited. Besides, a considerable number of them live in the rural area and are very poor. A considerable gap is exists between demand and supply for all financial service in our state too. The present formal financial sector is unable to bridge this gap because of its long and cumbersome formalities coupled with rules and regulations and their risk perception have been limiting factors. Consequently, many people living in rural areas, especially socially and economically weaker sections, have no access to credit due to lack of security. Some people are reluctant to access bank facilities because of their belief in the religion. Traditionally, banks have usually not provided financial service to clients with little or no cash income. Banks incur substantial cost to manage the client's accounts, regardless of how small the sum of money involved. Nevertheless, the fixed cost of processing loan of any size is considerable; assessment of potential borrowers, their repayment prospectus and security: administration of outstanding loan and collecting from delinquent borrower create headache to banks. Moneylenders will exploit this vulnerable situation and it will make an awful end of the poor people, by charging exorbitant interest to poor people than others. Therefore, poor people are born in debt, live in debt and die in debt. To avoid this situation, Financial inclusion has emerged as the most suitable and practical alternative in reaching the hitherto untapped poor population and will improve the standard of living of the downtrodden section of the society.

Thus, it is essential to explore the outcome of the financial inclusion in the overall improvement of the society in Kerala, especially of the weaker and oppressed sections. Unless financial and collective inclusion takes place in an effective way, our State cannot attain affluence in its true sense. This can be accomplished through the provision of thrift, credit and other financial services and products of very small amount to the poor in rural, semi-urban and urban areas for enabling them to raise their income levels, and improve their living standard in the State of Kerala. How far it has been successful among the beneficiaries? How far the present financial inclusion schemes benefited this cause? What are the hurdles, if any, in achieving this objective? What are the corrective actions to be taken for the smooth and paced accomplishment of these schemes? A meaningful study undertaken through a detailed analysis can throw light on the shortcomings of the effectiveness of financial inclusion in Kerala.

WHAT IS FINANCIAL INCLUSION?

Financial inclusion is delivery of banking services at an affordable cost to the vast sections of disadvantaged and low income groups.

Unrestrained access to public goods and services is the *sine qua non* of an open and efficient society. As banking services are in the nature of public good, it is essential that availability of banking and payment services to the entire population without discrimination is the prime objective of the public policy. Economic history reveals that broad-based financial inclusion is a precondition for the transition of an agrarian system to industrial system. Access to financial services helps to the poor to-insure them against income shock and equip them to meet emergencies like illness or loss of employment. It enables to obtain a range of appropriate financial products and financial services to under privileged sections at an affordable cost. Also financial inclusion is necessary for generating equitable sustainable inclusive growth and thereby economic opportunity can be equally divided to the downtrodden sections of the mass.

THE SCOPE OF FINANCIAL INCLUSION

When bankers do not give the desired attention to certain areas, the regulators have to step in to remedy the situation. This is the reason why the Reserve Bank of India is placing a lot of emphasis on financial inclusion. In India the focus of the financial inclusion at present is confined to ensuring a bare minimum access to a savings bank account without frills, to all. Internationally, the financial exclusion has been viewed in a much wider perspective. Having a current account/savings account on its own, is not regarded as an accurate indicator of financial inclusion. There could be multiple levels of financial inclusion and exclusion. At one extreme, it is possible to identify the 'super-included', i.e., those customers who are actively and persistently courted by the financial services industry, and who have at their disposal a wide range of financial services and products. At the other extreme, we may have the financially excluded, who are denied access to even the most basic of financial products. In between are those who use the banking services only for deposits and withdrawals of money. But these persons may have only restricted access to the financial system, and may not enjoy the flexibility of access offered to more affluent customers.

CONSEQUENCES OF FINANCIAL EXCLUSION

Consequences of financial exclusion will vary depending on the nature and extent of services denied. It may lead to increased travel requirements, higher incidence of crime, general decline in investment, difficulties in gaining access to credit or getting credit from informal sources at exorbitant rates, and increased unemployment. The small business may suffer due to loss of access to middle class and higher-income consumers, higher cash handling costs, delays in remittances of money. According to certain researchers, financial exclusion can lead to social exclusion.

STEPS TOWARDS FINANCIAL INCLUSION

In the context of initiatives taken for extending banking services to the small man, the mode of financial sector development until 1990's was characterized by a hugely expanded bank branch coupled with cooperative network and new organizational forms like RRBs;a greater focus on credit rather than other financial services like savings and insurance. Although the banks and cooperatives did provide deposit facilities; lending the target groups as directed in the 'priority sectors' like agriculture and other allied sectors were not satisfactory. Hence, priority sector lending especially to weaker sections of the population, coupled with interest rate ceilings; significant government subsidies channeled through the banks and cooperatives, as well as through related government programmes; a dominant perspective that finance for rural and poor people was a social obligation and not a potential business opportunity. The following table shows No. of Kisan Cards issued by Cooperative banks and RRBs against the amount of loan disbursed.

From the table it is clear that the performance of cooperative

Number of Kisan Cards Distributed and Amount Disbursed by Banks

Year	*Cooperatives*		*RRBs*	
	No. of cards issued (Lakhs)	*Amount (Lakhs)*	*No. of cards issued (Lakhs)*	*Amount (Lakhs)*
2005 -06	25.98	20339	12.49	8483
2006 -07	22.98	13141	14.06	7373
2007 -08	20.91	20492	17.73	9074
2008 -09	13.44	13172	14.14	7632
2009 -10	15.67	18654	15.22	8214

Source: SLBC, Kerala.

banks and RRBs in terms of cards issued and amount issued are only satisfactory. Therefore, steps should be taken to accelerate the pace of the banking function in this regard.

The banks should come out of inhibited feeling that very aggressive competition policy and social inclusion are mutually exclusive. As demonstrated elsewhere, the mass banking with no-frills account can become a win-win situation for both. Basically banking services need to be "marketed" to connect with large population segments and these may be justifiable promotional costs. The opportunities are plenty especially in the context of India becoming one of the largest micro-finance markets in the world. The following table shows change in bank deposit in Kerala.

From the table it is clear that the amount of bank deposit in

Change in Bank Deposit in Kerala

Deposit (crore)	*2007*	*2008*	*2009*	*2010*
Domestic Deposit	60581	76793	96781	109333
NRI Deposit	31995	31865	37983	38036
Total	92576	108658	134764	147369
% of share of Domestic Deposit	65.44	70.69	71.82	74.19

Source: SLBC, Kerala.

Kerala is on increase throughout the period under study. From the year 2007 it is 65.44% of the total deposit, whereas in the period 2010 the amount of bank deposit in Kerala has been ascended to 74.19%, a growth of 9.85%.

The IBA may explore the possibility of a survey about the coverage in respect of financial inclusion keeping in view the geographical spread of the banks and extent of financial services available to the population so as to assess the constraints in extension of financial services to hitherto unbanked sections and for initiating appropriate policy measures.

It may be useful for banks to consider franchising with other segments of financial sector such as cooperatives, RRBs and Postal Department so as to extend the scope of financial inclusion with minimal intermediation cost. Sector wise no-frills accounts opened in banks are shown below.

From the table it is clear that Sector-wise No. of No-frills

Sector-wise Number of No-frills Accounts Opened in Banks

Banks	*March 2006*	*March 2007*	*March 2008*	*March 2009*
Public Sector Banks	332875	5865419	13909935	18407516
Private Sector Banks	156388	860997	1845869	2487569
Foreign Banks	231	5919	33115	55618
Total	489097	6732335	15788919	20950703

Source: SLBC, Kerala.

accounts opened in Banks in Kerala is on increase throughout the period under study. This shows the active involvement by commercial banks with respect to no-frills accounts.

Since large sections of low income groups transactions are related to deposits and withdrawals, with a view to containing transaction costs, 'simple to use' cash dispensing and collecting machines akin to ATMs, with operating instructions and commands in vernacular would greatly facilitate financial inclusion of the semi-urban and rural populace. In this regard, it is worthwhile to emulate the example of 'e-Choupal' project brought forth through private sector initiative.

CONCLUSION

It is becoming increasingly apparent that addressing financial exclusion will require a holistic approach on the part of the banks in creating awareness about financial products, education, and advice on money management, debt counseling, savings and affordable credit. The banks would have to evolve specific strategies to expand the outreach of their services in order to promote financial inclusion. One of the ways in which this can be achieved in a cost-effective manner is through forging linkages with micro-finance institutions and local communities. Banks should give wide publicity to the facility of no frills account. Technology can be a very valuable tool in providing access to banking products in remote areas. ATMs cash dispensing machines can be modified suitably to make them user friendly for people who are illiterate, less educated or do not know English. To sum up, banks need to redesign their business strategies to incorporate specific plans to promote financial inclusion of low income group treating it both a business opportunity as well as a corporate social responsibility. They have to make use of all available resources including technology and expertise available with them as well as the MFIs and NGOs. It may appear in the first instance that taking banking to the sections constituting "the bottom of the pyramid", may not be profitable but it should always be remembered that even the relatively low margins on high volumes can be a very profitable proposition. Financial inclusion can emerge as commercial profitable business. Achievement of inclusive growth depends on the attainment of dependency of financial inclusion. Bring one and all under the ambit of banking services irrespective of caste, class creed and occupation. Saving tendency can be augmented only when they learn the lessons of creating a surplus after the day-to-day subsistence and banks can chalk out credit schemes to such sections for creating a surplus after meeting their subsistence. Only the banks should be prepared to think outside the box!

References

Banerjee, Amalesh (1993), The impact of new economic policy on agricultural labour, *Indian Journal of Agricultural Extension*, 48(3), 471-76.

Bansil, P.C. (1971), Short-term credit requirement at the end of the Fourth Plan, 1973-74. *Indian Journal of Agricultural Economics*, 26: 467-73.

Bhagyalekshmi, J. (2001), New initiatives for poverty alleviation, *Yojana*, 45: 12-13.

Birdar, B.R., and Jayasheela (2000). Rural finance: A village study, *Kurukshetra*, 43: 19-25.

Christabell, P.J. (2001), Role of micro-finance institutions in development process, Department of Economics, University of Kerala, Kariavattom.

Gulati, Leela (1990), Agricultural workers' pension in Kerala: An experiment in social assistance, *Economic and Political Weekly*, 339-43.

NABARD (2001), NABARD and micro-finance, Micro-Credit Innovations Department, NABARD, Mumbai.

13

Financial Inclusion for Inclusive Growth: Role of Commercial Banks

PROMOD GOPAL

ABSTRACT

The inclusive growth as a strategy of economic development received attention owing to a rising concern that the benefits of economic growth have not been equitably shared. Growth is inclusive when it creates economic opportunities along with ensuring equal access to them. Financial Inclusion is integral to the inclusive growth process and sustainable development of the country. Financial inclusion denotes delivery of financial services at an affordable cost to the vast sections of the disadvantaged and low income groups. The objective of the financial inclusion is to extend the scope and activities of organized financial system. It should be capable to eradicate the poverty among poor people. Then only the development is possible.

Financial Inclusion is intended to connect people with banks. Banks play an important role in inclusive growth. Banks are the key pillars of India's financial system. Commercial banks are now slowly coming to appreciate the business potential in financial inclusion and also the need for better involvement. Commercial Banks providing basic banking services to the rural people through these low cost devices, without the concomitant costs associated with setting up of an Extension Counter/ATM or a Branch and thus aiming to bring down significantly the transaction costs in rural banking. The Bank developed the new operating model to cover a large number of un-banked villages.

Mr. Janamejava Sinha (Chairman, CII task force on Financial Inclusion) set a five-point agenda for financial inclusion, which called for:

(i) increasing overall consciousness of the need for financial inclusion;
(ii) increase in wireless and broadband connectivity in the rural areas to support rural banking;
(iii) spread of financial literacy programmes;
(iv) greater experimentation for financial inclusion through business correspondents, self-help groups, etc.; and
(v) greater collaboration between the key stakeholders in the banking system.

We have moved a long way from the time when the bank was mere deposit taking and money lending institutions and managed by people whose aim was maximum profit with minimum risk. This old concepts and methods replaced and new strategies are developed by the Commercial Banks. This also paved the way for industrial development.

As the dream of Mahatma Gandhi, Commercial banks give greater considerations to the rural areas. As a result, number of branches established in rural areas. Here we have separately considered the Public Sector banks and Private Sector banks. We have 27 public sector banks that constitute strong public sector Indian commercial banking. They include SBI and 7 subsidiaries. These controlled 85% of total deposit of our country. Private sector banks cover 32 scheduled and 3 non-scheduled banks that control 10% of total deposits. All these banks are established as per the special guidelines issued by RBI. In order to expand Banking services, Commercial banks started number of branches in different regions of our country.

Number of Branches of Scheduled Commercial Banks, March 2009

Bank	*Group population group*				
	Rural	*Semi-urban*	*Urban*	*Metropolitan*	*Total*
SBI and Associates	5562	4858	3407	2931	16758
Nationalised Banks	13388	8732	9487	9177	40784
Foreign Banks	4	4	53	234	295
Regional Rural Banks	11636	2833	823	100	15392
Other Scheduled					
Commercial Banks	1114	2664	2841	2591	9210
All Scheduled Banks	31704	19091	16611	15033	82439

Source: RBI Branch Banking Statistics, March 2009.

Effect of Nationalisation of Commercial Bank

After nationalisation Commercial Banks started playing an inevitable role in the economic development of a country. Nationalisation enabled to channalise bank credit to priority sectors like agriculture, S.S.I., exports, extend banking facilities to unbanked rural areas. It gives a professional bent to bank management. After nationalization commercial banks have been successfully in establishing branches even in remote and backward areas of the country. Improved banking habits of people led to generation of more deposit by commercial bank. Commercial banks adopted a new policy known as social banking to meet socio-economic obligation of the country. After nationalization commercial banks started investing their funds in government and other approved securities to meet their liquidity requirements. Through this, banks made their funds available to government for meeting the plan requirements. The Government of India has used the public sector banks to finance its pet programmes such as Village Adoption Scheme, IRDP, Swarnajayanthy Gram Swarosgar Yojana (SGSY), etc.

Innovative Services Provided by Commercial Bank

For the effective financial and economic development banks develops wide veriety of innovative services.

Core Banking is the product of revolution in IT Sector. WAN encouraged banking sector to introduce core banking with a view to improve customer service. Under core banking, the database for the whole bank is maintained at Central point. The customers can transact their business through any branch of the Bank. The data can be accessed from any part of the world through internet. Customers can save their valuable time.

Tele Banking considers customers queries and responded over telephone with voice processing facility. In this system, computers at the bank are connected to a telephone link with the help of modem. Voice printing facility is provided in the software. This software identifies the voice of the caller and provides suitable reply.

E-cheque is an electronic image of a paper cheque. It is signed compulsorily using digital signals of drawer. It can be forwarded by the drawer to any person for payment. It is an anytime cheque. It is a boon to e-banking. It facilitates performing of banking transactions around the clock.

ATM Cards was introduced for 24 hours banking services to customers. It is a computerised telecommunications device that provides the clients of a financial institution with access to financial transactions in a public space without the need for a cashier. This is a plastic card which bears the customer's name, signature and card number. It provides update statements immediately after every transaction. Banks have started dispensing Railway Tickets, Air Tickets, Movie Tickets, etc. through ATMs. Voice activated ATMs, ATMs with finger print scanning technology etc are on the move. In future, a bank's ATM would function like a kiosk delivering more on non-cash transactions,thereby reducing fixed and operating costs.

The acronym 'RTGS' stands for Real Time Gross Settlement, which can be defined as the continuous (real-time) settlement of funds transfers individually on a order by order basis. Under RTGS system payments are cleared singly and bilaterally as they occur. When a payment message is moved through the clearing house, the paying bank's account with the RBI is simultaneously debited and credited in the receiving Bank's account. There is a certainty of payment and the receiving Bank can credit the beneficiary's account immediately and allow full use of funds. Faster fund transfer fecilitates better fund transfer and inventory management.

National Electronics Funds Transfer System (NEFT) is an electronic fund transfer system that operates on a Deferred Net Settlement (DNS) basis which settles transactions in batches. In DNS, the settlement takes place with all transactions received till the particular cut-off time. These transactions are netted (payable and receivables) in NEFT. It is a Nationwide system that facilitates individuals, Firms and Corporate to electronically transfer funds from any branch bank to pay any individual, Firms and Corporate having an account with any other bank branch in the country. It is possible only through NEFT enabled bank branches.

A debit card (also known as a bank card or check card) is a plastic card that provides the cardholder electronic access to his or her bank account(s) at a financial institution. Some cards have a stored value with which a payment is made, while most relay a message to the cardholder's bank to withdraw funds from a designated account in favour of the payee's designated bank account. The card can be used as an alternative payment method to cash when making purchases.

A credit card is a small plastic card issued to users as a system of payment. It allows its holder to buy goods and services based on the holder's promise to pay for these goods and services. The issuer of the card creates a revolving account and grants a line of credit to the consumer (or the user) from which the user can borrow money for payment to a merchant or as a cash advance to the user.

E-Payment system enabled the tax payers to pay tax directly from their accounts without approaching the tax authorities' office.

All these services are performed with the help of core banking system. Now even a layman can easily operates the banking transactions.

Commercial Banks in Financial Inclusion—Indian Scenario

The first-ever Index of Financial Inclusion to find out the extent of reach of banking services among 100 countries, India has been ranked 50. Only 34% of Indian individuals have access to or receive banking services. In order to increase this number the Reserve Bank of India had the Government of India take innovative steps. One of the reasons for opening new branches of Regional Rural Banks was to make sure that the banking service is accessible to the poor. With the directive from RBI, our banks are now offering "No Frill" Accounts to low income groups. These accounts either have a low minimum or nil balance with some restriction in transactions. The individual bank has the authority to decide whether the account should have zero or minimum balance. With the combined effort of financial institutions, six million new 'No Frill' accounts were opened in the period between March 2006-07. Banks are now considering Financial Inclusion (FI) as a business opportunity in an overall environment that facilitates growth.

The main reason for financial exclusion is the lack of a regular or substantial income. In most of the cases people with low income do not qualify for a loan. The proximity of the financial service is another fact. The loss is not only the transportation cost but also the loss of daily wages for a low income individual. Most of the excluded consumers are not aware of the bank's products, which are beneficial for them. Getting money for their financial requirements from a local moneylender is easier than getting a loan from the bank. Most of the banks need collateral for their loans. It is very difficult for a low income individual to find collateral for a bank loan. Moreover, banks give more importance to meeting their financial targets. So they focus on larger accounts. It is not profitable for banks to provide small loans and make a profit.

Financial inclusion mainly focuses on the poor who do not have formal financial institutional support and getting them out of the clutches of local moneylenders. As a first step towards this, some of our banks have now come forward with general purpose credit cards and artisan credit cards which offer collateral-free small loans. The RBI has simplified the KYC (Know your customer) norms for opening a 'No frill' account. This will help the low income individual to open a 'No Frill' account without identity proof and address proof.

In such cases banks can take the individual's introduction from an existing customer whose full KYC norm procedure has been completed and the introducer must have a satisfactory transaction with the bank for at least 6 months. This simplified procedure is available to those who intend to keep a balance not exceeding Rs. 50,000 in all accounts taken together. With this facility we can channel the untapped, considerable amount of money from the low income group to the formal economy.

Banks are now permitted to utilize the service of NGOs, SHGs and other civil society organizations as intermediaries in providing financial and banking services through the use of business facilitator and business correspondent models.

Self-Help Groups (SHG) are playing a very important role in the process of financial inclusion. SHGs are usually groups of women who get together and pool money from their savings and lend money among them. Usually they are working with the support of an NGO. The SHG is given loans against the group members' guarantee. Peer pressure within the group helps in improving recoveries. Through SHGs nearly 40 million households are linking with the banks. Micro-finance is another tool which links low income groups to the banks.

Yet, banks are fighting to fulfil the Financial Inclusion dream. The main reason is that the products designed by the banks are not satisfying the low income families. The provision of uncomplicated, small, affordable products will help to bring the low income families into the formal financial sector. Banks have limitations to reach directly to the low income consumers. Correspondents can be considered to be an excellent channel which banks can use to distribute their product information. Educating the consumers about the financial benefits and products of banks which are beneficial to low income groups will be a great step to tap their potential.

Banks are now using new technologies like mobile phones to reach low income consumers. It is possible that the telephone providers themselves will start basic banking services like savings and payments. Indian telecom consumers have few links to financial institutions. So without much difficulty telecom providers can win the battle with banks. Banks should therefore be proactive about transferring this technology into an opportunity.

The Indian Government has a long history of working to expand financial inclusion. Nationalization of the major private sector banks in 1969 was a big step. In 1975, Government of India (GoI) established RRBs with the same aim. It encouraged branch expansion of bank branches especially in rural areas. The RBI guidelines to banks shows that 40% of their net bank credit should be lent to the priority sector. This mainly consists of agriculture, small scale industries, retail trade, etc. More than 80% of our population depends directly or indirectly on agriculture. So 18% of net bank credit should go to agriculture lending. Recent simplification of KYC norms are another milestone.

Almost half the population in the country do not have deposit accounts in banks. Less than 10 per cent have loan accounts with banks. The extent of financial exclusion in India is staggering. But some change in these depressing numbers is underway.

India has ambitious plans to bring everyone under the formal banking network within the next few years. It seems to have made rapid strides in the past year if the villages covered under the financial inclusion programme are any indication. Now at least one-sixth of the six lakh plus villages in the country have a channel to access banking network.

The number of villages under the formal banking network, which was around 54,000 in March 2010, doubled in a span of one year. At the end of June 2011, the banks in the country had covered nearly 1.07 lakh villages under the financial inclusion programme.

The share of brick-and-mortar network of branches in a country with a total of more than 93,000 branches remains at 36 per cent. According to RBI statistics, all commercial banks in the country had a total branch network of 93,080 branches at the end of March 2011. Of them, 33,602 were in rural areas.

In such a situation, most banks prefer using a Business Correspondent (BC) model for expanding their network in the un-banked areas in the country.The BC units more than doubled during 2011. Of the more than 1.07 lakh villages that came under banking network during the year, 84,274 were covered through BCs till June 2011. This was 32,684 villages at the end of March 2010.

It was not that brick-and-mortar model was given a go-by during the year. More than 1,300 brick-and-mortar branches were opened in the un-banked villages of the country in 2011. Other channels such as mobile vans made a huge jump from mere 99 in March 2010 to more than 460 during this calendar year.

While speaking at a seminar on financial inclusion in New Delhi in October this year, Dr K.C. Chakrabarty, Deputy Governor of Reserve Bank of India, had said that 2.20 lakh un-banked villages will be covered by banking network by March 2012, and 3.52 lakh villages by March 2013. He also hoped to add more than 2100 brick-and-mortar outlets by March-end. (*Source*: *The Hindu-Business Line*)

Our assessment is that the economy is operating slightly below trend. The second consideration is the moderation in inflation—headline inflation, which ruled around 9 per cent for much of 2011, has come down to a shade below 7 per cent for March 2012, and non-food manufactured inflation has come down from a peak of 8.4 per cent in November last year to 4.7 per cent, which is close to the average of 4.5 per cent over the last six years.

We are delicately balanced in the growth-inflation balance. And that if we grow as expected at 7.3 per cent this year, we will be growing close to the trend. The scope for policy rate adjustment in the future will depend on how the growth-inflation dynamics evolve. But purely on growth consideration, the output gap is nearly closed or will get closed shortly.

There has been a rapid growth in gold loans. There was a concentration risk. It is not as if the business model or activity of a particular motivated this concern. This concern arose from concerns about systemic instability that could potentially arise. So, to avoid concentration risk and systemic instability, we have taken these measures.

Challenges of Commercial Banks in Inclusive Growth

A broad financial strategy for financial inclusion in India in relation to banking system has been developed. It covers uses highly sophisticated technology, emphasis on financial literacy and credit counseling, advising banks to open zero balance account, etc. Even though number of strategies are developed, it is not free from challenges. Major challenges are:

1. From the perspective of the banks, providing such services would have various risk associated with it. The major risks to the banks are legal, reputation and operational risks. These risks are to be managed with tight and regular monitoring, developing systems and procedures and by developing effective risk mitigating tools and matrix.
2. The banks are faced with high operating cost in extending the financial services to the remote areas. High maintenance cost of these accounts as well as small ticket size of the transactions is also adding to the problem.
3. People may not have adequate knowledge in bank dealings. Financial Literacy programmes need to be implemented.
4. Even though the number of branches established in under developed, the commercial banks could not be able to mobilize maximum targeted deposit because of the scattered population and poor savings habits of residents. The Bank observed that many of the villages were reluctant to visit the bank branches for various reasons like long distance to be travelled, time lost, difficulty in following procedures and reluctance to visit branches for small value transactions.
5. Poor recovery of loans and advances increases the amount of Non-Performing Asset (NPA). Effective policy implementation is required in this area.

CONCLUSION

The whole process of financial inclusion will not be possible without the contribution of Commercial Banks. Public have immense faith in Commercial Banks. Share of bank deposits in the total financial assets of households has been steadily rising. Financial inclusion initiatives strengthening the banking system. Commercial banks with experience in technical innovations could help reduce the costs of operating in rural areas and improve services provided to rural clients by introducing new technology. Adoption of innovative technology in banking makes banks more approachable to poor people. Commercial Banks could be able to mobilize the savings of people and channalise it to investment and productive purposes. Here the commercial bank became an effective Piller for industrial and economic development. A strong and sound monitory policy of government and effective participation of Banks will surely make the economic development possible. Extending services of banking to every people is a key factor towards inclusive growth.

References

Banking Law and Practice, P.N. Varshney.

Banking: State Co-operative Union.

Banking Theory and Practice, S.N. Maheswary, R.R. Paul.

Banking Theory: Law and Practice, K.P.M. Sundaram, P.M. Varshney.

The Hindu-Business Line.

Financial Inclusion and its Impacts

SARITHA, P. AND RINCY JAMES

ABSTRACT

The term financial inclusion has gained importance since the early 2000s. Financial inclusion or inclusive financing is the delivery of financial services at affordable cost to sections of disadvantaged and low income segments of society. Financial inclusion is generally defined in terms of exclusion from the financial services. Financial inclusion mainly focuses on the poor who do not have formal financial institutional support and getting them out of the clutches of local moneylenders. One of the reasons for opening new branches of Regional Rural Banks was to make sure that the banking service is accessible to the poor. Banks are now considering Financial Inclusion as a business opportunity in an overall environment that facilitates growth.

INTRODUCTION

Financial inclusion or inclusive financing is the delivery of financial services at affordable costs to sections of disadvantaged and low income segments of society. Unrestrained access to public goods and services is the *sine qua non* of an open and efficient society. It is argued that as banking services are in the nature of public good, it is essential that availability of banking and payment services to the entire population without discrimination is the prime objective of public policy. The term "financial inclusion" has gained importance since the early 2000s, and is a result of findings about financial exclusion and its direct correlation to poverty.

Concept

Defining financial inclusion is considered crucial from the viewpoint of developing a conceptual framework and identifying the underlying factors that lead to low level of access to the financial system. A review of literature suggests that there is no universally accepted definition of financial inclusion. As measuring inclusion is perceived to be difficult, financial inclusion is generally defined in terms of exclusion from the financial system. Early discussion on financial exclusion was preceded by social exclusion and focused predominantly on the issue of geographical access to financial services, in particular banking outlets (Leyshon and Thrift, 1993). However, financial exclusion is not just about physical access caused by the changing topography of financial services. Therefore, the debate has now broadened to include all types of people who make little or no use of financial services and the processes of financial exclusion (Ford and Rowlingson, 1996; Kempson and Whyley, 1998).

Definition of Financial Inclusion

Financial Inclusion is the process of ensuring access to appropriate financial products and services needed by all sections of the society in general and vulnerable groups such as weaker sections and low income groups in particular at an affordable cost in a fair and transparent manner by mainstream institutional players.

RBI Changes Financial Inclusion Definition

The Reserve Bank of India (RBI) today said that financial inclusion is not restricted merely to opening of bank accounts and should imply provision of all financial services like credit, remittance and overdraft facilities for the rural poor. "The accounts must be operational to provide benefits beyond deposit of money like availability of credit, remittance facility and overdraft among others". D. Subbarao, Governor of RBI said here. "I have already requested to the commercial banks in this regard and going to pursue with them", Subbarao said. Talking to the media after meeting the Orissa chief minister, Naveen Patnaik in the state secretariat, he said, a pilot project for financial inclusion has been launched in Karnataka. Though RBI is trying to push the pilot project across the country, it favours learning through intensive experiment in Karnataka. The bank is encouraging all the states to take the financial inclusion process forward. Referring to his discussion with the chief minister, Subbarao said, he had urged the state government to include financial literacy in the curriculum of schools and colleges in the state.

The chief minister has assured to take this proposal forward. Asked whether the RBI intends to intervene for controlling inflation when the food inflation has reached 17.47 per cent, fuelled by rise in the prices of potato, onions and other essential items, the Governor refused to comment. He also refused to forecast the growth rate of Gross Domestic Product (GDP) for the third quarter stating that the RBI will revisit the subject in its January policy. Sources said, the state government made a presentation before the RBI Governor on the progress of banking in the state. It was pointed out that the per capita bank credit in Orissa is Rs. 11,381 compared to Rs. 27,824 for the nation as a whole. This compares very unfavourably with state like Maharashtra (Rs. 94,300), Andhra Pradesh (Rs. 28,018) and Punjab (Rs. 32,774). Declining credit-deposit (CD) ratio, identification of un-banked areas, opening of bank branches in those areas, inadequate flow of credit to agriculture, MSMEs, handicrafts and handloom sectors were cited as areas of concern. "During the discussion with the RBI Governor we sought more loans for farmers, agriculture, small scale industries and branches in rural areas so that people can take benefit out of various state and Central government schemes", Patnaik told the media.
www.business-standard.com

Financial Inclusion in India

The Reserve Bank of India has set-up a commission (Khan Commission) in 2004 to look into financial inclusion and the recommendations of the commission were incorporated into the mid-term review of the policy (2005-06). In the report RBI exhorted the banks with a view of achieving greater financial inclusion to make available a basic "no-frills" banking account. In India, Financial Inclusion first featured in 2005, when it was introduced, that, too, from a pilot project in UT of Pondicherry, by K.C. Chakraborthy, the chairman of Indian Bank. Mangalam Village became the first village in India where all households were provided banking facilities. In addition to this KYC (Know Your Customer) norms were relaxed for people intending to open accounts with annual deposits of less than Rs. 50,000. General Credit Cards (GCC) were issued to the poor and the disadvantaged with a view to help them access easy credit. In January 2006, the Reserve Bank permitted commercial banks to make use of the services of non-governmental organizations (NGOs/SHGs), micro-finance institutions and other civil society organizations as intermediaries for providing financial and banking services. These intermediaries could be used as business facilitators (BFs) or business correspondents (BCs) by commercial banks. The bank asked the commercial banks in different regions to start a 100% financial inclusion campaign on a pilot basis. As a result of the campaign states or U.T.s like Pondicherry, Himachal

Pradesh and Kerala have announced 100% financial inclusion in all their districts. Reserve Bank of India's vision for 2020 is to open nearly 600 million new customers' accounts and service them through a variety of channels by leveraging on IT. However, illiteracy and the low income savings and lack of bank branches in rural areas continue to be a road block to financial inclusion in many states. Apart from this there are certain in current model which is followed. There is inadequate legal and financial structure. India, being a mostly agrarian economy, hardly has schemes which lend for agriculture. Along with micro-finance we need to focus on micro-insurance too.

RBI is currently working on a three-year financial inclusion plan and is discussing this with each bank to see how to take this forward, K.C. Chakrabarty, deputy governor, RBI said.

"Nearly forty years after nationalization of banks, 60% of the country's population does not have bank accounts and nearly 90% do not get loans," he pointed out.

Despite heightened focus on financial inclusion, Indian banks still somewhat failed to bring the under- and un-banked into the mainstream banking fold.

India has currently the second-highest number of financially excluded households in the world. Approximately, 40% of India's population have bank accounts, and only about 10% have any kind of life insurance cover, while a meager 0.6% have non-life insurance cover.

According to UNITED NATIONS, "A financial sector that provides 'access to credit for all' "bankable" people and firms and to savings and payments services for everyone. Inclusive finance does not require that everyone who is eligible use each of the services, but they should be able to choose use them if desired.

REPORT OF THE COMMITTEE ON FINANCIAL INCLUSION IN INDIA (Chairperson : C. Rangarajan) (2008) "The process of ensuring access to financial services and timely and adequate credit where needed by vulnerable groups such as weaker sections and low income groups at an affordable cost."

As per TREASURY COMMITTEE, HOUSE OF COMMONS, UK, (2005) "Ability of individuals to access appropriate financial products and services."

'Major Three Aspects of Financial Inclusion' make people to Access Financial Markets:

- Access Credit Markets
- Learn Financial Matters (financial education)

Financial Inclusion Includes Accessing of Financial Products and Services like,

- Savings facility
- Credit and debit cards access
- Electronic fund transfer
- All kinds of commercial loans
- Overdraft facility
- Cheque facility
- Payment and remittance services
- Low cost financial services
- Insurance (Medical insurance)
- Financial advice
- Pension for old-age and investment schemes
- Access to financial markets
- Micro-credit during emergency
- Entrepreneurial credit

Financially Excluded People The financially excluded sections largely comprise:

- Marginal farmers
- Landless labourers
- Oral lessees
- Self-employed and unorganised sector enterprises
- Urban slum-dwellers
- Migrants
- Ethnic minorities and socially excluded groups
- Senior citizens
- Women

The North-East, Eastern and Central regions contain most of the financially excluded population.

Factors Affecting Access to Financial Services

Legal identity: Lack of legal identity like voter id, driving license, birth certificates, employment identity card, etc.

Limited literacy: Particularly financial literacy and lack of basic education prevent people to have access from financial services.

Level of income: Level of income decides to have financial access. Low income people generally have the attitude of thinking that banks are only for rich.

Terms and conditions: While getting loans or at the time of opening accounts banks places many conditions, so the uneducated and poor people find it very difficult to access financial services.

Complicated procedures: Due to lack of financial literacy and basic education, it is very difficult for those people who lack both to read terms and conditions and account filling forms.

Psychological and cultural barriers: Many people voluntarily excluded themselves due to psychological barriers and they think that they are excluded from accessing financial services.

Place of living: As the name suggests that commercial banks operate only in commercially profitable areas and they set-up branches and main offices only in that areas. People who lived in under developed areas finds it very difficult to go to areas in which banks are generally reside.

Lack of awareness: Finally, people who lack basic education do not know the importance of the financial products like Insurance, Finance, Bank Accounts, cheque facility, etc.

Consequences of Financial Exclusion Major Two Threats

Losing opportunities to grow: In the absence of finance, people who are not connected with formal financial system lack opportunities to grow.

Country's growth will retard: Due to vast unutilized resources that is in the form of money in the hands of people who lack financial inclusive services.

Other Consequences

Business loss to banks: Banks will loss business if this condition persists for ever due to lack of opening of bank accounts.

Exclusion from mainstream society: The people who lacks financial services, presumed that they are excluded from mainstream society.

All transactions cannot be made in cash: Some transactions can be made in cash. In this technological world everybody wants to have electronic cash system like debit and credit cards and also EFT.

Loss of opportunities to thrift and borrow: Financially excluded people, may lose chances to save their some part of livelihood earnings and also to borrow loans.

Employment barriers: Nowadays all salary and other financial benefits from various sources like Governments scholarships, any compensation, grants, reliefs, etc. are paid through bank accounts.

Loss due to theft: Banks provide various schemes of safety locker facility. It mitigates the risk due to thefts.

Other allied financial services: People who do not have bank accounts may not go to bank as for as possible. So they lack basic financial auxiliary services like DD, Insurance cover and other emergency need loans, etc.

Benefits of Inclusive Financial Growth

Growth with equity: In the path of super power we the Indians will need to achieve the growth of our country with equality. It is provided by inclusive finance.

Get rid of poverty: To remove poverty from the Indian context all everybody will be given access to formal financial services. Because if they borrow loans for business or education or any other purpose they get the loan will pave way for their development.

Financial Transactions Made Easy: Inclusive finance will provide banking-related financial transactions in an easy and speedy way.

Safe savings along with financial services : People will have safe savings along with other allied services like insurance cover, entrepreneurial loans, payment and settlement facility, etc.

Inflating National Income: Boosting up business opportunities will definitely increase GDP and which will be reflected in our national income growth.

Becoming Global Player: Financial access will attract global market players to our country that will result in increasing employment and business opportunities.

Relationship between Financial Inclusion and Development Indicators

Economic growth follows financial inclusion. In order to achieve the objective of growth with equity, it is imperative that infrastructure is developed with financial inclusion.

- *Savings and credit accounts*—indicators of financial inclusion.
- *Per capita income*—indicator of economic development.
- *Electricity consumption and road length*—indicators of infrastructure development.

All the above influence economic development which follows adequate financial and credit facilities:

- Expectations of poor people from financial system Taking into account their Seasonal Inflow of Income from agricultural operations,
- Migration from one place to another,
- Seasonal And Irregular Work Availability and Income; the existing financial system needs to be designed to suit their requirements,
- Security and safety of deposits,
- Low transaction cost,

- Convenient operating time,
- Minimum paper work,
- Frequent deposits,
- Quick and easy access, and
- Product suitable to income and consumption.

CONCLUSION

The first-ever Index of Financial Inclusion to find out the extent of reach of banking services among 100 countries, India has been ranked 50. Only 34% of Indian individuals have access to or receive banking services. In order to increase this number the Reserve Bank of India had the Government of India take innovative steps. One of the reasons for opening new branches of Regional Rural Banks was to make sure that the banking service is accessible to the poor. With the directive from RBI, our banks are now offering "No Frill" Accounts to low income groups. These accounts either have a low minimum or nil balance with some restriction in transactions. The individual bank has the authority to decide whether the account should have zero or minimum balance. With the combined effort of financial institutions, six million new 'No Frill' accounts were opened in the period between March 2006-07. Banks are now considering FI as a business opportunity in an overall environment that facilitates growth.

Financial inclusion mainly focuses on the poor who do not have formal financial institutional support and getting them out of the clutches of local moneylenders. As a first step towards this, some of our banks have now come forward with general purpose credit cards and artisan credit cards which offer collateral-free small loans. The RBI has simplified the KYC (Know Your Customer) norms for opening a 'No frill' account. This will help the low income individual to open a 'No Frill' account without identity proof and address proof.

15

Financial Exclusion and Fisherwomen in Kollam District

INDHU, L. AND DR. BIJU, T.

ABSTRACT

Financial Exclusion is the unavailability of banking service to people living in poverty. It is believed to be one factor preventing poor people from existing poverty, by forcing them to manage their finances on cash only basis and restricting their access to equitable source of credit. Low income, illiteracy are the important causes of exclusion from the financial services. Lack of banking knowledge, insufficiency of knowledge on banking products, etc., prevent the fisherwomen from knocking the door steps of banks. Lacks of organized women group, ignorance of modern processing technology, exclusion from decision-making are the major problems of financial exclusion of fisherwomen in Kollam. Even after spending crores and implementing several projects and programmes, the fisher folk especially the womenfolk are out of the purview of financial inclusion. For an inclusive growth more planned, scientific and systematic measures for financial inclusion is to be put forth by considering the ground realities. More scientific and systematic studies are essential for this. Strengthening of Co-operative societies and other NGOs and social service institutions of churches and other groups is necessary for providing an adequate coverage.

INTRODUCTION

Financial Exclusion is the unavailability of banking service to people living in poverty. It is believed to be one factor preventing poor people from existing poverty, by forcing them to manage their finances on cash only basis and restricting their access to equitable source of credit. Access to finance especially by the poor and vulnerable group is a prerequisite for a employment, economic growth, poverty reduction and social cohesion. Further, access to finance will empower the vulnerable group by giving them an opportunity to have a bank account to save and invest, to insure their homes or to partake of credit, thereby facilitating them to break the chain of poverty. The banking industry in India recognized this imperative and has undergone certain fundamental changes over the last two decades. The reforms in the early 90's in the banking sector have facilitated, increasing competition, the development of new generation private sector banks as well as technological breakthrough in diverse financial products, services and delivery channels. With the recent developments in technology, both delivery channels and access to financial service have transformed banking from the traditional brick and mortar infrastructure like staffed branches, to a system supplemented by other channel like ATM, Credit/Debit card, Internet banking, on line money transfer, etc. The point however, is that access to such technology is restricted only to certain segments of society. Indeed some trends, such as increasingly sophisticated customer segmentation technology allowing for example more accurate targeting of section of the market, have led to restricted access to financial services for some groups. There is a growing divide with an increase range of personal finance options, for a segment of high and upper, middle income population and significantly large section of population who lack access to even the most basic banking services. This is termed as financial exclusion. The people particularly those living on low income, cannot access main stream financial products such as bank account, low cost credit, remittance and payment services, financial advisory services, insurance facility, etc.

Women Workers in Kerala

The status of women in a complex society like Kerala is not uniform. According to census 2011, more than 110 million women are engaged as workers in rural areas, 36.5% of them are cultivator and 43% work as agricultural labourers. In rural Kerala agricultural workers are subject to worst ill effects of poverty. In Kerala agriculture and allied sections employ 89.5% of total female labour. Women work extensively in livestock maintains, forest-resource use and fish processing. Women provide 50% of the labour in fish processing.

Fisher Women and Financial Exclusion

No saving, No insurance, No access money adverse, no avoidable credit, no bank account and asset are called financial exclusion. The fisherwomen have limited access to bank and financial services. Low income, illiteracy are the important causes of exclusion from the financial services. Lack of banking knowledge, insufficiency of knowledge on banking products, etc., prevent the fisherwomen from knocking the door steps of banks. Lack of organized women group, ignorance of modern processing technology, exclusion from decision-making is the major problems of financial exclusion of fisherwomen in Kollam district.

The present paper examines the extent and causes of financial exclusion among fisherwomen in Kollam district.

The state of Kerala comprising of 14 districts, of which nine are marine districts. Among them the leading districts are Thiruvananthapuram, Kollam, Alappuzha, Ernakulam and Kozhikkode. The Kollam district enjoys a pivotal position as it is the pioneer of mechanized fishing through the implementation of Indo-Norwegian pilot project. The fishing sector in Kollam consisting of two major sectors namely Inland sector and Marine sector. The marine sector was again classified in to traditional sector and modern or mechanized sector. The district comprising of 140,425 fish workers of which 51055 are women and 30,707 are children. The men usually engaged in the catching activity, while women are engaged in various activities like fish vending, fish processing and so on. The condition of the poor women workers is so pathetic and they do not enjoy any freedom with regard to social or economic spheres. Hence, the present study was proposed to evaluate the causes and extent of financial exclusion among fisher women in Kollam district.

The study was conducted among 60 fisher women selected 30 each from inland and marine sectors by applying judgment sampling technique. The required data were collected from them through survey technique with the help of an interview schedule. The data were collected during the first week of December 2011. The primary data so collected were analysed by applying simple percentages. The data analysis part was discussed below.

Extend of Financial Exclusion among Fisherwomen in Kollam District

The extend of financial exclusion was examined by analyzing the accessibility of selected financial products to the womenfolk of Kollam District. For that variables like the accessibility of savings bank account, loan account etc from public sector commercial banks and co-operative banks, accessibility to life insurance policy and health insurance, etc. were selected. The data were presented in Table. 1

TABLE I

Accessibility to Various Financial Products

(Percentage)

	Inland		*Marine*		*Total*	
	Yes	*No*	*Yes*	*No*	*Yes*	*No*
Saving bank account with Co-op. Bank	10 (33.33)	20 (66.67)	15 (50)	15 (50)	25 (41.67)	35 (58.33)
Account with Commercial Bank	5 (16.67)	25 (83.33)	7 (23.33)	23 (76.67)	12 (20)	48 (80)
Loan account with Co-op. Bank	16 (53.33)	14 (46.67)	17 (56.67)	13 (43.33)	33 (55)	27 (45)
Loan account with Commercial Bank	6 (20)	24 (80)	8 (26.67)	22 (73.33)	14 (23.33)	46 (76.66)
Life insurance policy	4 (13.33)	26 (86.67)	6 (20)	24 (80)	10 (16.67)	50 (83.33)
Medical insurance (Govts. Health Card)	17 (56.66)	13 (43.33)	16 (53.33)	14 (46.67)	33 (55)	27 (45)

Source: Primary Data.

The data revealed that even after implementing several measures by Government and other agencies for total financial inclusion of the poor and vulnerable sections of the community almost 50% of the fisher women are out of the purview of financial inclusion. With regard to savings bank account, even after the introduction of no frills account by commercial banks 80 percent are not having such as account with commercial banks. But at the same time the coverage made by co-operative bank was much better as 41.67 percent are having savings bank account with co-operative banks. This may be due to more accessibility provided by co-operative banks rather than commercial banks in to the rural areas. The major factor to be noticed here is that the number of members having SB account is less than of the number of members availing loan account. This reveals the indebtedness of poor fisherwomen. Even the financially excluded fisherwomen are indebted to the local moneylenders and all due to several reasons as explained earlier. In the field of life insurance also the position of poor fisher women is not that hopeful. Of the 60 women selected for the study 46 were out of the purview of life insurance. But the Health insurance implemented by the Government enabled more coverage than any other products. But that too not covered the entire fisherwomen in the costal Kollam. This reveals that more measures are essential for the financial inclusion of the women folk in the fishing sector. There is no significant difference between the fisher women from inland sector and marine sector with regard to different variables included here such as Savings Bank account, Loan account, Life insurance, etc. Therefore, a comprehensive plan for including the fisherwomen is essential with regard to the causes of financial exclusion, some of the leading causes pointed out by rural fisherwomen were ranked and given in Table 2.

TABLE 2

Causes of Financial exclusion

Rank	*Cause*	*Percentage*
1	Lack of Awareness	72%
2	Lack of Accessibility	63%
3	High cost of financial products	54%
4	Complexity in dealing with banks	53%
5	Lack of understanding of forms & procedures	51%
6	Attitude of Bank personal	43%

Source: Primary Data.

This study revealed that more extensive financial literary programmes to be mooted among the fisher folk to make them more aware about the financial products and services. Mean time more rural branches should be opened either by Public Sector Commercial Banks or by Regional Rural Banks or by strengthening the Co-operative Banks. The RBI already insisted opening of No-frills account by Banks, more such measurers be initiated for reducing the cost of financial products. More flexibility, friendliness, etc. from the part of Bank personnel are also needed to make them accessible to fishermen. The Government initiated several measures for financial inclusion of the fishing community. Some important ones are enlisted below :

Major Development Programmes

The major developmental programmes implemented during the 11th plan period in the State include inland fishers development, development of fishing harbours and landing centers and programmes ensuring social and livelihood security of fisherwomen. Some of them are enlisted below.

Society for Assistance to Fisherwomen

Societies for assistance to fisherwomen are a registered society for encouraging and strengthening the locally organized social organization among fisherwomen in coastal areas. More than 5000 women SHGS were organized in the coastal districts of Kerala with SAF under the micro-enterprise scheme upto March 2010 training on capacity building were given for 252 units through SAF. About 40,000 fisherwomen were given assistance in the form of revolving fund for fisher vending. Major achievements of projects implemented through SAF are given in a Table 3.

TABLE 3

Projects Implementary through Society for Assistance to Fisherwomen

Sl. No.	*Name of Projects*	*No. of units completed*	*No. of Beneficiaries*
1.	Economic empowerment of fisherwomen	819	7414
2.	Construction and modernization of fish market	31 (progressing)	
3.	Development of micro-enterprises	1282	6628
4.	Dressed/dry Fish unit	57	285
5.	Handmade toiletry	26	130
6.	Rural marketing executive	55	220
7.	Sustainability of Micro-enterprises	1800 (Progressing)	12000
8.	Establishment of value added fish products unit	90 progressing	450

Source: Economic Review (SHGS–Self-Help Groups), (SAF–Society for Assistance Fisherwomen).

Matsya Fed

Matsya fed is an Apex federation of 666 primary levels of fisherman Development welfare co-operative societies of which 34 numbers are in marine sector, 192 numbers are in inland sector and 133 women co-operative societies. The total membership in these societies is more than 3 lakhs.

In order to provide social security and livelihood support to the fishermen community the programmes like saving-*cum*-relief scheme, Group insurance to fishermen, insurance coverage for fishing implements, etc. were under implementation.

CONCLUSION

Even after spending crores and implementing several projects and programmes, the fisher folk especially the womenfolk are out of the purview of financial inclusion. For an inclusive growth mere planned, scientific and systematic measures for financial inclusion is to be put forth by considering the ground realities. More scientific and systematic studies are essential for this. Strengthening of Co-operative societies and other NGOs and social service institutions of churches and other groups is necessary for providing an adequate coverage.

REFERENCES

Govt. of Kerala, *Economic Review*, 2010, State Planning Board, Thiruvananthapuram, 2011.

Govt. of Kerala, *Facts and Figures*, 2010, Fisheries Department, Thiruvananthapuram.

Govt. of Kerala, *Annual Report*, 2010, Fisheries Department, Thiruvananthapuram.

Marine Fisheries Statistics of Kerala, 2010, Fisheries Department, Thiruvananthapuram.

www.google.com

16

Role of Life Insurance Corporation of India in Inclusive Growth

JISSY, S.G.

ABSTRACT

By financial inclusion, we mean the delivery of financial services, include access to savings, loans, insurance, payments and remittance facilities offered by the formal financial system, banking services and credit, at an affordable cost to the vast sections, disadvantaged and low income groups who tend to excluded. Among the key financial services that are risk management or risk mitigation services *vis-a-vis* economic shocks. Such shocks may be an income shock due to adverse weather conditions or natural disasters or an expenditure shock due to health emergence or accidents, leading to a high level of unexpected expenditure. This aspect of financial inclusion is of vital importance in providing economic security to individual and families. LIC should ensure to provide security to their customers. LIC as a responsible Corporate Citizen has been fulfiling its social responsibilities from time to time. In fact, most of our investments are geared towards industrial growth, infrastructure growth and national development.

INTRODUCTION

Financial inclusion may be defined as the process of ensuring access to financial services and timely and adequate credit where needed by vulnerable groups such as weaker sections and low income groups at an affordable cost. The financial services include the entire gamut-savings, loans, insurance, credit, payments, etc. The financial system has to provide its function of transferring resources from surplus to deficit units but both deficit and surplus units are those with low incomes, poor backwards, etc.

Finance has come a long way since the time when it wasn't recognized as a factor for growth and development. It is now attributed as the brain of an economic system and most economies strives to make their financial systems more efficient. It also keeps policy-makers on their toes as any problem in this sector could freeze the entire economy and even lead to a contagion.

Financial services such as savings, loans, remittance and insurance services by the vast majority of the population in the rural and urban areas are believed to be the constraint to the enlargement of the livelihood opportunities and empowerment of the section. Currently LIC has no other great role than making life insurance business successful in India. This is the only role an Insurance company needs to and can play in a civilized open economy. Once the insurance business is undertaken, investments have to take place automatically. This will help economic growth sentences that lead to the relevance of insurance, and institutions leading insurance can play a good role in inclusion efforts. LIC, a government owned institution is a model in financial inclusion process. Life Insurance Corporation of India plays an important role in inclusive growth. Some of their roles are as follows:

Role 1: Life Insurance as an "Investment"

Insurance is an attractive option for investment. While most people recognize the risk hedging and tax saving potential of insurance, many are not aware of its advantages as an investment option as well. Insurance products yield more compared to regular investment options, and this is besides the added incentives (read bonuses) offered by insurers.

Role 2: Life Insurance as "Risk Cover"

First and foremost, insurance is about risk cover and protection—financial protection, to be more precise—to help outlast life's unpredictable losses. Designed to safeguard against losses suffered on account of any unforeseen event, insurance provides you with that unique sense of security that no other form of investment provides. By buying life insurance, you buy peace of mind and are prepared to face any financial demand that would hit the family in case of an untimely demise. To provide such protection, insurance firms collect contributions from many people who face the same risk. A loss claim is paid out of the total premium collected by the insurance companies, who act as trustees to the monies.

Role 3: Life Insurance as "Tax Planning"

Insurance serves as an excellent tax saving mechanism too. The Government of India has offered tax incentives to life insurance products in order to facilitate the flow of funds into productive assets. Under Section 88 of Income Tax Act, 1961, an individual is entitled to a rebate of 20 per cent on the annual premium payable on his/her life and life of his/her children or adult children. The rebate is deductible from tax payable by the individual or a Hindu Undivided Family. This rebate is can be availed up to a maximum of Rs. 12,000 on payment of yearly premium of Rs. 60,000. By paying Rs. 60,000 a year, you can buy anything upwards of Rs. 10 lakh in sum assured. (Depending upon the age of the insured and term of the policy) This means that you get a Rs. 12,000 tax benefit. The rebate is deductible from the tax payable by an individual or a Hindu Undivided Family. To the extent LIC makes money by helping people do what has been written above, it plays a role. And, that's it.

The history of life insurance in India dates from1818 when this instrument was conceived means to provide risk cover to the families. The Bombay Mutual Life Insurance Society, the first Indian owned life insurance company, was established in 1870. The insurance business grew at a faster pace after independence in 1947. Indian companies strengthened their hold on this business but, despite the growth, insurance remained primarily an urban phenomenon. In 1956, the Government of India brought together over 240 private life insurers and provident societies under one nationalized monopoly corporation and the Life Insurance Corporation of India (LIC) was born with the enactment of Life Insurance Corporation Act, 1956. Nationalization was justified on the ground that it would generate the much needed funds for rapid industrialization. This was in conformity with the Government's chosen path of state led planning and development.

FINANCIAL INCLUSION AND LIFE INSURANCE CORPORATION

LIC of India started micro-insurance initiative immediately after the IRDA Micro-insurance regulations were issued by IRDA in November 2005. the purpose of giving prime importance to micro-insurance and opening a separate vertical for their channel was that, it is through only micro-insurance, i.e. small ticket policies, that the most vulnerable section of society can be given the risk cover which has eluded them so far. One of the main objectives of promoting financial inclusion packages is to economically empower those sections of society who are otherwise denied access to financial services, by providing banking and credit and risk cover services thereby focusing on bridging the rural financial security gap. The banking sector is focusing on financial inclusion on a priority basis. Vulnerability to various risk factors is one of the fundamental attributes of these sections of the society. Lack of protective elements may not serve the objective of promoting financial inclusion packages as the targeted section may fall back into the clutches of poverty in the event of unforeseen contingencies. Hence, to provide a hedge against these unforeseen risks, micro-insurance is widely accepted as one of the essential ingredients of financial inclusion packages. The prime object of LIC is to spread life insurance widely and in particular to the rural areas and to the socially and economically backward classes, with a view to reaching all insurable persons in the country and providing them adequate financial cover against death at a reasonable cost. Micro-insurance is a financial arrangement to protect low income people against specific perils in exchange for regular premiums payable proportionate to the likelihood and the cost of the risk involved. As individuals it is inherent to differ. Each individual's insurance needs and requirements are different from that of the others. LIC's Insurance Plans are policies that talk to you individually and give you the most suitable options that can fit your requirement. Some of their insurance plans are as follows:

1. Jeevan Arogya Plan

Health has been a major concern on everybody's mind, including yours. In these days of skyrocketing medical expenses, when a family member is ill, it is a traumatic time for the rest of the family. As a caring person, you do not want to let any unfortunate incident to affect your plans for you and your family. So why let any medical emergencies shatter your peace of mind. LIC has launched LIC's Jeevan Arogya, a unique non-linked Health Insurance plan which provides health insurance cover against certain specified health risks and provides you with timely support in case of medical emergencies and helps you and your family remain financially independent in difficult times.

LIC's Jeevan Arogya gives you:

- Valuable financial protection in case of hospitalisation, surgery, etc.
- Increasing Health cover every year.
- Lump sum benefit irrespective of actual medical costs.
- No claim benefit.
- Flexible benefit limit to choose from flexible premium payment options.

2. Bima Account Plan

Bima Account-I

As the name explains "LIC's Bima Account-I" is a simple non-linked plan under which you can be covered without undergoing any medical examination subject to certain conditions.

This plan offers you everything you think of an insurance plan should provide:

Simplicity
Liquidity
Guaranteed minimum return
No medical examination
Transparent charges
Risk cover

Under this plan, the premiums paid by you, after deduction of charges, will be credited to the Policyholder's Account maintained separately for each policyholder. The risk cover will be provided by deduction of mortality charges from the Policyholder's Account. If all due premiums are paid, the amount held in your Policyholder's Account will earn an annual interest rate of 6% p.a. which will be guaranteed for whole of the policy term. In addition to this guaranteed return, if all due premiums are paid, your account may earn an additional return depending upon the experience under this plan.You will also have an option to pay additional (Top-up) premiums without any increase in risk cover. Loan facility will also be available immediately after first policy anniversary

Bima Account-II

Under this plan, the premiums paid by you, after deduction of charges, will be credited to the Policyholder's Account maintained separately for each policyholder. The risk cover will be provided by deduction of mortality charges from the Policyholder's Account. If all due premiums are paid, the amount held in your Policyholder's Account will earn an annual interest rate of 6% p.a. which will be guaranteed for whole of the policy term. In addition to this guaranteed return, if all due premiums are paid, your account may earn an additional return depending upon the experience under this plan. You will also have an option to pay additional (Top-up) premiums without any increase in risk cover. Loan facility will also be available immediately after first policy anniversary.

3. Endowment Plan

In this policy, the investment risk in investment portfolio is borne by the policyholder. This is a unit linked Endowment plan which offers investment-*cum*-insurance cover during the term of the policy. You can choose the level of insurance cover within the limits, which will depend on the mode and level of premium you agree to pay. You have a choice of investing your premiums in one of the four types of investment funds available. Premiums paid after deduction of allocation charge will purchase units of the Fund type chosen. The Unit Fund is subject to various charges and value of units may increase or decrease, depending on the Net Asset Value (NAV).

4. Jeevan Anurag

LIC's Jeevan ANURAG is a with profits plan specifically designed to take care of the educational needs of children. The plan can be taken by a parent on his or her own life. Benefits under the plan are payable at pre specified durations irrespective of whether the Life Assured survives to the end of the policy term or dies during the term of the policy. In addition, this plan also provides for an immediate payment of Basic Sum Assured amount on death of the Life Assured during the term of the policy.

5. Jeevan Kishore

This is an Endowment Assurance Plan available for children of less than 12 years of age. The policy may be purchased by any of the parent/grand parent. The risk commences either after 2 years from the date of commencement of policy or from the policy anniversary immediately following the completion of 7 years of age of child, whichever is later. Premiums are payable yearly, half-yearly, quarterly or monthly throughout the term of the policy or till earlier death of child, or single premium. This is a with-profits plan and participates in the profits of the Corporation's life insurance business. It gets a share of the profits in the form of bonuses. Simple Reversionary Bonuses are declared per thousand Sum Assured annually at the end of each financial year. Once declared, they form part of the guaranteed benefits of the plan. A Final (Additional) Bonus may also be payable provided policy has run for certain minimum period.

6. Marriage Endowment or Educational Annuity Plan

This is an Endowment Assurance Plan that provides for benefits on or from the selected maturity date to meet the Marriage/Educational expenses of the named child. Premiums are payable yearly, half-yearly, quarterly, monthly or through Salary deductions, as opted by you, throughout the term of the policy or earlier death. This is a with-profit plan and participates in the profits of the Corporation's life insurance business. It gets a share of the profits in the form of bonuses. Simple Reversionary Bonuses are declared per thousand Sum Assured annually at the end of each financial year. Once declared, they form part of the guaranteed benefits of the plan. Such bonuses are to be added till maturity even if the life assured dies before the maturity date. Final (Additional) Bonus may also be payable provided a policy is of a certain minimum term.

7. Child Future Plan

This plan is specially designed to meet the increasing educational, marriage and other needs of growing children. It provides the risk cover on the life of child not only during the policy term but also during the extended term (i.e. 7 years after the expiry of policy term). A number of Survival benefits are payable on surviving by the life assured to the end of the specified durations.

8. Jeevan Adhar

This plan may be offered to a person who has a handicapped dependant satisfying conditions as specified in Section 80DDA of Income Tax Act, 1961. The plan provides life insurance cover throughout the lifetime of the purchaser. The benefits under the plan are for the handicapped dependant which are partly in lump sum and partly in the form of an annuity. The premiums paid under this plan are eligible for Income Tax relief under Section 80DDA of Income Tax Act.

9. The Endowment Assurance Policy

This policy not only makes provisions for the family of the Life Assured in event of his early death but also assures a lump sum at a desired age. The lump sum can be reinvested to provide an annuity during the remainder of his life or in any other way considered suitable at that time. Premiums are usually payable for the selected term of years or until death if it occurs during the term period.

10. Jeevan Shree-I

This is an Endowment Assurance plan offering the choice of many convenient premium paying terms. It provides financial protection against death throughout the term of plan with the payment of maturity amount on survival to the end of the policy term. The policy provides for the Guaranteed Additions at the rate of Rs. 50 per thousand Sum Assured for each completed year for first five years of the policy. The Guaranteed Additions are payable along with the Basic Sum Assured at the time of claim.

11. Jeevan Pramukh

Insurance Regulatory and Development Authority (IRDA) requires all life insurance companies operating in India to provide official illustrations to their customers. The illustrations are based on the investment rates of return set by the Life Insurance Council (constituted under Section 64C(a) of the Insurance Act, 1938) and is not intended to reflect the actual investment returns achieved or may be achieved in future by Life Insurance Corporation of India (LICI). This is an Endowment Assurance plan offering the choice of three premium paying terms. It provides financial protection against death throughout the term of the plan with the payment of maturity amount on survival to the end of the policy term.

12. Jeevan Bharathi-I

LIC's Jeevan Bharati-I is a plan exclusively for women. It is a with profit plan having special features considering the needs of women. The plan also provides for Accident Benefit, Critical Illness Benefit and Congenital Disability Benefit as Optional Riders.

13. The Whole Life Policy

This plan is mainly devised to create an estate for the heirs of the policyholder as the plan basically provides for payment of sum assured plus bonuses on the death of the policyholder. However, considering the increased longevity of the Indian population, the Corporation has amended the above provision, thereby providing for payment of sum assured plus bonuses in the form of maturity claim on completion of age 80 years or on expiry of term of 40 years from date of commencement of the policy whichever is later.

The premiums under the policy are payable up to age 80 years of the policyholder or for a term of 35 years whichever is later. If the payment of premium ceases after 3 years, a paid-up policy for such reduced sum assured will be automatically secured provided the reduced sum assured exclusive of any attached bonus is not less than Rs. 250. Such reduced paid-up policy is not entitled to participate in the bonus declared thereafter but the bonuses already declared on the policy will remain attach, provided the policy is converted in to a paid-up policy after the premiums are paid for 5 years.

14. Jeevan Saathi

This is an Endowment Assurance Plan issued on the lives of husband and wife. The plan provides financial protection against death of both the lives. It pays the maturity amount on survival of one or both the lives to the end of the policy term. The plan provides financial protection against death of both the lives. It pays the maturity amount on survival of one or both the lives to the end of the policy term.

LIC has taken a very positive and facilitative approach adopted in the spirit of the micro-insurance regulations, thereby extending insurance penetration to vulnerable segments of society. LIC's first Micro-Insurance Product "Jeevan Madhur" was launched on 28.09.2006 by Dr. A.P.J. Abdul Kalam, targeting to cover low income group, and especially those who have no fixed and stable income. This policy was intended for individuals in age group of 18 to 60 yrs and offered and with minimum and maximum sum assured of Rs. 5000 and Rs. 30,000 respectively with rates of premium as low as Rs. 25 per week to Rs. 100 per month.

JEEVAN MADHUR was introduced by LIC as the first initiative in this field as a simple savings related life insurance plan, wherein premiums are payable regularly at weekly, fortnightly, monthly, and quarterly, and half-yearly and annual intervals. On surviving the date of maturity, payment of maturity sum is paid along with vested bonus, if any. On death of the policyholder, an amount equal to total premiums payable during the entire term of the policy will be paid along with vested bonus, if any. On death arising as a result of an accident during the term of the policy, an additional amount equal to sum assured shall be payable. In Sept. 2009, LIC brought out its second Micro-Insurance Product "Jeevan Mangal"—A Term Assurance Policy with return of premium on maturity. The policy provides for Sum assured ranging from minimum of Rs. 10, 000 to maximum of Rs. 50,000. Mode of premium payment ranges from weekly to yearly and with single premium facility as well. The minimum premium installment is Rs. 15 per week. By taking a Jeevan Mangal policy together with earlier Jeevan Madhur policy, low income policy holder can now avail the life coverage benefit of upto Rs. 80,000. These policies have been sold through a distribution channel comprising Non-Government Organizations, Self-Help Groups, Micro-Finance Institutions, Non-Profit Associations, Corporate Agents, Brokers and Non-Profit Societies including Companies registered under section 25 of Companies Act, who have been appointed as Micro-Insurance Agents by LIC.

Currently, there are more than four crore policyholders under the Jana Shree Bima Yojana, Aam Aadmi Bima Yojana and Micro-Insurance Schemes who will stand to benefit from the financial inclusion initiative that will play a critical role in enabling financial inclusion and is expected to transform the way benefit under social welfare programs are delivered, by making the process more inclusive of communities now cut-off from such benefits. LIC intends to use this platform for disbursement of benefits. LIC intends to use this platform for disbursement of benefits under the Social Security Schemes and to collect renewal premiums on regular policies. LIC has entered into this partnership with the aim of providing best-in-class services to its customers and also fulfiling its commitment of extending insurance coverage to each and every Indian. LIC already has a Data Warehouse consisting of the complete details of all its customers, which it intends to leverage for the allocation of UIDs to LIC customer. LIC has implemented many customer relationship management initiatives over the last 5 years. LIC today has more than 260 million policyholders. There are other private insurers also operating for last 10 years. Even then, an estimated 290 million people who are in proximity to the BPL mark are totally devoid of any insurance. The fact that 60% of the world population does not have any cover. In the Banking World for the similar exclusion phenomenon, noble laureate Prof. Md. Yunus wrote, "It's not people who is not credit worthy. It's not people who are not credit worthy. It's the Banks that are not people worthy.

CONCLUSION

Financial inclusion is the availability of financial services at an affordable cost to disadvantaged and low-income groups. In India the basic concept of financial inclusion is having a saving or current account with any bank. In reality it includes loans, insurance services and much more. Banks are now considering FI as a business opportunity in an overall environment that facilitates growth. Financial inclusion mainly focuses on the poor who do not have formal financial institutional support and getting them out of the clutches of local moneylenders. Micro-insurance is an important tool which links low income groups to the financial sector. The services designed by the insurance companies are satisfying the low income families. The provision of uncomplicated, small, affordable services will help to bring the low income families into the formal financial sector. LIC has an eminent role in financial inclusion. It also helps to develop the growth of the economy. In India Financial inclusion will be good business ground in which the majority of her people will decide the winners and losers.

REFERENCES

Indian Financial Market Review, 2012—BSE, NSE.
Life Insurance Corporation of India.
The Economic Times.
www.licindia.in

17

Urban Poverty Alleviation through Micro-Enterprises and Micro-Finance

KRISHNAVENI, S.

ABSTRACT

Recently urban poverty alleviation is a challenging task before the policy-makers in our country. Urban unemployment in Kerala is the second highest in India. This paper is concerned with exploring the relationship between urban economic growth and poverty reduction. Poverty alleviation is possible only through income generation. Improving incomes of the poor is possible through improving skills and investment for self-employment. For that poor should have an access to the financial services and products. Most of the financial institutions, being commercial institutions, do not find it commerceially feasible to lend to the poor. In that context, to alleviate poverty and bring economic prosperity to the urban economy, micro-finance has engaged as a powerful tool. Micro-finance can encourage the micro-enterprises by providing capital and knowledge asset at lower cost.

INTRODUCTION

Recently Urban poverty alleviation is a challenging task before the policy-makers in our country as the urban population in the country is a growing phenomenon. In order to meet these challenges, entrepreneurship development has to be given a priority. Thus the need of the hour is to improve the entrepreneur skills of the urban poor and to assist them to set-up micro-enterprises for generating employment and thereby promote economic growth and contribute to the urban economy.

Kerala is believed to be a rural-urban continuum and there are arguments suggesting that there is little difference between rural and urban Kerala. 21% of the urban population of the State is classified as 'poor' by the Planning Commission. Urban unemployment in Kerala (10%) is the second-highest in India. To alleviate poverty and bring economic prosperity to the urban economy, micro-finance has emerged as a powerful tool.

SIGNIFICANCE OF THE MICRO-ENTERPRISES

Micro-finance enterprises extend credit as well as other financial services to low income persons, weaker sections and informal business to facilitate economic development in urban areas. Even though micro-enterprises are recognized as an important constituent of the national economies, contributing significantly to employment expansion and poverty alleviation by the government, however, due to several bottlenecks these enterprises find it difficult to expand or grow as expected. Therefore, it is indeed necessary for the government to take more pro- active measures in effective implementation of policies and schemes.

India has enormous challenge of addressing the issues of poverty, unemployment and inclusive growth but at the same time the country is a land of million opportunities. Therefore, there is a need for the government, banks/financial institutions, corporate sector, micro-finance institutions and other civil society institutions to join hands to promote micro-enterprise to enable the job-seekers to become job creators.

FINANCIAL INCLUSION IN THE URBAN CONTEXT

Financial inclusion in the urban areas is a rising problem. The country's urban population is increasing at a faster rate than the total population. Much of this population comprises of migrants. Migrant workers seldom have steady employment and by extension, do not have a regular employer.

Financial Inclusion is firmly established as a policy objective of Government of India and the Reserve Bank of India (RBI). The Committee on Financial Inclusion defined financial inclusion as "the process of ensuring access to financial services and timely and adequate credit where needed by vulnerable groups such as weaker sections and low income groups at an affordable cost". In India Urban people have not been able to get an account as they don't have a proof of address and can't fulfil the norms, essential for opening a bank account. In order to realize the vision of financial inclusion, there is an urgent need for an approach that acknowledges and addresses the urban-specific challenges. Proper access to finance by the rural people is a key requisite to employment, economic growth and poverty reduction which are primary tools of economic development.

OBJECTIVES OF THE STUDY

The overall aim of this paper is to study the role of micro-finance in urban micro-enterprise development, for the urban poverty alleviation. The specific objectives of the study are:

1 To examine the role of micro-finance in developing the micro-enterprises in urban area
2. To study the need of providing training and skill development to develop entrepreneurs among urban poor
3. To examine the significance of knowledge asset management for urban micro-entrepreneurs
4. To analyze the role of micro-enterprises in empowering the community to tackle the issues of urban poverty

METHODOLOGY

The study has been undertaken to analyse the role of micro-finance in empowering the urban poor with through the development of entrepreneurship and micro-enterprises. The present study is based on both primary and secondary sources of data. The primary data was collected with the help of interview schedule, observation and discussion with members of Neighborhood Groups (SHGs) from the urban area of Thiruvananthapuram District, the capital of Kerala State. Secondary data are collected from the records of Urban Poverty Alleviation cell, Thiruvananthapuram, State Poverty Eradication Mission, Thiruvananthapuram and also from website of Ministry of Housing and Urban Poverty Alleviation (India).

MICRO-FINANCE AND FINANCIAL INCLUSION

The Reserve Bank of India defines micro-finance as "the provision of thrift, credit, and other financial services and products of very small amounts to the poor in rural, semi-urban and urban areas for enabling them to raise their income levels and improve their living standards". Urban poor need micro-finance for livelihoods.

Formal financial institutions were not designed to help those who don't already have financial assets. Financial Inclusion is enabling access to or delivery of banking services at an affordable cost to the vast sections of disadvantaged and low-income groups. Unrestrained access to public goods and services is the *sine qua non* of public policy of a nation. As banking services are in the nature of public service, provision of banking and payment services to the entire population without discrimination should be the prime objective of the public policy. Micro-finance enterprises are being considered as a promising alternative for expanding the base of financial services to the poor and weaker sections especially in developing economies. Financial inclusion is more than micro-finance.

KNOWLEDGE MANAGEMENT FOR URBAN POVERTY ALLEVIATION

Knowledge Management is the ability to evaluate weaknesses and provides training and development strategies to strengthen the weaker skills in the team. Unless micro-finance providers pay attention towards effective knowledge management, the performance of poverty alleviation projects couldn't attain success. Proper awareness of knowledge asset and knowledge management is essential for the micro-entrepreneurs to manage the business efficiently and effectively.

Productive capability is no longer completely dependent on capital and equipment along with that information and knowledge assets are increasingly important. Knowledge assets are the knowledge regarding markets, products, technologies and organisations, that a business owns or needs to own and which enable its business processes to generate profits. The ability of a locality to supply knowledge assets for an enterprise's need has become paramount in economic development. Hence micro-finance providers must pay attention to identify the local needs and knowledge and try to impart training for developing the knowledge asset, so as to enable them to start micro-enterprises by providing capital at lower cost.

Micro-entrepreneurs seeking fund from micro-finance for job creation, often experiences difficulties in managing its activities regarding marketing, accounting, new technology, dealing the legal requirements, etc. while expanding its business in due course. Each Enterprises must realise clearly "what they actually know and what they need to know" in order to keep the track and make use of their knowledge to get maximum return. There are many problems associated with finding out these knowledge assets and being able to use them in an efficient and cost-effective manner. Some of the reasons for lack of micro-entrepreneurship in Kerala are aversion for taking risks and preference for secured employment, lack of confidence to innovate, poor self-esteem of entrepreneurs, lack of business culture built on mutual trust, unsympathetic and unsupportive bureaucracy, delay in sanctioning of loans, the labour laws, lack of training and knowledge, etc.

Urban poverty alleviation programs, in Kerala support not only provide knowledge regarding loan facilities to borrowers either in group or individual, but also they provides knowledge assets like marketing, accounting and other technical support as per the requirements of the prospective entrepreneurs through arranging trainings and workshops.

MICRO-ENTERPRISE FORMATION FOR URBAN POVERTY ALLEVIATION

In February 1997, as per the recommendations of the Hashim Committee Report, all the Urban Poverty Alleviation Schemes were subsumed in a new scheme namely Swarna Jayanti Shahari Rozgar Yojana (SJSRY), and which was launched with effect from 1.12.97. The Swarna Jayanti Shahari Rozgar Yojana (SJSRY) is primarily an employment generation programme for the urban to set-up small enterprises. Local skills and local crafts are encouraged for this purpose.

Institutional Arrangements for the Implementation of SJSRY

The Urban Local Government (ULG), Community Development Society (CDS), Kudumbasree Mission and the District Planning Committee (DPC) are the institutions that play important roles in the implementation of SJSRY in Kerala. Kudumbasree District Mission shall be responsible for district-level facilitation and monitoring of SJSRY. Banks play a very important role in helping to achieve the objectives of SJSRY.

The success of the programmes designed by the government depends upon the training they impart to the prospective entrepreneurs Anyone who is interested to know about self-employment opportunities, can approach Urban Poverty Alleviation cell for SJSRY scheme loans for micro-enterprise related activities, and they need to undergo following trainings during the various stages.

Self-Employment Training for new entrepreneurs from BPL families has the following components:

- *General Orientation Training (GOT)*: One-day orientation provided to all persons desirous of becoming entrepreneurs.
- *Entrepreneurship Development Programme (EDP)*: Two or more days of training Programme to develop entrepreneurial abilities of beneficiaries who have completed GOT and continue to be interested in forming enterprises
- *Skill Training*: Skill development programme for developing ability to start and run enterprises in a specific sector. The

skill training provided will be specific to the business chosen by the individual/group entrepreneurs.

Micro-enterprise Creation training aims at developing entrepreneurial competence and confidence on potential entrepreneurs to help them start new ventures, whereas Micro-enterprise Assistance programme is for existing entrepreneurs to support them to successfully run their enterprises.

DETAILS OF MICRO-ENTREPRISES

According to the information provided by State Poverty Eradication Mission there are nearly 700 micro-enterprise units functioning in Thiruvananthapuram.

According to the information provided by Urban Poverty Alleviation cell Thiruvananthapuram three types of training are provided to the beneficiaries belonging to NHGs as per their request. Only after providing the general orientation training the members are considered to be eligible for providing micro-finance loan with subsidy from the

TABLE 1

Total Number of Micro-Enterprises

No. of Units of Micro Entreprises in Urban Area—2009-10		
Type	*Thiruvananthapuram*	*Subsidy Granted upto-2009*
Individual	688	4935306
Group	250	27342063
Total	938	32277369

TABLE 2

Total Number of Micro-Enterprises

New Microenterprise Units in Thiruvananthapuram during 2009-10					
Nature of Units	*CDI*	*%*	*CDII*	*%*	*Total*
Manufacturing	5	28	7	29	11
Trading	4	22	8	33	12
Service	6	33	5	21	11
Agriculture	2	11	3	13	5
Dairy Farm	1	6	1	4	2
Total	18	100	24	100	42

Government for starting new enterprises. But during the year 2010 training is given to 1190 beneficiaries including existing micro-enterprises by the UPA CELL

DETAILS OF SAMPLE

Thirty one NHGs members belong to urban area of Thiruvananthapuram corporation have been selected and interviewed from different units like manufacturing trading service and agriculture for the purpose of this study. The responses are taken in order to analyse the impact of micro-finance and entrepreneurship training in urban micro-enterprise development and urban poverty alleviation.

DATA ANALYSIS

Respondent's opinion about the level of awareness about the micro-finance is very high. The Local Self-Governments (LSGs), NHGs, the banks, and Non-Government Organisations play their role effectively to create awareness about micro-finance and vocational training among the urban poor. The paper seeks to examine the impact of training on urban poor of selected NHGs from Thiruvananthapuram District in the state of Kerala. It has also attempted to examine the impact of micro-enterprises on poverty by empowering women.

The Table 3 shows all the respondents of the study are undergone the GOT and EDP training. During the year and also running micro-enterprises. Their products are exhibited in the festival fair.

The Table 4 clearly describes the major reasons for joining the NHGs and training. Monetrary benefit is main inspiration of the urban poor to join this activities. 7% of the respondent joined only for getting loan while 10% were joined to enhance their knowledge. 16% of the respondents joined with the intention to get loan and save money while 61% to start business, with loan. It reveals that they are interested to start business with this micro-credit.

Savings creates self-confidence in life. The above table reveals that 85% of the respondent did not have sufficient income or savings before starting business. But the training enables them to gain self-employment, so as to keep their family out of poverty. 94% of the respondent opinioned that after starting micro-enterprises, they have sufficient income and 87% have the debt repaying capacity, only 6% of the total sample tended to express dissatisfaction about the income even after starting business.

The above Table 6 reveals that 19% have very high satisfaction regarding the training given to them. 61% have high satisfaction. Only 7% expressed low satisfaction. Thus, the greater part of the total sample

TABLE 3

The Nature of Training Received by the Respondents

Type of Training Received by the Respondents in Urban Area Under Urban Self-Employment Programme					
	Type	*GOT*		*EDP*	
		No.	*%*	*No.*	*%*
Manufacturing					
	Umbrella-making	0	0	0	0
	Soap, Lotion-making, etc.	1	3.23	1	3.23
	Ornaments and Jewellary-making	2	6.46	2	6.46
	Readymade Dress-making	2	6.46	2	6.46
	Doll-making	0	0	0	0
	Food Processing	6	19.36	6	19.36
	Handicraft	2	6.46	2	6.46
Trading					
	Bags, Chapels, etc.	2	6.46	2	6.46
	Fish Marketing	0	0	0	0
	Textile Goods	4	12.91	4	12.91
Service					
	Clean Well Unit	6	19.36	6	19.36
	Nursing	0	0	0	0
	Beauty Parlor	0	0	0	0
	Tailoring	2	6.46	2	6.46
	Screen Printing	1	3.23	1	3.23
Agriculture Dairy Farming					
	Gardening	2	6.46	2	6.46
	Dairy Farming	1	3.23	1	3.23
	Poultry Farming	0	0	0	0
		31	100	31	100

Source: Computed from field data.

TABLE 4

Reasons for Joining the NHGs and Training

Inspiration to Join the Training	*No. of Respondents*	%
To Get Loan	2	7
To Get Training	3	10
To Move with People	2	6
To Get Loan and Save	5	16
To Get Loan and to Get Help to Start Business	19	61
Total	31	100

Source: Primary Data.

TABLE 5

Sufficiency of Income to meet their Needs and Capacity to Repay the Debts after Starting Micro-Enterprises

Monthly Savings	*Before Starting*	%	*After Starting*	%
Sufficiency of Income—Yes	5	15	29	94
Sufficiency of Income—No	26	85	02	6
Repaying Capacity of Debt—Yes	0	0	27	87
Repaying Capacity of Debt— No	31	100	4	13

Source: Primary Data.

TABLE 6

Opinion about the Training Provided by the UPA CELL

Satisfaction Level	*No. of Respondent*	%
Very High	6	19
High	19	61
Moderate	4	13
Low	2	7
Very Low	0	0
Total	31	100

Source: Computed from field data.

tended to express full satisfaction about the training provided to them and stated that it is the training that enable them to start certain business activities.

This table reveals after starting micro-enterprises with the help of micro-finance and training 77% of the respondent have increase in

TABLE 7

Impact of Micro-Enterprises on Economic Empowerment

Indicators	*No Change*	%	*Increased*	%
Improvement in Income	7	23	24	77
Increase in Savings	4	13	22	71
Increase in Employment	3	10	25	81
Increase in Access to Credit	3	10	28	90

Source: Computed from field data.

TABLE 8

Impact of Micro-Enterprises on Knowledge Management

Indicators	*Very High*	*High*	*Average*	*Low*	*Nil*
Chance to Develop Own Knowledge	9	15	6	0	1
Ability to Adapt to Market Needs	6	8	12	4	1
Chance for New Skill Development	8	9	14	0	0
Ability to Deal with Legal Business Requirement	4	11	9	6	1
Ability to take Decision after Training	7	16	3	5	0
Ability to Lead Independent Life	7	17	5	2	0
Improvement in Self-Confidence	9	18	4	0	0
Ability to Manage Business Activities	8	17	4	1	1

Source: Computed from field data.

income, but 71% got the chance to increase their savings. 81% have the opinion that employment opportunities improved and 90% of the respondent expressed that their access to credit also increased to large extent. Thus the contribution of micro-enterprise to total family income is found to be significant which shows micro-enterprises have a significant role in economic empowerment among urban poor.

The analysis reveal that training provides to develop own knowledge as well as new skill for a creative purpose. They got the courage to start micro-enterprise units and to understand how to market the products. For that micro-finance institutions as well as the CDS provides trade fares, exhibition stalls, etc. It is observed that majority of the respondent attained the ability to manage business activities through the training. It enables them to create self-confidence, decision-making capacity and also helps them to lead independent life. The ability to evaluate own weaknesses and to develop own strategies to strengthen the weaker skills in the team, leads the micro-entrepreneurs towards effective knowledge management and thereby reduce the urban poverty.

MAJOR FINDINGS

It is found that the majority of the respondents were unemployed and after receiving the training they started their own business. Micro-finance provides funds for micro-enterprises and facilitates to generate income and urban poverty reduction. Major findings are:

The study shows that the flow of micro-finance is a pushing factor for the promotion of micro-enterprises and facilitates to generate income and urban poverty reduction.

The study reveals that through proper training entrepreneurial skill can be developed which facilitates the micro-entrepreneurs to enrich their knowledge regarding latest developments and improve the marketing potential of their products and services.

Age, educational qualification or marital status is not the basis of getting training and any person who is unemployed can become a member in NHGs and can apply for training.

Majority of the individual women micro-entrepreneurs in the study areas belong to younger age group with average education and were self-starters in their business or trade.

Training is given as per the requirement and demand of the applicants and all the trained members are not in a position to start micro-enterprises just after completing the training.

Active intervention of government urban poverty alleviation schemes can provide proper knowledge asset management skill for the successful micro-enterprises.

Through micro-finance urban poor can become entrepreneurs and can increase social status and economic empowerment which leads to the reduction of the urban poverty.

Loan availability and loan repayment are easy and economic to the urban poor through micro-finance.

Entrepreneurship Skill Development Training Programme enables the trainees to start new business to a great extent and trainees express great satisfaction about the training. Some members take up more than one training and engaged in more than one activity (e.g. food processing and tailoring).

The increased incomes from business activities have helped to supplement the family income which facilitates to reduce the levels of poverty to a great extent in several families. Most of the entrepreneurs in the study area in respect of occupational activity prefer miscellaneous activities to earn something and this trend indicates that they are unskilled and have no serious intention to take more business risk.

SUGGESTIONS

Based upon the above findings it is suggested that there is a need to address the issue of urban poverty alleviation in a systematic, scientific and a time-bound manner. More micro-finance is needed to the urban poor to create confidence to start new business. There is a need to have more focus on the skill up gradation of the urban poor to improve their "employability" and to facilitate their employment. Alleviation of rural poverty can be achieved by identifying income-generating activities with focus on micro-finance as the basic input for socio-economic development. Through proper knowledge management micro-enterprises can achieve better result which will lead to create more self-employment opportunities.

CONCLUSION

Micro-finance can encourage the micro-enterprises by providing capital and knowledge asset at lower cost. Kudumbasree's work in urban Kerala is excellent for urban poverty alleviation in the state with the help of micro-finance. Self-employment through setting up of micro-enterprises and skill development is now considered as a better remedy for under-employed and unemployed urban youth. Local knowledge is the human capital of both the urban and rural people. It is the main asset they invest in the struggle for survival. Hence, micro-enterprises must give importance to develop and utilize the local knowledge continuously for a gradually changing environment. Micro-manufacturing units need knowledge about market opportunities, on what support resources are available and how to use these resources productively and efficiently. Therefore, a need has arisen to develop micro-enterprises as urban poverty reduction tool so as to manage urban poverty in a systematic manner.

REFERENCES

Boekema F., K. Morgan, S. Bakkers, R. Rutt (Editors) (2000), Knowledge, Innovation and Economic Growth: The Theory and Practice of Learning Regions, Edward Elgar.

Boekema, F., K. Morgan, S. Bakkers, R. Rutt (Editors) (2000), Knowledge, Economic Review, State Planning Board, Thiruvananthapuram.

C.A.K. Yesudian, Tata Institute of Social Sciences, Mumbai, India (2007), "Poverty alleviation programmes in India: A social audit".

Censes of India, 2001.

Dr. Jaya, S. Anand, Addressing Poverty through Self-Help Groups: A Case Study of Kerala.

Dr. Jitendra Ahirrao and Suryakant Chaugule (2010), Micro-finance for rural Entrepreneurship development &rural industrialization.

K.S. Mohindra, A report on women Self-Help Groups (SHGs) in Kerala State, India: a public health perspective, March 2003.

NABARD and Local Administration Department (1997), Poverty Eradication Mission, Kerala State, Thiruvananthapuram.

Oommen, M.A. (1999), The Community Development Society of Kerala, Institute of Social Sciences, New Delhi.

www.Kudumpashree.org

www.mhupa,gov.in

18

Financial Inclusion and Inclusive Growth

ARUN KUMAR, T.T.

ABSTRACT

Financial inclusion is the delivery of financial services at affordable costs to vast sections of disadvantaged and low income groups. It is argued that as banking services are in the nature of public good, it is essential that availability of banking and payment services to the entire population without discrimination is the prime objective of public policy. The term "financial inclusion" has gained importance since the early 2000s, and is a result of findings about financial exclusion and its direct correlation to poverty. Financial inclusion is now a common objective for many central banks among the developing nations. The first priority for banks is to adopt core banking solution (CBS), including all regional rural banks (RBS). Next, a multi-channel approach using handheld devices, mobiles, cards, micro-ATMs, branches and kiosks can be used. However, it should be ensured that the transactions put through such front-end devices should be seamlessly integrated with the banks' CBS.

Financial inclusion is the delivery of financial services at affordable costs to vast sections of disadvantaged and low income groups. It is argued that as banking services are in the nature of public good, it is essential that availability of banking and payment services to the entire population without discrimination is the prime objective of public policy. The term "financial inclusion" has gained importance since the early 2000s, and is a result of findings about financial exclusion and its direct correlation to poverty. Financial inclusion is now a common objective for many central banks among the developing nations.

To just sum up "the process of ensuring access to financial services and timely and adequate credit where needed by vulnerable groups such as weaker section and low income groups at an affordable cost given by Rangarajan who headed Committee on Financial Inclusion.

The first priority for banks is to adopt core banking solution (CBS), including all regional rural banks (RBS). Next, a multi-channel approach using handheld devices, mobiles, cards, micro-ATMs, branches and kiosks can be used. However, it should be ensured that the transactions put through such front-end devices should be seamlessly integrated with the banks' CBS.

In rural areas, where accessibility is a problem, banks are sing the micro-finance network and business correspondents and facilitators to bring more people under the ambit of banking services, said a report of PwC prepared for the CII's banking summit, Capitalising on the huge untapped potential in smaller towns and cities and rendering financial services to this segment of people poses a big challenge. "Few banks have explored technology solutions to increase the scale of their micro-finance portfolios, with the use of smart cards and core banking solutions".

FINANCIAL INCLUSION IN INDIA

Reserve Bank of India has set-up a commission (Khan Commission) in 2004 to look into financial inclusion and the recommendations of the commission were incorporated into the mid-term review of the policy (2005-06). In the report RBI exhorted the banks with a view of achieving greater financial inclusion to make available a basic "no-frills" banking account. In India, Financial Inclusion first featured in 2005, when it was introduced, that, too, from a pilot project in UT of Pondicherry, by K.C. Chakraborthy, the chairman of Indian Bank. Mangalam Village became the first village in India where all households were provided banking facilities. In addition to this KYC (Know Your Customer) norms were relaxed for people intending to open accounts with annual deposits of less than Rs. 50,000. General Credit Cards (GCC) were issued to the poor and the disadvantaged with a view to help them access easy credit. In January 2006, the Reserve Bank permitted commercial banks to make use of the services of non-governmental organizations (NGOs/SHGs), micro-finance institutions and other civil society organizations as intermediaries for providing financial and banking services. These intermediaries could be used as business facilitators (BF) or business correspondents (BC) by commercial banks. The bank asked the commercial banks in different regions to start a 100% financial inclusion campaign on a pilot basis. As a result of the campaign states or U.T.s like Pondicherry, Himachal Pradesh and Kerala have announced 100% financial inclusion in all their districts. Reserve Bank of India's vision for 2020 is to open nearly 600 million new customers' accounts and service them through a variety of channels by leveraging on IT. However, illiteracy and the low income savings and lack of bank branches in rural areas continue to be a road block to financial inclusion in many states. Apart from this there are certain in Current model which is followed. There is inadequate legal and financial structure. India, being a mostly agrarian economy, hardly has schemes which lend for agriculture. Along with micro-finance we need to focus on micro-insurance too.

In its platinum jubilee year, the Reserve Bank of India (RBI) wants to connect every Indian to the country s banking system.

RBI is currently working on a three-year financial inclusion plan and is discussing this with each bank to see how to take this forward, K.C. Chakrabarty, Deputy Governor, RBI said.

"Nearly forty years after nationalization of banks, 60% of the country's population does not have bank accounts and nearly 90% do not get loans."

Despite heightened focus on financial inclusion, Indian banks still somewhat failed to bring the under and un-banked into the mainstream banking fold.

India has currently the second-highest number of financially excluded households in the world. Approximately, 40% of India s population has bank accounts, and only about 10% have any kind of life insurance cover, while a meager 0.6% has non-life insurance cover.

According to UNITED NATIONS, "A financial sector that provides access to credit for all "bankable" people and firms and to savings and payments services for everyone. Inclusive finance does not require that everyone who is eligible use each of the services, but they should be able to choose use them if desired.

REPORT OF THE COMMITTEE ON FINANCIAL INCLUSION IN INDIA (Chairperson: C. Rangarajan) (2008), "The process of ensuring access to financial services and timely and adequate credit where needed by vulnerable groups such as weaker sections and low income groups at an affordable cost."

'Major Three Aspects of Financial Inclusion' make people to:

- Access financial markets
- Access credit markets
- Learn financial matters (financial education)

Financial Inclusion includes Accessing of Financial Products and Services like,

- Savings facility
- Credit and debit cards access
- Electronic fund transfer
- All kinds of commercial loans
- Overdraft facility
- Cheque facility
- Payment and remittance services
- Low cost financial services
- Insurance (Medical insurance)
- Financial advice
- Pension for old age and investment schemes
- Access to financial markets
- Micro-credit during emergency
- Entrepreneurial credit

Financially Excluded People, the financially excluded sections largely comprise:

- Marginal farmers
- Landless labourers
- Oral lessees
- Self-employed and unorganised sector enterprises
- Urban slum-dwellers
- Migrants
- Ethnic minorities and socially excluded groups
- Senior citizens
- Women

The North, East, Eastern and Central Regions contain most of the financially excluded population.

Factors affecting access to financial services:

- *Legal identity*: Lack of legal identity like voter id, driving license, birth certificates employment identity card, etc.
- *Limited literacy*: Particularly financial literacy and lack of basic education prevent people to have access from financial services.
- *Level of income*: Level of income decides to have financial access. Low income people generally have the attitude of thinking that banks are only for rich.

- *Terms and conditions*: While getting loans or at the time of opening accounts banks places many conditions, so the uneducated and poor people find it very difficult to access financial services.
- *Complicated procedures*: Due to lack of financial literacy and basic education, it is very difficult for those people who lack both to read terms and conditions and account filling forms.
- *Psychological and cultural barriers*: Many people voluntarily excluded themselves due to psychological barriers and they think that they are excluded from accessing financial services.
- *Place of living*: As the name suggests that commercial banks operate only in commercially profitable areas and they set-up branches and main offices only in that areas. People who lived in under developed areas find it very difficult to go to areas in which banks are generally reside.
- *Lack of awareness*: Finally, people who lack basic education do not know the importance of the financial products like Insurance, Finance, Bank Accounts, cheque facility, etc.

Consequences of Financial Exclusion Major Two Threats:

- *Losing opportunities to grow*: In the absence of finance, people who are not connected with formal financial system lack opportunities to grow.
- *Country's growth will retard*: Due to vast unutilized resources that is in the form of money in the hands of people who lack financial inclusive services.

Other Consequences:

- *Business loss to banks*: Banks will loss business if this condition persists for ever due to lack of opening of bank accounts.
- *Exclusion from mainstream society*: The people, who lack financial services, presumed that they are excluded from mainstream society.
- *All transactions cannot be made in cash*: Some transactions can be made in cash. In this technological world everybody wants to have electronic cash system like debit and credit cards and also EFT.
- *Loss of opportunities to thrift and borrow*: Financially excluded

people, may lose chances to save their some part of livelihood earnings and also to borrow loans.

- *Employment barriers*: Nowadays all salary and other financial benefits from various sources like Government scholarships, any compensation, grants, reliefs, etc. are paid through bank accounts.
- *Loss due to theft*: Banks provide various schemes of safety locker facility. It mitigates the risk due to thefts.
- *Other allied financial services*: People who do not have bank accounts may not go to bank as for as possible. So they lack basic financial auxiliary services like DD, Insurance cover and other emergency need loans, etc.

Benefits of Inclusive Financial Growth:

- *Growth with equity*: In the path of super power we the Indians will need to achieve the growth of our country with equality. It is provided by inclusive finance.
- *Get rid of poverty*: To remove poverty from the Indian context everybody will be given access to formal financial services. Because if they borrow loans for business or education or any other purpose they get the loan will pave way for their development.
- *Financial Transactions made easy*: Inclusive finance will provide banking-related financial transactions in an easy and speedy way.
- *Safe savings along with financial services*: People will have safe savings along with other allied services like insurance cover, entrepreneurial loans, payment and settlement facility, etc.
- *Inflating National Income*: Boosting up business opportunities will definitely increase GDP and which will be reflected in our national income growth.
- *Becoming Global Player*: Financial access will attract global market players to our country that will result in increasing employment and business opportunities.

Relationship between Financial Inclusion and Development Indicators

Economic growth follows financial inclusion. In order to achieve the objective of growth with equity, it is imperative that infrastructure is developed with financial inclusion.

- Savings and credit accounts—indicators of financial inclusion.

- Per capita income—indicator of economic development.
- Electricity consumption and road length—indicators of infrastructure development.
- All the above influence economic developments which follows adequate financial and credit facilities.
- Expectations of poor people from financial system taking into account.
- Seasonal Inflow of Income from agricultural operations,
- Migration from one place to another.
- Seasonal And Irregular Work Availability and Income; the existing financial system needs to be designed to suit their requirements.
- Security and safety of deposits.
- Low transaction cost.
- Convenient operating time.
- Minimum paper work.
- Frequent deposits.
- Quick and easy access.
- Product suitable to income and consumption.

References

Government of India (2008), The Committee on Financial Inclusion (Chairman: C. Rangarajan).

Government of India (2007), 11th Five Year Plan Document, Planning Commission.

Reserve Bank of India (2008), Report on Currency and Finance, 2006-08.

Reserve Bank of India (2009), "100 percent Financial Inclusion—Evaluating by External Agencies Board Findings", Circular dated January 22.

Financial Inclusion for Inclusive Growth—Role of New Generation Banks

ABY, R.L. AND SHIJUMON, K.J.

ABSTRACT

Financial inclusion is a burning topic in India. Government had introduced many programmes through different financial institutions including both banking and non-banking, for the promotion of financial inclusion all over the country. Delivery of financial services at an affordable cost to the vast sections of disadvantaged and low income groups is called financial inclusion. Financial inclusion gives stress on availability of banking and payment services to entire population without discrimination. Financial inclusion may be—state driven that is, state may take actions for exercising financial inclusion services or voluntary effort by the banking community. To ensure financial inclusion in the lower level of economy new generation banks and non-banking statutory financial organisations are playing an important role. They have mostly set-up by Government, ICICI, NHB, RRB, NABARD, NCDC are some of the new generation banks or NBSFOs working on the principle of financial inclusion. Now-a-days, new generation banks and NBSFOs provide many services to attract both rural and urban people towards banking. These services include credit to agriculturists and weaker sections of the society, micro-finance, No-frills account and digital banking services through mobile as well as internet banking.

Financial inclusion is a ablaze topic of the present India, having a stable and high growth economy. For the promotion of financial inclusion Government has introduced many programmes through different banking and non-banking financial institutions. According to RBI financial inclusion is the delivery of banking services at an affordable cost to the vast sections of disadvantaged and low income groups who tend to be excluded from the formal financial system. Its target is essentially the poor people who have not yet been brought in to the mainstream of formal banking culture, i.e. financial inclusion gives stress on availability of banking and payment services to entire population without discrimination.

Access to finance, especially by the poor in rural area, is an essential requisite for employment, economic growth, poverty alleviation, increased standard of living and social upliftment of our country. Further, financial inclusion will enable the poor and the rustics of our country to open a bank account to save and invest, to borrow and to repay, to insure and to take part in the credit. This will enable them to break the chain of poverty. Most of the Indians are not aware about basic services provided by financial institutions. According to RBI monthly bulletin 2007 only around 59% of Indians are having bank account. The following table makes it clear that there exist a regional imbalance also; Northern region people have a highest of 80% and North-Eastern region having the lowest of only 37%.

Percentage of Savings Bank Account

Area	*Percentage of SB account*
Southern region	66
Western region	60
Central region	52
Eastern region	41
North-eastern region	37
Northern region	80
India	59

To ensure financial inclusion in the lower level of economy Non-Banking Statutory Financial Organizations (NBSFOs) or new generation banks play an important role. They are usually special or specialized institutions mostly set-up by Goverment but some sort of private participation is also there. ICICI, NHB, IDBI, NABARD, NCDC, etc.

are some of the Non-Banking statutory financial organizations working on principle of financial inclusion.

Now-a-days new generation banks provide many services to attract both rural and urban people towards banking. Through an inclusive programme new generation banks promote the development of innovative and cost effective approach in banking sector. These services provided by new generation banks include.

- Credit to agriculturists and weaker sections of the society.
- Micro-finance.
- No-frills account.
- Digital Banking through mobile, etc.
- Credit to agriculturists and weaker sections of the society.

New generation banks in India are ready to roll out variety of financial products for villagers and farmers in rural areas. The ability to access appropriate financial services shows the development of a society. Despite considerable expansion in the banking system, the rural people in India particularly farmers do not have access to the formal financial services such as bank account and low cost loans. It is mainly because of farmer's small and frequent credit requirements and also due to their incapability to offer sufficient collateral securities. None of the private sector banks have achieved the separate individual target for the priority sector and target for agriculture and weaker sector. The Non-Banking statutory financial organizations like NABARD is the only player in this market. In related with lending to agriculture sector NABARD offers credit to state Co-operative banks from there it reaches to district Co-operative and from to primary Co-operatives. These primary Co-operative societies provide short-term frequent loans to agriculturists. RRB's are also these for the development of backward rural areas. The new food security bill and need for food, there is a possibility of subsidies and other supports to agriculture sector. The new generation banks are now aiming this vast market segment with technology baking.

No-Frills Account

The basic problem is that today less than half of Indians have a bank account. The No-frills bank account is an innovative instrument launched in 2005 to introduce the concept of banking to the under privileged rural people of India. These are bank accounts either with nil or very minimum balance. New generation banks are providing no frills account facility for example one of the new generation bank ICICI is offering this facility in 18 states and around 3 million such account-holders are there.

Digital Banking through Mobile

Financial inclusion refers to the policy goal of providing a full range of formal financial services like savings, credit, insurance, remittance, etc. to all financially excluded groups. In India for a population of 1.21 billion people only 200 million people (16.52%) have access to bank account, while 811 million (67%) have a mobile phone. This suggests how best mobile phone potential can be used for achieving financial inclusion in our country. New generation banks like ICICI and IDBI provide mobile access facility to their account-holders and thus participate in our countries financial inclusion programme. As compared with other players in banking sector new generation bank are the major users of digital banking and this may help them to offer low cost services every effectively to the rural untapped areas and act as a director in the financial inclusion process. New Generation Banks allow its customers to avail the following bank's services through Internet:

- Online Payments.
- Conduct Banking Operations from House or Office.
- Service available for 24 hours and 365 days a year.
- Accessible from anywhere in the world using Internet.

Financial Education

Financial literacy plays a significant role in the efficient allocation of household savings and the ability of individuals to meet their financial goals. It also means the ability to seek sound financial advices. Financial literacy has assumed greater importance in recent years as financial markets have become increasingly complex and the common man finds it very difficult to make informed decisions. Financial literacy is considered as an important adjunct for promoting financial inclusion and ultimately financial stability. Financial inclusion can be achieved only through transfer of knowledge. New generation banks like IDBI, ICICI, SFCs, NBSFOs and other volunteers for educating the poor provide credit counselling, financial education programs in regional languages, awareness programs, etc. Financial education helps to avoid complexities in banking services.

CONCLUSION

It is to be concluded that, in India new generation banks plays a vital role for achieving financial inclusion and there by resulting inclusive growth. With a view to reaching poor people in backward areas banks have to launch new programmes. For better result unwillingness of banks to serve low income group of people will be changed. A public-private partnership for financial advice and general help can increase financial inclusion. RBI should ensure transparency of financial institutions.

References

Agenda for Banking in the New Millennium —Jalan, B.
Financial Inclusion: A Challenging Target for India—V.V Georgekutty.
Financial Inclusion: Role of Micro-Finance Institution—Devendra Prasad Pandey.
Micro-finance Muddle—Bajaj, Kapil.
WTO and Indian Banking Sector: An Overview—Jayalekshmi and A. Ashok.

20

Financial Inclusion—A Myth or Reality

DR. NIMI DEV, R. AND RANI, L.

ABSTRACT

It is commonly understood that poverty can be reduced through Financial inclusion. It is the availability of banking services at an affordable cost to disadvantaged and low-income groups. The first-ever Index of Financial Inclusion to find out the extent of reach of banking services among 100 countries, India has been ranked 50. Only 34% of Indian individuals have access to receive banking services. In order to increase this number the Reserve Bank of India had the Government of India take innovative steps like starting regional rural banks, offering 'no frills' account. Inspite of these efforts from the part of commercial banks, there are chances of financial exclusion. The reach of financial inclusion is a big worry even though we say that there is 100% financial inclusion in Kerala. The main reason is that the products designed by the banks are not satisfying the low income families. The provision of uncomplicated, small, affordable products will help to bring the low income families into the formal financial sector. Banks have limitations to reach directly to the low income consumers. Correspondents can be considered to be an excellent channel which banks can use to distribute their product information. Educating the consumers about the financial benefits and products of banks which are beneficial to low income groups will be a great step to tap their potential.

INTRODUCTION

Financial inclusion is the availability of banking services at an affordable cost to disadvantaged and low-income groups. In India, the basic concept of financial inclusion is having a saving or current account with any bank. In reality it includes loans, insurance services and much more.

The RBI recently came up with a State-wise Index of Financial Inclusion and the results were rather surprising. While Kerala topped the index, followed closely by Maharashtra, Gujarat lagged far behind. In this survey, RBI considered three basic dimensions of an inclusive financial system — banking penetration, availability of the banking services and usage of the banking system.

The first-ever Index of Financial Inclusion to find out the extent of reach of banking services among 100 countries, India has been ranked 50. Only 34% of Indian individuals have access to receive banking services. In order to increase this number the Reserve Bank of India had the Government of India take innovative steps. One of the reasons for opening new branches of Regional Rural Banks was to make sure that the banking service is accessible to the poor. With the directive from RBI, our banks are now offering "No Frill" Accounts to low income groups. These accounts either have a low minimum or nil balance with some restriction in transactions. The individual bank has the authority to decide whether the account should have zero or minimum balance.

The Indian Government has a long history of working to expand financial inclusion. Nationalization of the major private sector banks in 1969 was a big step. In 1975 GOI established RRBs with the same aim. It encouraged branch expansion of bank branches especially in rural areas. It can be stated that bank nationalization was the first step towards financial inclusion in India. Public Sector banks make use of the services of non-governmental organizations (NGOs/SHGs), micro-finance institutions and other civil society organizations as intermediaries for providing financial and banking services. These intermediaries are used as business facilitators (BF) or business correspondents (BC) by commercial banks.

SUCCESS STORIES

So far, 344 districts have been identified by State Level Bankers Committee for 100 per cent financial inclusion. As a result of the campaign of the public sector banks, 175 districts in 21 States and 7 Union Territories have reported having achieved the target. The self-help group (SHG)-bank linkage programme has emerged as the major micro-finance programme in the country and is being implemented by commercial banks, RRBs and co-operative banks.

RRBs are a powerful instrument for financial inclusion. RRBs have more reach compared to scheduled commercial banks especially in rural areas. The SHG-Bank Linkage Programme can be regarded as another initiative since Independence for delivering financial services to the poor in a sustainable manner. The programme has been growing rapidly and the number of SHGs financed increased to 29.25 lakhs on 31 March 2007.

NGOs have played a commendable role in promoting SHGs and linking them with banks. NGOs, being local initiators with their low resources, are finding it difficult to expand in other areas and regions. There is, therefore, a need to evolve an incentive package which should motivate these NGOs to diversify into other backward areas. The SHG-Bank Linkage Programme is now more than 15 years old. There are a large number of SHGs in the country which are well established in their savings and credit operations. The members of such groups want to expand and diversify their activities with a view to attain economies of scale. SHG-bank linkage has emerged as an effective credit delivery channel to the poor clients. However, there are segments within the poor such as share croppers/oral lessees/tenant farmers, whose loan requirements are much larger but who have no collaterals to fit into the traditional financing approaches of the banking system. To service such clients, Joint Liability Groups (JLGs), an up-gradation of SHG model, could be an effective way. Micro-Finance Institutions (MFIs) could play a significant role in facilitating inclusion, as they are uniquely positioned in reaching out to the rural poor. Many of them operate in a limited geographical area, have a greater understanding of the issues specific to the rural poor, enjoy greater acceptability amongst the rural poor and have flexibility in operations providing a level of comfort to their clientele. Micro-insurance needs a further push and guidance as it is a key element in the financial services package for people at the bottom of the pyramid. Evidences are there showing that Financial literacy is the only panacea for quick financial inclusion.

After Goa and Himachal Pradesh, Kerala, which earlier had a distinction of first state to achieve total literacy, has now become a total banking state. Every single household in Kerala has been brought under banking network with at least one member of each family having a bank account. All such persons will now be eligible for a general purpose loan up to Rs. 25,000. Palakkad district of Kerala is the first district in India to achieve one hundred percent financial inclusion.

Gray Areas of Financial Inclusion

The two types of financial exclusion normally seen are: (i) exclusion from payment system : not having access to bank accounts, (ii) exclusion from formal credit markets leading to approaching informal/exploitative markets. There are problems from the part of banks and people. The ambiance, products, rules, formalities, documents, notice etc support that it is exclusively for the elite class in the economy. We can call it as supply side problems. That is why Citizen believes that the banks are for rich people. Banks are in a falls belief that the poor people are not a profitable market segment, we can call it as demand side problems The main reason for financial exclusion from the demand side is the lack of a regular or substantial income. In most of the cases people with low income do not qualify for a loan. The proximity of the financial service is another fact. The loss is not only the transportation cost but also the loss of daily wages for a low income individual. Most of the excluded consumers are not aware of the bank's products, which are beneficial for them. Getting money for their financial requirements from a local moneylender is easier than getting a loan from the bank. Most of the banks need collateral for their loans. It is very difficult for a low income individual to find collateral for a bank loan. The supply side problems also the banks responsibility towards shareholders. So the management give more importance for meeting their financial targets. So they focus on larger accounts. It is not profitable for banks to provide small loans and make a profit. Technology, absence of coverage, improper delivery mechanism, priority of banks, etc. are other supply areas need special attention. The banks show concerns towards agricultural credit, MGNREGs account opening, rural area branches, etc. due to government pressure and not the commitment towards social responsibility. So the government should shoulder the sole responsibility of financial inclusion.

Financial inclusion mainly focuses on the poor who do not have formal financial institutional support and getting them out of the clutches of local moneylenders. As a first step towards this, some of our banks have now come forward with general purpose credit cards and artisan credit cards which offer collateral-free small loans. The RBI has simplified the KYC norms for opening a 'No- Frill' account. This will help the low income individual to open a 'No- Frill' account without identity proof and address proof.

In such cases banks can take the individual's introduction from an existing customer whose full KYC norm procedure has been completed. And the introducer must have a satisfactory transaction with the bank for at least 6 months. This simplified procedure is available to those who intend to keep a balance not exceeding Rs. 50,000 in all accounts taken together. With this facility the banks can channel the untapped, considerable amount of money from the low income group to the formal economy. Banks are now permitted to utilize the service of NGOs, SHGs and other civil society organizations as intermediaries in providing financial and banking services through the use of business facilitator and business correspondent models.

ROAD AHEAD

Yet, banks are fighting to fulfil the 'Financial Inclusion' dream. The main reason is that the products designed by the banks are not satisfying the low income families. The provision of uncomplicated, small, affordable products will help to bring the low income families into the formal financial sector. Banks have limitations to reach directly to the low income consumers. Correspondents can be considered to be an excellent channel which banks can use to distribute their product information. Educating the consumers about the financial benefits and products of banks which are beneficial to low income groups will be a great step to tap their potential.

Banks are now using new technologies like mobile phones to reach low income consumers. It is possible that the telephone providers themselves will start basic banking services like savings and payments. Indian telecom consumers have few links to financial institutions. So without much difficulty telecom providers can win the battle with banks. Banks should therefore be proactive about transferring this technology into an opportunity.

The RBI guidelines to banks show that 40% of their net bank credit should be lent to the priority sector. This mainly consists of agriculture, small scale industries, retail trade, etc. More than 80% of our population depends directly or indirectly on agriculture. So a major share of net bank credit should go to agriculture lending. Recent simplification of KYC norms are another milestone of governments efforts in this inclusion process.

Financial inclusion is a great step to alleviate poverty in India. But to achieve this, the government should provide a less perspective environment in which banks are free to pursue the innovations necessary to reach low income consumers and still make a profit. Financial service providers should learn more about the consumers and new business models to reach them.

To conclude commercial banks act as spokes in the wheels for drive to achieve 100% financial inclusion in India. Financial inclusion through commercial banks shall wipe out the last tear from the face of most deprived person on the Indian soil.

References

K.C. Chakrabarty, Pushing Financial Inclusion—Issues, Challenges and Way Forward, A Presentation by Deputy Governor, RBI at 20th SKOCH Summit 2009, Mumbai, on July 17, 2009.

M.K. Samantaray, Reserve Bank of India, Guwahati, Financial Inclusion: Perspective of Reserve Bank of India.

Manoj Sreela, www.chillibreeze.com

Pawar Ganesh, Kumar Sushil, Joshi Chawla, Deepak, Inclusive growth—Role of Banks as Credit provider in the Economy and Credit delivery models.

Report of the Committee on Financial Inclusion, January 2008.

Report of the Committee on Financial Inclusion, January 2008.

www.redif.com/business/financial inclusion, Financial Inclusion: India's Top States; Gujarat Lags, 24th August 2011.

www.redif.com/business/financial inclusion, Financial Inclusion: India's Top States; Gujarat Lags, 24th August 2011.

21

Micro-Financing and the Dimensions of Inclusive Growth

KAIKASY, V.S.

ABSTRACT

Financial sector policies in India have long been driven by the objective of increasing financial inclusion, but the goal of universal inclusion is still a distant dream. Financial inclusion is conceived as a major driving force to achieve self-sustained inclusive economic growth. Financial inclusion is the process of ensuring access to financial services and timely availability of adequate credit where needed by vulnerable Groups such as weaker sections and low income groups at an affordable cost. Micro-finance refers to a broad range of financial services, primarily credit, made available to people who don't have access to formal banking services. It fulfils small financial needs of poor and assists in strengthening and developing rural activities, employment, support economic growth, financial susceptibility and also eradication of global poverty. To ensure inclusive growth, three dimensions of micro-finance—a relationship to the poor, a reliance on permanent institution and a connection with the financial system of a country—needs to be reinforced.

INTRODUCTION

Financial sector policies in India have long been driven by the objective of increasing financial inclusion, but the goal of universal inclusion is still a distant dream. For a financial system to be truly inclusive, it should meet the needs of everyone who can fruitfully use financial services, including the poor. For the developing countries like India, micro-finance has come as a breakthrough in the philosophy and practices of poverty eradication, economic empowerment and inclusive growth. Yet given the enormity of economic compulsions and complexities in developing countries, micro-finance is an unfinished agenda. However, over the last several years, the Indian micro-finance industry has undergone considerable evolution. It helped the poor to catch up with the rest of the economy as it grows. It also helped the poor to increase income, build viable businesses, and reduce their vulnerability to external shocks.

Micro-finance refers to a broad range of financial services, primarily credit, made available to people who don't have access to formal banking services. Normally, these services would be required in areas with small population and 'ticket-size' entailed would also be relatively smaller, i.e. factors making banks' presence unviable. Therefore, Micro-financial institutions (MFIs) facilitate the reach of financial services at a more 'micro' level.

"Inclusive growth" is one of the important objectives of eleventh Fivr Yrar Plan in India. Inclusion of each and every section of the society in the process of economic development and achieving growth with equity is the basic objective of "inclusive growth". Financial inclusion is conceived as a major driving force to achieve self-sustained inclusive economic growth. Financial inclusion can be defined as the process of ensuring access to financial services and timely availability of adequate credit where needed by vulnerable Groups such as weaker sections and low income groups at an affordable cost. Achieving financial inclusion through formal banking system is a cumbersome task. Unavailability of adequate financial services like credit, insurances, and remittances to majority population at an affordable cost is a major roadblock for the growth of financial sectors. In this context, Micro-finance approach can be considered as an alternative solution to provide financial services to common section of the society. Micro-finance is the provision of thrift, credit and other financial services and products of very small amounts to the poor for enabling them to raise their income levels and improve their living standards. Micro-finance has profound implications not just from a finance perspective, but also from the perspective of economic development. Micro-finance consisting of micro-credit, micro-savings and micro-insurance, is regarded as an important tool to reduce risk, poverty and vulnerability of common people. Micro-finance is one of the most remarkable socio-economic developments in the present era. The micro-finance sector started getting recognition in India after the launch of the self-help group linkage model in the year 1992. Self-Help group linkage model is one of the indigenously developed and successfully operated models of Micro-finance in India. Under this model, the SHGs are financed by bank without any collateral, peer group pressure is considered as collateral by the lenders. SHG led micro-finance approach also helps to reduce the burden of heavy transaction cost faced by formal financial institution in India. Further, various empirical studies also found that micro-finance through SHG bank linkage programme has enabled the SHG members to improve their socio economic status through the availability of various micro-finance services. Thus, Micro-finance through self-help group bank linkage model can provide sustainable mechanism to meet the unmet financial needs of un-banked poor.

Micro-finance has benefited the beneficiaries by several ways, e.g. by enhancing decision-making capacity affecting family, generating self-respect, self-confidence, leadership quality, consumption pattern and asset purchase and bringing change in the perception regarding nutrition health, family planning, decisions relating to monetary matters, mobility, educational development, access to health services and family income, improving quality of life and education. To make the micro-finance more accessible, enhancing the capacity building among women so as to ensure timely repayment capacity by optimal utilization of money is needed.

RATIONALE FOR FINANCIAL INCLUSION IN INDIA

Impeded and higher cost of access to adequate financial services like credit, insurances, and remittances to majority population are major roadblocks for the growth of primary sectors like agriculture. Financial inclusion can create win-win environment for both customer and financial institution in an economy. It enables customer to avail various kind of financial products for productive purposes. It also helps customers in availing micro-remittance facilities, micro-credit at an affordable cost. The Government also can use the bank accounts of people for providing various social security services for the vulnerable section of society. Thus, financial inclusion can be considered as prerequisite to achieve inclusive growth which would further helps in achieving sustainable economic growth.

Significance of Micro-Financing

Cost-effectiveness

Moneylenders charge exorbitant rates (50-100% p.a.) and the lending too is normally secured by land or property; so if crops fail, the farmer loses his income as well as his asset, i.e. land. Commercial Banks charge much low rates officially, viz. 6-8% p.a. but the overall cost to the borrower far exceeds this number. Loans can be rarely availed without kickbacks to credit officers. Borrower has to make multiples visits to the distantly located bank branches.

A normal process would require him to visit the bank, once each for understanding the process, completing the documentation, getting disbursement and subsequently for each drawdown or repayment.

Better Monitoring of End-use of Funds; Improved Credit Discipline

M.S. Swaminathan Committee highlighted that defining end-use of funds was crucial to ensuring farmers' prosperity. When a farmer takes a loan to buy seeds/fertilizers/tractor, he can still use the credit to fund his daughter's wedding or dowry, i.e. debt fueling consumption. The SHG model of lending used by MFIs ensures that funds are used for the purpose that they were first availed and therefore foster improved credit discipline. More than 99% of the outstanding MFI-generated credit is still categorized under 'standard' or performing loans, much higher than corresponding ratios for any banks.

Vital tool for Financial Inclusion

Financial Inclusion is a key to inclusive growth and the role played by MFIs in the process leading to employment generation and sustenance cannot be over-emphasized. Banks lend to MFIs to fulfil their Priority Sector Lending (PSL) targets—40% for Domestic Banks, 32% for Foreign Banks—and MFIs use those funds for onward lending. Ministry of Finance (MoF) and RBI's credit policies constantly pressurize as affirmative action has resulted in all banks preparing a 3-year target-driven roadmap for enhancing and strengthening financial inclusion. This development is also in sync with RBI/MoF's views that the banks reach out to the segment which is currently being served by MFIs and the MFIs start targeting those who are now dependant on private moneylenders. Although Micro-credit commands the lion's share, Micro-finance also includes Micro-savings (generates income for savers and channels savings into productive uses) and Micro-insurance (Crop insurance, cattle insurance, etc.) both of which are vital tools in financial intermediation and consequently financial inclusion.

Financial Inclusion is a process which leads to a system wherein every individual has access to financial services, primarily credit and savings; alternatively, a system where no one is excluded from basic financial services. Greater access to financial services enables more effective and efficient availability or deployment of capital thereby generating livelihood, alleviating poverty, improving access to basic health & education requirements and fostering entrepreneurship – the tenets of sustainable growth. Micro-finance is a significant and sustainable way of bringing greater financial inclusion and, consequently, more inclusive and sustainable growth.

CONCLUSION

Micro-finance is a critical tool in addressing the issues of financial and social exclusion. It fulfills small financial needs of poor and assists in strengthening and developing rural activities, employment, support economic growth, financial sustainability and also eradication of global poverty. Financial inclusion ensures ease of availability, accessibility and usage of formal financial system to all members of the economy. Financial inclusion has been widely recognized as important means to achieve inclusive growth on India. To ensure inclusive growth, three dimensions of micro-finance—a relationship to the poor, a reliance on permanent institution and a connection with the financial system of a country—needs to be reinforced.

Role of MGNREGS on the Empowerment of Rural Women

REMYAKRISHNAN, G.R., DR. ZAJO JOSEPH, AND MITHESH MADHAVAN

ABSTRACT

A society can be said to be progressed only if the fruits of development have reached all the sections of that society. Women is one of the major sections that is being neglected by most of the societies. No country can achieve its potential without adequately investing in developing the capabilities of women. Mobilization of women into group and organization is one of the very important tools for the empowerment of women. The Government of India established several Schemes for the development of lower class women. One among such is Mahatma Gandhi National Rural Employment Guarantee Act (MGNREGA). It is a job guarantee scheme which provides hundred days of employment in every financial year to adult members of any rural household willing to do public work related unskilled manual work Since 80 per cent among the workforce is women, it must be a scheme which helps in the empowerment of the rural women. The progress of the scheme has been hindered by numerous challenges including the unavailability of work, delay in wage payments, etc.. Keeping in view' the pragmatic importance of the participation of women in this scheme, the study examines the role of MGNREGS in the socio-economic empowerment of rural women beneficiaries.

INTRODUCTION

The condition of women in emerging democratic India is not very different from other countries of South Asia. For an Indian woman the group in which she is born often determines the whole pattern of her life. Her position, status and freedom depend on the laws and characteristics of her ethnic group. Although tradition and customs still play an important role in the lives of Indian women, of late many new developments have taken place. They have now access to education, more opportunities in the field of employment, health, etc. The response of Indian women towards changes in political, social, economic and technological scenario has been very positive; and they have made maximum use of new opportunities in order to improve their own lives and the lives of their children.

Empowerment is a process which aims at challenging and changing existing ideologies, the set of ideas, attitudes, beliefs and practices in which gender and social biases are embedded. There is an urgent necessity to improve the status of women by well conceived, planned developmental programmes which would have active community participation based on the women's needs in order to emancipate and empower them. The transformation has to bring changes in the ideological system, in access to resources and in institutions and structures at several levels, such as the family and the household, the village and the community, the state and the market, etc. In the light of the notion of empowerment and the constraints prevailing all around in the different walks of life, the pertinent question is the identification of target areas and the ways of achieving it.

Mobilization of women into group and organization is one of the very important tools for the empowerment of women. The Government of India established several Schemes for the development of lower class women. One among such is Mahatma Gandhi National Rural Employment Guarantee Act (MGNREGA). It is a job guarantee scheme which provides hundred days of employment in every financial year to adult members of any rural household willing to do public work related unskilled manual work. It is one of the most progressive legislations enacted since independence. Its significance is evident from a variety of perspectives. First, it is a bold and unique experiment in the provision of rural employment—in India and indeed in the world at large. Second, it is the first expression of the right to work as an enforceable legal entitlement. In a country where labour is the only economic asset for millions of people, gainful employment is a prerequisite for the fulfilment of other basic rights—the right to life, the right to food, and the right to education. There is much that the MGNREGS promises from the perspective of women's empowerment as well. Most boldly, in a rural milieu marked by stark inequalities between men and women—in the opportunities for gainful employment as well as reasonable wage rates—MGNREGS represents action on both these counts. The act stipulates that wages will be equal for men and women. It is also committed to ensuring that at least 33% of the workers shall be women. By generating employment for women at fair wages in the village, MGNREGS can play a substantial role in economically empowering women and laying the basis for greater independence and self-esteem. By putting cash incomes into their hands, MGNREGS is beginning to create a greater degree of economic independence among women. As mentioned, this was one of MGNREGS's main aims: with the increased participation of women in household income-generation a positive contribution to gender relations can be made.

All this taken together seems to sketch out the beginnings of a marked shift from the previous role of women. While women's labour (farm and non-farm) has always been an essential component in the functioning of rural households, it has been made invisible due to the absence of any monetary remuneration. By putting cash earnings in women's hands, MNREGS has both increased and diversified the contributions that women are making to household incomes as wage-earners.

Empowerment could take place at two levels, individual and collective. Individual empowerment is a process of personal empowerment involving self-esteem, dignity, self-respect and self-perception. The problem of securing better access to education and skills employment, material resources and political power can be tackled only at collective level. The empowerment of women especially in rural area is one of the economic empowerment of any country all over the world. In India majority of the women in rural areas are poor, illiterate and deprived sections of the society due to various restrictive social norms and culture. They are facing problems like very low wages for casual works, lack of employment opportunities, bad working conditions and other barriers. But no country can achieve its potential without adequately investing in developing the capabilities of women. As the central government implemented this scheme for the entire rural society for their development, 80 per cent among the workforce is women. Hence, it must be the scheme which helps in the empowerment of rural women. But still the progress of this scheme has been hindered by numerous challenges including the unavailability of work, delay in the payment of wages, matching labourers with physical work, etc. Keeping in view the pragmatic importance of the participation of women in this scheme, the study examines the role of MGNREGS in the socio-economic empowerment of rural women beneficiaries.

REVIEW OF LITERATURE

Osmani (1996) in his paper 'The Grameen Bank Experiment: Empowerment of Women through Credit' found that access to credit has improved women's break down position in terms of increased income and ownership of asset building land and their perceived contribution to the family compared with men. Borrowers have gained greater autonomy in certain spheres of decision-making and feel that they have gained better access to food and health care.

Joshi (1999) points out that the proxy measures are important and are ideally associated with empowerment, they may not capture all aspects of the multidimensional concept of empowerment. Recently, scholars have turned from using indirect proxies to quantify autonomy/ empowerment to using more direct measures. These direct measures consist of a combination of observable items or indicators that are categorized into different dimensions of autonomy, such as access to and control over resources, participation in economic and child-related decisions, self-esteem, mobility, freedom from domestic violence, and political awareness and participation

Smitha (2000) in her study presented a framework for assessing the level empowerment of the targeted group of the programme. He concluded that irrespective of context, empowerment has a few key elements such as power autonomy and self-reliance, entitlement participation, awareness development and capacity building. Thus, for assessing empowerment at the group and individual levels one need to assess each of these elements.

An earlier study by Jose Chathukulam and Gireesan (2007) on their impact of NREGS in 37 Grama Panchayats in two Districts—Wayanad and Palakkad—in the state of Kerala points out the active involvement of LSGs in programme planning and implementation. Several micro-level institutions have been formed at the Panchayat level for the smooth functioning of NREGS; but their sustainability has not been ensured. Although the registration of workers and issuance of job cards was accomplished, there have been lapses in providing employment to the registered workers. There is impressive participation of women not only as workers but also as supervisors. Flood control, renovation of traditional water bodies, micro-irrigation works and water conservation and harvesting are the major areas of intervention in NREGS, with lower priority given to rural connectivity. NREGS activities are not integrated with other developmental programmes. Although many workers are eligible for unemployment allowances, they were not paid these allowances. According to this study, in spite of the many problems resulting from NREGS work being executed during agricultural seasons, this scheme has been largely beneficial for socially and financially backward population groups.

Mihir Shah (*EPW*, December 2009) points out, this is especially important in view of intra-household gender discrimination. The right for work as guaranteed by the NREGA has been restricted to households, rather than to each individual of the household. The limiting of work to hundred days a year is also a lacuna in the Act. Although there is a provision in the Act to raise the household work entitlement beyond 100 days or extend to every adult, unfortunately this has not been given due attention. As Mihir Shah says there could be seasons and areas when and where the requirement of work would be more or less. Each state should ideally be allowed to dovetail the financial allocation for annual schemes to suit specific needs. The GoK insists that 10 percent of the funds should go towards rural connectivity. This study has attempted to assess whether this focus on rural connectivity was strictly followed by the Grama Panchayats. The Grama Panchayats have skillfully included the maintenance of drainages and roads in flood control and land development categories and the construction of new roads alone has been categorized as rural connectivity. Hence, the use of the categories to justify expenditure is often misleading.

OBJECTIVES OF THE STUDY

To study the role of MGNREGS in the socio-economic empowerment of rural women beneficiaries.

Methodology

The present study is descriptive in nature using primary and secondary data. Primary data were collected by using a structured interview schedule from the women workers of MGNREGS. Secondary data were collected from various published research reports relating to women empowerment and journals like Economic and Political Weekly, Southern Economist and various websites.

Sample Size was 120. The three Grama Panchayaths in Trivandrum district such as Edava, Vellanadu and Madavoor were selected randomly. From this Grama Panchayaths, Judgement sampling was used for selecting the samples of 40 each. The criteria for selecting the sample were on the basis of women workers who had been working for atleast one year under this scheme. The study covers the period of four years from 2007 to 2010. The collected data were analysed by using simple arithmetical tool like percentage.

Findings

The three Gram Panchayaths in Trivandrum district such as

Edava, Vellanadu and Madavoor were selected for the study. Among the total respondents 33% were found to be in the age group of 26-40 years, 44% in the age group of 41-60 years and 15% in the age group of 21-25 years. 8% were over 60 years of age. These indicate that the need for employment is greater even for those women who are above the age of 60. The workers' awareness level about the provisions of MGNREGS revealed that the respondents who have awareness about the scheme do not know all the provisions of MGNREGS. Some of the respondents above the age of 55 do not know this is a demand driven scheme and other provisions like unemployment allowance, Compensation for delayed payment, Right to get payment within a fortnight and some institutional mechanism for making complaints or seeking redressal of grievance, etc.

The most noticeable feature was the number of women that took part in this scheme. About 80% out of the total work forces were women. This was remarkable in another way when we came to know that now rural women are not merely silent watchers but active participators in the decision-making of their family affairs. The MGNREGS Act states that the main objective of the scheme is to enhance livelihood security in rural areas by providing atleast 100 days of guaranteed wage employment, in a financial year to every household

TABLE I

Economic Empowerment of Women Beneficiaries

Grama Panchayats / *Factors*	*Number of respondents*			*Total*
	Edava	*Vellanadu*	*Madavoor*	
Income	33 (82.5)	35 (87.5)	26 (65)	94 (78.33)
Ownership of assets	15 (37.5)	18 (45)	14 (35)	47 (39.16)
Savings	5 (12.5)	10 (25)	11 (27.5)	26 (21.67)
Standard of living	21 (52.5)	19 (47.5)	17 (42.5)	57 (47.5)
Employment opportunities	32 (80)	34 (85)	33 (82.5)	99 (82.5)
Expenditure	20 (50)	23 (57.5)	19 (47.5)	62 (51.67)

Figures in the parenthesis represent the percentage to the total respondents.
Source: Field Survey.

whose adult members want to do unskilled manual work voluntarily. Table 1 reveals that MGNREGS have increased employment opportunities by 99 per cent per annum. Although there was increase in the income of the beneficiaries up to 94 per cent but the savings among them is considerably poor. More importantly, the payments to the labourers are done through the accounts in banks and post offices. Hence, its helps in inculcating the saving habits in the minds of the women beneficiaries

Figures in Table 2 shows that with the greater involvement of women in the scheme has made improvement in their standard of living to an extent and betterment in the decision-making power (79 per cent) and the social awareness too after joining MGNREGS, which resulted in contribution and nourishment of their families. Participation in this scheme helped to improve the interpersonal relationship and communication skill of the beneficiaries.

TABLE 2

Social Empowerment of Women Beneficiaries

Grama Panchayats / *Factors*	*Number of respondents*			*Total*
	Edava	*Vellanadu*	*Madavoor*	
Decision-making power Within the family	25 (62.5)	28 (70)	26 (65)	79 (65.83)
Improvement in inter-personal relationship	19 (47.5)	22 (55)	27 (67.5)	68 (56.67)
Social awareness	29 (72.5)	33 (82.5)	27 (67.5)	89 (74.17)
Communication skills	30 (75)	34 (85)	31 (77.5)	95 (79.17)

Figures in the parenthesis represent the percentage to the total respondents.
Source: Field Survey.

SUGGESTIONS AND CONCLUSION

On the basis of the study the following suggestions are made.: - Awareness among the women workers should be improved and their participation in making and implementing the scheme should be ascertained. The beneficiaries should be allowed to express their suggestions. So that the loop-holes in the scheme may be rectified. Efforts should be made to reduce the time gap between work done and payment received by rural labourers in MGNREGS. Proper worksite facilities like drinking water, period of rest and first aid facilities should be ensured.

References

Chathukulam, Jose and K. Gireesan, "Impact Assessment of NREGS in Kerala: An Evaluation of Systems and Processes", Center for Rural Management, Kottayam, September 2007.

Joshi, S.T., Women and Development—The Changing Scenario, New Delhi: Mittal Publications., 1999.

Osmani, L.N.K., 'The Grain Bank Experiment: Empowerment of Women Through Credit', Derwent College, University of Newyork, 1996.

Shah, Mihir, 'Structures of Power in Indian Society: A Response', *Economic and Political Weekly*, 43(46): 78-83, 2009

Smitha, Mishra Panda, Women Empowerment through NGO Interventions: A Framework for Assessment. Working paper 145, Anand: Institute of Rural Management, 2000.

www.nrega.nic.in

www.mnrega.in

www.mnrega.com

Role of Micro-Credit on the Socio-Economic Development of Fisherwomen

ASWANI, S.P., DR. ZAJO JOSEPH, AND SUBA KURIAKOSE

ABSTRACT

Microfinance is one of the practical development strategies and approaches that has been discovered and implemented for sustainable development and has been used as a means to foster inclusive growth in the Indian economy. Credit is an important part of microfinance. It is one of the diverse financial services that poor people need to improve their lives. Apart from providing micro-credit Microfinance aims to provide a broad range of financial services like: deposits, loans, payment services, money transfers, insurance to poor and low-income households and their micro-enterprises. Women constitute the majority of microfinance clients, primarily because of their better repayment records. A major target group of microfinance activities is fishing communities. Women are involved in productive activities directly related to fisheries production, processing and marketing as well as in non-fisheries livelihood activities that are very important in augmenting household income during periods of scarcity and seasonality often experienced in fishing communities. Targeting women in micro-finance programmes in fisheries is like investing for their empowerment and improving the \\well-being of their families and communities. But the reality is that, this loans/credit is improperly utilized among fisherwomen. So the study is essential to find out how far micro credit is channelized to productive activities by these beneficiaries. The study revealed that though micro-finance programmes have helped in improving the social status of women, it has not helped in improving their economic status.

INTRODUCTION

Micro-finance is a financial model specially designed for serving the poor. Micro-finance programmes provide tiny loans to poor people for self-employment projects. The system is for "Building financial systems that serve the poor"

"Micro-finance is a provision of thrift, credit and other financial services and products of very small amounts provided to the poor in rural areas, semi-urban areas and urban areas. The concept that micro-finance is an income producing tool rather than consumption aid is an appropriate way of bringing social changes and transforming the society in the new and developed world. That is why micro-finance and micro-credit do not provide consumers with loans to simply increase their consumption. Instead, they provide loans for the specific purpose of creating self-employment for the poor, thereby enabling the poor to build their own micro-enterprises and with the passage of time, they can become the owners of large size business houses and can create employment opportunities for needy and help them to beat the poverty.

The focus of micro-finance on "poor" client is one innovative approach to the bridge gap between haves and have nots. A balanced society depends upon the balanced pillar and micro-finance is an effective tool to strengthen the weaker pillar.

Micro-Finance includes financial producers like Micro-credit, Micro-savings, Micro-insurance, etc. Besides, technical assistance, capacity building, social and cultural programmes can also be considered as supporting activities. The term "Micro" is used differently, it may be understood according to size of target users or deployment of funds for small goals or it may be due to easy and flexible terms and conditions. Micro-finance is not limited to micro-credit but also aims to provide a broad range of financial services like: deposits, loans, payment services, money transfers, insurance to poor and low-income households and their micro-enterprises.

Women constitute the majority of micro-finance clients, primarily because of their better repayment records which a particular target group of micro-finance activities in fishing communities. It is recognized that women play an important role in fishing communities. Women are involved in productive activities directly related to fisheries production, processing and marketing as well as in non-fisheries livelihood activities that are very important in augmenting household income during periods of scarcity and seasonality often experienced in fishing communities.

Targeting women in micro-finance programmes in fisheries is like investing for their empowerment and improving the well being of their families and communities

Statement of the Problem

Micro-finance is one of the practical development strategies and approaches that has been discovered and implemented for sustainable development and has been used as a means to foster inclusive growth in the Indian economy. Credit is an important part of micro-finance; it is just one of the diverse financial services that poor people need to improve their lives by providing them with micro-credit loans. But the reality is that, this loans/credit is improperly utilized among fisher women. So the study is essential to find out how far micro-credit is channelized to productive activities by these beneficiaries. Hence, the present study is conducted to find out the extent of micro-credit utilization and Socio-economic development of fisher women residing in coastal area.

Significance of the Study

Some of the main stream financial Institutions involved in extending Micro-finance are NABARD, Small Industries development bank of India (SIDBI), housing development corporation (HDFC), commercial banks, regional rural banks (RRBs) and credit co-operative societies, etc. Alternative Micro-finance institutions are those which have come up to fill the gap between the demand and supply for Micro-finance. These institutes have been structured with the main aim of providing thrift, credit and other financial services and products of very small amounts mainly to the poor, in rural, semi-urban or urban areas for enabling them to raise their income level and improve living standards. This study is to identify weakness of present Micro-finance program and make suggestions to facilitate capacity building and proper utilization.

Review of Literature

The working group, RBI (1996) observed that, SHGs had helped to generate and collect small thrift amounts from a cross-section of people hitherto considered incapable of saving. The essential difference between thrift and savings was that while thrift was generated out of deferred consumption, the savings were generated out of surplus. SHGs have facilitated the rural poor in fulfiling their credit requirements, both for emergent consumption needs as well as for small production requirements. SHGs have been able to meet successfully the credit requirements of the rural poor as per their choice, unlike in the case of borrowing under other programs of formal credit institutions. The high recovery rates of the SHGs are in sharp contrast to the poor recovery performance of banks in respect of various activities under rural credit. Since credit/finance was seen as management of the participants' own funds and enterprises, a feeling of ownership and responsibility was generated. The entire cycle of assessing need, disbursement, recovery, monitoring, and supervision shifted closer to the scene of action under SHGs, and therefore the transaction cost of the loans was relatively less.

NABARD (2001) in publication their article women were emerging as an effective medium of delivery of credit, state that besides creating social awareness, SHGs also paved the way for empowerment of rural people through the concept of regular saving and linkage to the financial sector. This, in turn helps in improving the standard of life and as such SHGs could be supported by those agencies concerned with rural development and poverty alleviation programme.

According to Chatnani and Thakur (2006) micro-finance provides an important way to balance the outreach among the rural poor while keeping the cost of lending low. These credits allow people living in financial difficulties to set-up small business capable of being generating income through micro-enterprises.

According to Rangarajan (2008) the financial inclusion attained through SHGs is sustainable and scalable on account of its various positive features. One of the distinctive features of the SHGBLP has been the high recovery rate. However, the spread of SHGs is very uneven and is more concentrated in southern states. This regional imbalance needs to be corrected and special efforts in this regard may have to be made by NABARD. SHGs also needed to graduate from mere providers of credit for non-productive purposes to promoting micro-enterprises.

Anuradha and Ganesan (2010) in their study 'Sustainable Development and Fostering Inclusive Growth through Micro-finance in the Indian Economy', observed that Micro-finance is expected to play a significant role in poverty alleviation and development. Micro-finance is an attempt to break this deadlock, by providing the poor with the financial means to engage in new forms of economic activity and so improve their lives. Equitable gain from development on a sustainable basis and ensuring viability of financial services are key elements in strategy of poverty reduction by means of credit support.

OBJECTIVES OF THE STUDY

To study the credit utilization pattern among fisher women.

To study the Socio-economic development of fisher women through Micro-Credit.

Methodology

Both primary and secondary data were used for this study. It is descriptive in nature. Primary data were collected from the fisher women in the coastal area through structured interview schedule. Secondary data were collected from published research reports relating to Women

Empowerment, Working Papers of Institute of Rural Management, Published reports of Reserve Bank of India, Journals like Indian Journal of Finance, Indian Management, Journal of Micro-Finance, XIMB Journal of Management, Kurukshetra and subject related to Newspapers, Websites, etc.

The sample size was 150. The samples were selected from Anjuthengu, Puthenthopu, Vetukadu, Adimalathura, and Poovar. Judgement sampling was used for this study. The criteria for judgement sampling was the places selected from the clusters of Matsyafed.

FINDINGS, SUGGESTIONS AND CONCLUSION

TABLE 1

Credit-Utilization Pattern

(In Percentage)

Variable / *Opinion*	*Yes*	*No*
Lending money for interest	26	74
Income generating activity	48	52
Purchase equipment	29	71
Socio-cultural equipment	34	66
Personal debt	92	8
Insurance	13	87
Child education	27	73
Hospital expenses	12	88

Source: Primary Data.

TABLE 2

Economic Development

(In Percentage)

Variable / *Opinion*	*Highly Agree*	*Agree*	*Neutral*	*Disagree*	*Highly Disagree*
Savings	20	40	18	2	10
Income	27	45	18	8	2
Investment	23	38	17	12	10
Employment	13	20	34	13	20
Expenditure	22	33	27	15	3

Source: Primary Data.

TABLE 3

Social Development

(In Percentage)

Opinion / Variables	Very High	High	Moderate	Low	Very Low
Increased Status and Decision-making power	20	39	20	11	10
Ability to solve family problem	28	46	16	5	5
Improvement in Communication Skill	38	33	15	9	5
Ability to solve social issue	45	39	8	6	2

Source: Primary Data.

Findings

Credit utilization pattern among fisher women mainly in lending money for interest, income generating activity, purchase equipment, socio-cultural expense, personal debt, insurance, children education, hospital expenses. Credit utilization of micro-credit is mostly concentrated in personal debts payment and income generating activities. In case of social development, majority of the beneficiaries agreed that their decision-making power, ability to solve family problems and communication skills has increased. Though the income of majority of the respondents has increased due to the increased expenditure their savings has not increased. Hence, it can be concluded that the economic status of the fisher women has not undergone any major change.

Suggestions

Most of the beneficiaries utilize their fund for repayment of personal debt, if it channelize to income generating activities, it will lead to much improvement in socio-economic development.Proper awareness regarding income generating activities should be made among fisher women. Further they should be given suitable training for utilising the income properly. Government should appoint authorities for reviewing proper implementation of the schemes and should prevent the diversion of credit to other unproductive purposes.

Conclusion

Micro-credit is a powerful tool to fight against poverty. It builds financial system that serves the poor. In coastal areas women play an important role in the family, and take more risk compared to men. So it is very helpful to them. But due to improper utilization of the fund, they can't eliminate their poverty and improve the standard of living. If the fund is utilize for income generating activity and channelize in a proper way, it will brighten their lives, eliminate poverty and improve their Socio-economic status.

24

Financial Literacy—Essential for Inclusive Financing

PRIJI, L.P. AND SREELEKHA, R.G.

ABSTRACT

Financial Literacy is the ability to understand finance. More specifically, it refers to the set of skills and knowledge that allows an individual to make informed and effective decisions through their understanding of finances. The economic growth is always depending upon the financial literacy rate of our society. Therefore, financial literacy is an important element for inclusive economic growth. Financial inclusion is directly related to financial literacy. Thus, financial literacy is the first step in the process of financial inclusion and inclusive growth with blood and life. Kerala is an example for this. Kerala has become the first state in the country to achieve 'total financial inclusion' of the citizen families; at least one member from each family now had a bank account. Compared with other states in India standard of living of people in Kerala is very high. Obviously it is attributed to the high literacy rate and the educational standard of people. This paper shows the relevance of financial literacy for inclusive growth of financing and the role of financial institutions by way of providing various services in the area of banking. insurance, and alternative financial services, to achieve this growth in Kerala.

FINANCE

The word finance refers to matters of money, which is very important to the standard of living for an individual. The term finance means management of money for your expenses. In broad term finance is the science of funds management. Finance includes saving money and often includes lending money. The field of finance deals with how money is spent and budgeted. It also deals the concepts of time, money and risk and how they are interrelated. Finance is also a money budget management. Finance is the need of the today world economy.

The general areas of finance are:

- *Personal finance*—Finance used by individuals.
- *Business finance*—It means the finance used by business as well as by a wide variety of organizations including schools and non-profit organizations.
- *Public finance*—It means the finance used by Governments for the welfare of general public.

LITERACY

Literacy is "the quality or state of being literate." Literacy has been described as the ability to read for knowledge and write coherently and think critically about the written word. Literacy can also include the ability to understand all forms of communication such as someone's body language, pictures, video and sound.

A 'Literate' is any person who is able to read, write, speak, listen and view on his own.

FINANCIAL LITERACY

Financial Literacy is the ability to understand finance. More specifically, it refers to the set of skills and knowledge that allows an individual to make informed and effective decisions through their understanding of finances. Financial Literacy can broadly defined as the capacity to have familiarity with and understanding of financial market products, especially rewards and risks in order to make informed choices. It includes the tools and knowledge an individual needs in order to make informed decisions about money management. "It is well accepted that financial education can improve financial literacy and, more importantly, change financial behaviours" (Jacobs, Hudson and Bush, 2000).

FINANCIAL LITERCY IN KERALA

Kerala with a literacy rate of 90.90% stands first among other

Indian states. Recognizing the need for a literate population and provision of elementary education as a crucial input for nation-building, the state government with the backing of the central government, launched a number of plans and programmes over the past years to facilitate the provision of free and compulsory education with satisfactory quality to all children at least up to the age of 14 years. Apart from this, a number of government organizations and voluntary associations under various schemes and services conduct classes for the illiterate adults. As per the norms of National Literacy Mission, a literacy rate above 90% shall be treated as complete literacy. On this basis, Kerala was declared a, 'Fully Literate State', on April 18th, 1991.

Apart from providing general education, Govt. of Kerala has taken initiatives to provide computer education to all students and financial institutions also provide financial literacy to general public. This programme is being implemented at all schools and colleges throughout the state. Union Bank of India, lead bank in the Ernakulam district in the State of Kerala, established its first Financial Literacy and Credit Counseling Center (FLCCC) at Perumbavoor. The Concept of FLCCCs was recommended by Usha Thorat led High Power Committee on Lead Bank Scheme, under Reserve Bank of India's Financial Inclusion Program (FIP).

In every district, FLCCC is supposed to provide financial counseling service in order to disburse knowledge about various financial products and services among rural and urban people. The counseling will use face-to-face interaction approach, and other available media including e-mail, fax, mobile, etc. Financial inclusion program put financial literacy at a very high priority point. All the un-banked villages having population up to and above 2000 are to be covered in the first phase of the FIP.

Kerala has become the first State in the country to achieve 'Total Financial Inclusion' of the citizen families; at least one member from each family now has a bank account. The cooperative banks, government departments, Kudumbasree self-help groups, non-governmental organisations, several developmental agencies and the people's representatives at all levels were involved in the campaign to attain this goal. 'No frill' account facility is offered to the public to achieve this goal.

In Kerala at least one member from each family has a bank account. That means they included in financial matters. But Reserve Bank of India said that financial inclusion is not restricted merely to opening bank accounts and should imply provisions of all financial services like credit, remittance and overdraft facilities for the rural poor. That means the financial literacy is completed when people should understand all financial services offered by all types of financial institutions.

FINANCIAL SERVICES OFFERED BY FINANCIAL INSTITUTIONS

Financial services are the economic services provided by the finance industry, which encompasses a broad range of organizations that manage money, including credit unions, banks, creditcard companies, insurance companies, consumer finance companies, stock brokerages, investment funds and some government sponsored enterprises.

Banking Services

Keeping money safe and also allowing withdrawals when needed Issuance of checkbooks so that bills can be paid and other kinds of payments can be delivered by post:

- Provide personal loans, commercial loans, and mortgage loans.
- Issuance of credit cards and processing of credit card transactions and billing.
- Issuance of debit cards for use as a substitute for cheques Allow financial transactions at branches or by using Automatic Teller Machines (ATMs) provide wire transfers of funds and Electronic fund transfers between banks Facilitation of standing orders and direct debits, so payments for bills can be made automatically.
- Provide overdraft agreements for the temporary advancement of the Bank's own money to meet monthly spending commitments of a customer in their current account. Provide internet banking system to facilitate the customers to view and operate their respective accounts through internet. Provide Charge card advances of the Bank's own money for customers wishing to settle credit advances monthly. Provide a cheque guaranteed by the Bank itself and prepaid by the customer, such as a cashier's cheque or certified cheque.
- Notary service for financial and other documents.
- Accepting the deposits from customer and provide the credit facilities to them.

Foreign Exchange Services

- *Currency exchange*—where clients can purchase and sell foreign currency banknotes.
- *Foreign Currency Banking*—banking transactions are done in foreign currency.

- *Wire transfer*—where clients can send funds to international banks abroad.

Investment Services

- *Asset management*—the term usually given to describe companies which run collective investment funds. Also refers to services provided by others, generally registered with the Securities and Exchange Commission as Registered Investment Advisors.
- *Hedge fund management*—Hedge funds often employ the services of "prime brokerage" divisions at major investment banks to execute their trades.
- *Custody services*—the safe-keeping and processing of the world's securities trades and servicing the associated portfolios.

Insurance

- *Insurance brokerage*—Insurance brokers shop for insurance on behalf of customers. Recently a number of websites have been created to give consumers basic price comparisons for services such as insurance, causing controversy within the industry.
- *Insurance underwriting*—Personal lines insurance underwriters actually underwrite insurance for individuals, a service still offered primarily through agents, insurance brokers, and stock brokers. Underwriters may also offer similar commercial lines of coverage for businesses. Activities include insurance and annuities, life insurance, retirement insurance, health insurance, and property and casualty insurance.
- *Reinsurance*—Reinsurance is insurance sold to insurers themselves, to protect them from catastrophic losses.

Intermediation or advisory services, Private equity funds, venture capital, angel investment, retail banking, wholesale banking, investment banking, debt resolution, debt consolidation, debt settlement and refinancing, etc.

Alternative Financial Services (AFS)

Alternative financial services are financial services provided outside traditional banking institutions, on which many low-income individuals depend. In developing countries, these services often take the form of micro-finance. In developed countries, the services may be similar to those provided by banks, and include payday loans, rent-to-own agreements, pawnshops, refund anticipation loans, some subprime mortgage loans and car title loans, and non-bank cheque cashing, money orders, and money transfers. It also includes traditional moneylending by door-to-door collection, sometimes in the form of loan sharking. Alternative financial services are typically provided by non-bank financial institutions, although person-to-person lending and crowd funding also play a role.

CONCLUSION

It states that the financial literacy is an essential element for the inclusive financial growth in our country. Kerala is an example for this. Kerala is a full literate and fully financially literate state. In Kerala at least one member from each family has a bank account. That means they included in financial matters.

REFERENCES

www.financialinclusion.in

www.rediff.com›Business

en.wikipedia.org/wiki/Financial literacy

www.pfhub.com/financial-literacy

Role of Financial Inclusion as a Means of Inclusive Growth

VIJILA, V. AND ANILKUMAR, M.

ABSTRACT

Though our country's economy is growing around 9 percent, still the growth is not inclusive with the economic condition of the people in rural areas worsening further. One of the typical reasons for poverty is being financially excluded. Though there are few people who are enjoying all kinds of services from savings to net banking, but still in our country around 40% of people lack access to even basic financial services like savings, credit and insurance facilities. So an inclusive sector should not only serve the bankable clients, but also integrate the "un-bankable" clients by making them "bankable". Many actions taken by the Government like Nationalizing of Banks, 40% of credit targets to priority sector, opening of RRBs and LABs, etc. for past three decades are one form of financial inclusion, but still around 80% of rural households do not have access to credit from a formal source. Financial Inclusion is about delivery of banking services at an affordable cost to vast sections of disadvantaged, first step in FI is to facilitate people in getting basic facilities like food, shelter and clothing to the people and then comes the provision of bank account, wherein they can save whatever little they can. Financial Inclusion can be thought of in two ways. One is exclusion from the payments system, i.e. not having access to a bank account. The second type of exclusion is from formal credit markets, requiring the excluded to approach informal and exploitative markets.

INTRODUCTION

The broader concept of financial inclusion is delivery of banking services at an affordable cost to the vast sections of disadvantaged and low income groups. These banking are savings, deposits, loan, borrowings and, payment, settlement and remittance facilities. The insurance services come under savings facilities. Financial inclusion is intended to connect people to banks with consequential benefits. Ensuring that the financial system plays its due role in promoting inclusive growth is one of the biggest challenges facing the emerging economies. Out of these three above mentioned important services if any one of the service is absent the entire concept will be considered as incomplete, insufficient financial inclusion.

Commercial Banks, RRBs, Cooperatives, Government, M.F.I.s, SHGs, Post offices, NBFCs, NGOs, etc. are the provider of financial services and these have either adequate or inadequate presence in rural areas of the country. The operational definitions of financial inclusion, have also evolved from the underlying public policy concerns that many people, particularly those living on low income, cannot access mainstream financial products such as bank accounts and low cost loans, which, in turn, imposes real costs on them—often the most vulnerable people.

Definition

In the Indian context, Rangarajan Committee (Report of the Committee on Financial Inclusion in India (2008)) defines it as: "Financial inclusion may be defined as the process of ensuring access to financial services and timely and adequate credit where needed by vulnerable groups such as weaker sections and low income groups at an affordable cost." The financial services include the entire gamut—savings, loans, insurance, credit, payments, etc. By providing these services, the aim is to help them come out of poverty.

Statement of the Problem

The developed countries and the developing country like India are making effort for financial inclusion in order to improve the financial condition and standards of living of the poor and disadvantaged. The more developed the society the greater is the thrust on empowerment of the common person and marginal income groups in the lower strata of the society. In France it is a statutory right of the every citizen to have bank account. The financial inclusion Task Force in UK has identified three priority areas for the purpose of financial inclusion. These are: (i) access to banking, (ii) access to affordable credit, and (iii) access to free face-to-face money advice. Financial inclusion fund is established in

UK in order to promote financial inclusion and assigned responsibility to banks and credit unions to remove the barriers of financial exclusion. The study should focus on the different means by which the financial inclusion adopted for inclusive economic growth.

Objectives of the Study

- To know the concept of inclusive growth
- To understand the Initiatives for financial inclusion
- To identify the challenges to be faced for the effective financial inclusion
- To suggest adequate recommendation for the successful financial inclusion

Concept of Inclusive Growth

The "inclusive growth" as a strategy of economic development received attention owing to a rising concern that the benefits of economic growth have not been equitably shared. Growth is inclusive when it creates economic opportunities along with ensuring equal access to them. Apart from addressing the issue of inequality, the inclusive growth may also make the poverty reduction efforts more effective by explicitly creating productive economic opportunities for the poor and vulnerable sections of the society. The inclusive growth by encompassing the hitherto excluded population can bring in several other benefits as well to the economy. The concept "Inclusion" should be seen as a process of including the excluded as agents whose participation is essential in the very design of the development process, and not simply as welfare targets of development programmes (Planning Commission, 2007).

The Eleventh Five Year Plan (2007-12) envisions inclusive growth as a key objective. The Plan document notes that the economic growth has failed to be sufficiently inclusive particularly after the mid-1990s. The Indian economy, though achieved a high growth momentum during 2003-04 to 2007-08, could not bring down unemployment and poverty to tolerable levels. Further, a vast majority of the population remained outside the ambit of basic health and education facilities during this high growth phase.

INITIATIVES FOR FINANCIAL INCLUSION IN INDIA

The broad strategy for financial inclusion in India in recent years comprises the following elements:

Encouraging penetration into unbanked and backward areas and encouraging agents and intermediaries such as NGOs, MFIs, CSOs and business correspondents (BCs) focusing on a decentralised strategy by using existing arrangements such as State Level Bankers' Committee (SLBC) and district consultative committee (DCC) and strengthening local institutions such as cooperatives and RRBs using technology for furthering financial inclusion advising banks to open a basic banking 'no frills' account emphasis on financial literacy and credit counseling and Creating synergies between the formal and informal segments.

Constraints of Financial Inclusion

The requirements of documentary proof of identity and residential address are the most important barrier in opening not only the bank account but also in post offices for availing the financial services. The most sufferers are newly married women and migrants in rural areas. The women cannot borrow from the bank due to lack of pre-owned collateral (as the women do not have the property rights) despite having the bank account. Even an account holder in the bank cannot borrow if he fails to mobilize a guarantor. These are the numerous constraints of financial inclusion. The informal financial institutions are: (i) Money Landers, (ii) Relatives, (iii) Traders, (iv) Friends, and (v) Other professionals. If the rural households do not have any kind of transaction with formal financial institutions but have exclusive transaction with the informal financial institutions, these households will be considered under financial exclusion.

Issues and Challenges

India currently faces several issues and challenges in the area of Financial Inclusion for Inclusive growth. Salient among them are stated here below.

Balanced Distribution of Banking Services: Even though after often emphasized policy intervention by the government and the concerted efforts of Reserve Bank of India and the public sector banks there has been a significant increase in the number of bank offices in the rural areas; but it is not in tune with the large population living in the rural areas. For a population of 70% only 45% of bank offices provide the financial services.

Regional Distribution of Banking Services: The analysis by the authors brings to the fore that there has been uneven distribution of the banking services in terms of population coverage per bank office in the six regions viz., Northern, North-eastern, Eastern, Central, Western and Southern regions of the country.

Number of Bank Branches are required to be increased as it has a direct impact on the progress of financial inclusion. It is clearly established that as the bank branches increase number of bank accounts also increase significantly.

- Poverty levels are having direct relationship with the progress of financial inclusion. The authors have established in their study that as the poverty levels decrease financial inclusion also increase. As such, there should be multi-fold strategic approach in such poverty dominated areas for financial inclusion.
- *Overcoming Bankers' Aversion for Financial Inclusion*: Even though no banker openly expresses his aversion for the financial inclusion process, overtly it can be noticed that they are averse to it in view of the cost aspects involved in opening of no frill accounts.

RECOMMENDATIONS AND POLICY CHOICES

The following recommendations are made for the successful implementation of financial inclusion:

- *Formation of National Financial Inclusion Mission*: The authors recommend formation of National Financial Inclusion Mission on the lines of National Literacy Mission to carry out systematic and coordinated drive for financial inclusion.
- *Involvement of Education Sector for furthering Financial Inclusion:* Involving educational institutions, particularly college students for financial inclusion drive would not only be cost effective but also would create wide public awareness.
- *Building Client Capacities*: As the saying goes "teach him to fish instead of giving him fish", it should be the effort of all the concerned (particularly the financial institutions) to develop these poor people as prospective customers. Building client capacities would definitely help all the stakeholders and would to a vibrant financial system
- *Partnership with Dedicated NGOs and MFIs*: Partnering with trustworthy and acclaimed people's organisations would definitely accelerate the process of financial inclusion especially in the rural areas. Specific financial as well as non-financial incentives have to be designed for the spirited involvement of such organizations.
- *Financial Inclusion as a Part of Course Curriculum in High Schools*: Financial Inclusion should be imbibed into the course curriculum in high schools so that the students would understand the importance of financial inclusion for inclusive growth in the economy which in turn would motivate them to automatically participate in the financial system.

- *Digitise the Documentation Process for Opening of Bank Accounts*: One of the often stated reasons for slow pace of financial inclusion has been the hassles involved in opening of bank accounts and availing of loans from financial institutions due to the long process of documentation. To overcome this, there is a need to digitise the public records for dual purpose of easy accessibility and storage.
- *Strategize the Provision of Bank Credit*: Need is felt to strategize the provision of bank credit to the rural farmer households. Majority of the marginal farmer households are not at all covered by the formal finance. As such public sector banks and the co-operative banks in the rural areas have to sensitize about the need for provision of timely and cheaper credit to these segments. Reserve Bank of India in consultation with NABARD should come out with a comprehensive strategy for revitalizing the quiescent rural credit mechanism.
- *Exclusive Focus on the Socially Excluded and the Poor*: It is imminent to encompass the socially excluded sections and the poor like, tenant farmers, oral lessees and share croppers, marginal farmers with small economical land holdings, agricultural labourers, rural artisans and people involved in making handicrafts and also majority of weavers in handloom Sector.
- *Extensive use of Co-operatives*: PACS (Primary Agricultural Cooperative Societies) could provide valuable services to their members with a sense of belongingness. Accordingly, there is a need to revitalize these cooperatives as per the Vaidyanathan Committee recommendations and use them extensively for financial inclusion in the rural areas.
- *Undoubtedly a Greater Role for NABARD*: NABARD has to play a pro-active role by partnering with the rural credit institutions in the field and identify new initiatives that will contribute to effectively improving the extent of financial inclusion involving SHGs, MFIs, etc.
- *Procedural/Documentation Changes*: It is inevitable on the part of the regulators to find out an easy way of procuring the documents for opening of bank accounts and availing loans. The present guidelines are more tedious and result in huge costs for the poor in accessing the banks for any kind of services. Simplifying Mortgage Requirements, Exemption from Stamp Duty for Loans to Small and Marginal Farmers, Saral Documentation for Agricultural Loans.

- *Effective Use of Information Technology Solutions*: The use of IT enables banks to handle the enormous increase in the volume of transactions for millions of households for processing, credit scoring, credit record and follow up. The use of IT solutions for providing banking facilities at doorstep holds the potential for scalability of the Financial Inclusion initiatives.
- *Adequate Publicity for the Project of Financial Inclusion*: In a huge country like India, there needs to be huge publicity for popularizing the concept and its benefits to the common man. In this direction, a comprehensive approach has to be developed involving all the concerned at all levels to impress upon the need for financial inclusion for accelerating the economic growth in the country.
- *Financial Inclusion as a Corporate Social Responsibility of all the Banks and Financial Institutions*: It should be the endeavor of all the financial institutions to adopt financial inclusion as a corporate social responsibility and chalk out strategies in tune with the national policy on financial inclusion.
- *Role of RBI*: Reserve Bank needs to take a pro-active role in the accelerating financial inclusion by involving all the stakeholders in the financial system by using its power of moral suasion as well as regulatory powers.
- *Political Will*: Political will is an all important aspect in any developmental effort. Political leadership should accord adequate importance for financial inclusion in order to motivate and mobilise all the weaker sections of the society in favour of financial inclusion for their economic upbringing.

CONCLUSION

Financial inclusion is the key to empowerment of poor, underprivileged and low skilled rural households. Financial inclusion can truly lift the financial condition and improve the standards of living of the poor and the disadvantaged. Access to affordable financial services, especially credit and insurance, enlarges livelihood opportunities through adoption of different economic activities. Better financial inclusion would lead to increasing economic activities and self/wage employment opportunities for rural households. As a result, rural households will earn greater return/disposable income. A higher disposable income at the hands of rural households would lead to greater savings and would provide a wider deposit base to banks and other financial institutions to be helpful in undertaking variety of economic activities. Thus, financial inclusion provides monetary fuel for economic growth and it is considered critical for achieving inclusive growth.

References

H.M. Treasury (2007): "Financial Inclusion: the Way Forward", H.M. Treasury, UK, March.

Kempson, E. (2006): "Policy Level Response to Financial Exclusion in Developed Economies: Lessons for Developing Countries", Paper for Access to Finance: Building Inclusive Financial Systems, World Bank, Washington, May.

Kempson, E., J. Caskey, C. Whyley and S. Collard (2000): "In or Out?", London: Financial Services Authority.

Mohan, R. (2006): 'Agricultural Credit in India: Status, Issues and Future Agenda', *Economic and Political Weekly* (March), pp. 1013-23.

Peachy, S. and A. Roe (2004): "Access to Finance—What Does it Mean and How Do Savings Bank Foster Access?", Brussels: World Savings Bank Institute.

Report of the Committee on Financial Inclusion in India (Chairman: C. Rangarajan) (2008), Government of India.

Sen, Amartya (2000): 'Development as Freedom', Anchor Books, New York, 2000.

Financial Inclusion of the Urban Poor—Challenges and Solutions

JENIPHER CARLOS HOSANNA

ABSTRACT

The country's urban population is increasing at a faster rate than the total population. This will also lead to an increase in the number of urban poor, currently pegged at 80 million by NSSO in a report. It is this large section of the population that lacks access to even the most basic banking services: savings accounts, credit, remittances and payment services, financial advisory services, amongst others. Thus, technology and product innovation with a clear profitability objective can—like in the telecom sector—achieve the goal of amass-based and profitable service through economies of scale. However, the urban poor need to be clearly educated about the benefits of compulsory and forced savings and insurance. Insurance premium with no immediate benefit but a protective cover against financial shocks in the form of ill-health or death or accident or loss of productive assets is considered a wasteful expenditure that their incomes can ill-afford. A bank remittance product that saves time, cost-informal channels of money transfer charge large fees and risk of loss is the first step to get the urban poor and weaker sections introduced to the benefits of banking. This literacy would be a key turning point towards sustainable financial inclusion, especially in the urban poor. Further, new financial products should also be designed considering the credit needs, earning patterns, risk-bearing ability and bankability of the urban poor. In this context, this paper aims to analyze the challenges in realizing financial inclusion in urban India and possible solutions to address the same.

Even as we celebrate a booming economy, with its surplus jobs and employment opportunities, a section of our population is just waiting for a chance to earn their first salary—however, small it may be. Ironically, we also have the highest number of child labourers - close to 17 million. With just a days' salary, we can make available credit facility to the poor in India by funding for rural development in India. In this context, Financial Inclusion has been firmly established as a policy objective of Government of India and the Reserve Bank of India (RBI). The Committee on Financial Inclusion defined financial inclusion as "the process of ensuring access to financial services and timely and adequate credit where needed by vulnerable groups such as weaker sections and low income groups at an affordable cost."[1]

However, we are far from realizing the vision of universal financial inclusion. One of the key challenges has been that the debate of financial inclusion in India has largely been rural-centric. The analysis of the issues impeding inclusion and the subsequent strategy formulation has been based on, among other factors, challenges in making banking services accessible in rural areas. As mentioned in the abstract, this paper aims to analyze the challenges in realizing financial inclusion in urban India and possible solutions to address the same.

By 2030, about 40% of Indians will be living in cities and towns compared to the current proportion of 30%, according to a recent study by McKinsey Global Institute.[2] The 2001 Census puts the slum population at 42.6 million which forms 15 per cent of the country's total urban population and 23.1 per cent of population of cities and towns reporting slums.[3] The Census further reports that slums are an urban phenomenon confined to big-town and cities, supporting it with the fact that 41.6 per cent of the total slum population resides in cities with over one-million population. Informal settlements occupy one-third of the large city spaces: 34.5 per cent of the population of Mumbai, Delhi, Kolkata, and Chennai live in slum settlements. The slum settlements have a higher proportion (17.4 per cent) of scheduled castes compared to non-slum settlements.

Distribution of Slum Population in Cities and Different Size Groups City-size	*Number of cities and towns*	*Slum population (million)*	*% of total*
> 4 million	5	11.06	26.0
2-4 million	8	3.76	8.8
1-2 million	14	2.88	6.8
5,00,000 – 1 million	42	5.81	13.7
100,000 – 500,000	309	13.94	32.7
<100,000	262	5.13	12.0
Total	640	42.58	100.0

Source: Census of India 2001.

Significantly, the NSSO data shows 55 per cent of slum dwellers have been living in them for over 15 years and another 12 per cent between 10-15 years, establishing that slums are an integral part of the phenomenon of urbanization, and are contributing significantly to the economy of cities by being a source of affordable labour supply for production both in the formal and informal sectors of the economy" but are a reflection of the exclusionary socio-economic policies and planning in the country.

Number of Years Households have been living in slums (Years)	*Per cent of Slum Households*
< 5	22
5-10	10
10-15	12
> 15	55

Source: National Sample Survey, 2005.

Financial Inclusion in the Urban Context

Financial exclusion in the urban areas is a rising problem. The country's urban population is increasing at a faster rate than the total population. Much of this population comprises of migrants, who account for a substantial part of the 400 million people that comprise India's workforce work in the unorganized sector. According to McKinsey Global Institute, about 40% of Indians will be living in cities and towns by 2030 directly increasing in the number of urban poor.2 Providing financial services to the growing population will require addressing the following challenges.

Build a Network of Scalable Institutional Business Correspondents

One of the fundamental characteristic of the rural community is the availability of strong community networks. Given such community linkages, individual business correspondents who are part of the social network (kirana shop owners, for instance) can work effectively as financial intermediaries by leveraging their relationships with the community. However, in the urban context there are no such established community structures. Even among residents in a physical location, the engagement is limited. This is accentuated in the case of migrant workers, who are constantly on the move and do not integrate themselves with the community.

This impedes financial inclusion in three ways. Firstly, the identity of an individual is ascertained purely through a set of pre-defined documents, which workers more often than not do not possess. Secondly, business correspondents have to make substantial investments to build their network within the community. This is not feasible for individual business correspondents who consider the income generated through providing get the buy-in of the delivery ecosystem.

The promise of inclusion is realized only when the final delivery of the services, such as health and accident insurance is achieved. Today, the availability and engagement of the delivery ecosystem (E.g. hospitals) in the urban areas is assumed. However, in reality the urban poor do not have too many choices on the ground to address their needs.

Firstly, the design of the services does not consider the full circle of service and hence create process overheads for providers. For instance, in providing insurance products, the insurer do not account for the after-sales processes that the poor people need such as admitting workers to the hospital and helping workers at the hospitals get the correct set of documents so their claims are not rejected. In addition, claim processing for the workers was a major challenge. Moreover, a recent study by the Skoch Development Foundation shows that there is a huge need for savings, insurance and remittance products for the urban low-income and weaker sections.[2]

Secondly, hospitals do not find the urban poor a financially viable segment. The current schemes are not structured to be financially attractive to the service providers. In addition, these schemes do not attract sufficient workers and hence do not provide an attractive customer base to the hospitals creating a vicious circle impeding adoption among both parties.

Thirdly, the existing services do not address the most important needs of the customers. The outpatient care is where the workers spend the highest amount of money. However, there are no existing services that address this need even though workers are willing to pay for these services.

Invest in Awareness

Though financial education is an integral part of the financial inclusion mandate, today there are no systems in place in the urban context to provide financial education to the workers. This is especially crucial since there is a need to not only sell financial products where the customers have an explicit need (e.g. opening bank accounts) but also to evangelize products that do not have immediate benefit but provide a protective cover against unexpected shocks, e.g. Savings schemes, pensions. To do so will require a constant and consultative engagement with the workers and not just a transactional one. The need for awareness is also often underestimated while launching new products. The poor workers do not understand the need or urgency for a pension scheme. There is a strong need to have effective communication and training collaterals to effectively train the channels and raise awareness among the workers. However, the authorities wanted to invest in training and communication once the intermediaries start getting new customers.

Remove Operational Bottlenecks

Today, banks interpret the Know Your Customer (KYC) norms differently resulting in substantial differences in the banking practices. The intermediaries incur overheads in adapting to the differences in requirements and needs across banks. For instance, the poor people have to follow different guidelines when engaging with Canara Bank and Corporation Bank. Punjab National Bank has different guidelines for Haryana and Bangalore. Also, some banks mandate that Business correspondents have to be individuals. For instance, Corporation Bank only recognizes individuals as Business correspondents. It is important that the clear guidelines are defined across banks around standard operating practices. These guidelines should be based on the practices that have been implemented successfully today.

Move away from One-Size-Fits-All Approach

Urban poor is not a homogeneous group with similar needs and capacity. Today, the term encompasses the self-employed, the wage workers, and the paid workers all of whom have different saving and consumption patterns. By creating product offerings to customer segments divided by the poverty line the actual needs of the customers are not addressed. For instance, there are two health insurance products today in the market targeting those above poverty line and below poverty line respectively. However, if one considers the health risks, the saving patterns of the daily wage workers *vs.* the paid workers today it is clear that the packaging of the service should be different for these two segments. Providing market-aware choices to customers directly and positively impacts adoption. Doing so also makes it attractive to the delivery ecosystem such as hospitals since the overall mix of the customers becomes financially viable for them to serve.

CONCLUSION

There is a large and unmet demand for financial services among urban poor today. However, delivery of financial services to the poor is still far from reality. Replicating solutions that have been designed for rural areas will not be able to address challenges specific to urban areas. In order to realize the vision of financial inclusion, there is an urgent need for an approach that acknowledges and addresses the urban-specific challenges. Specifically, there is a need to identify and support institutional business correspondents who can provide the right scale and efficiency that is essential to deliver financial services in urban areas. It is important to tailor the financial products to the needs of various market sub-segments than adopt a one size-fits-all approach. Finally, it is important to co-opt the delivery ecosystem to ensure the full circle execution by making the solutions financially viable and attractive to them as well. It has been proved that the urban poor are willing to pay for services that improve their quality of lives. Bringing to market relevant solutions and delivering them effectively will create a win-win situation for all.

Notes and References

1. http://www.nabard.org
2. http://www.peerpower.com
3. The Census of India, 2001 collected the slum population data from cities and towns having population of 50,000 and more in 1991. There were a total of 743 cities and towns in that category, of which 640 reported slums. Admitting that it is the first time that the Census of India operations were extended to separately enumerate the slum population in the country, limiting the operations to firstly the notified and recognized slums, and secondly, those which had a threshold size of 60-70 households has considerably understated the size of the slum population. Moreover, count of slum population in several cities such as Patna (0.3 per cent of city's population), Lucknow (8.2 per cent of city's population) and many others *prima facie*, appears erroneous. It is also significant that while the Census collected data on the social composition of slum population, on literacy, and the structure of employment, it did not record the number and sizes of slum settlements.

References

Agrawal (2008): The need for Financial Inclusion with an Indian Perspective, IDBI, GILTS.

Anbarasan, R.S. and Ossie Fernandez (1986): Credit for fisherfolk: The experience in Adirampattinam, Tamilnadu, India, Food and Agriculture Organisation, United Nations, www.onefish.org.

Anderson, T.B and N. Malchow Moller (2006): Strategic Interaction in undeveloped credit markets, *Journal of Development Economics*, 80(2): 275-98.

Anjani Kumar, Dhiraj, K. Singh and Prabhath Kumar (2007): "Performance of Rural Credit and Factors affecting the choice of credit sources", *Indian Journal of Agricultural Economics*, Vol. 62, No. 3, July-Sept. 2007.

Aravind Aswathi (2007): "Production and Investment Credit of Scheduled Commercial banks in India: Need for a systematic Approach", *Indian Journal of Agricultural Econoimics*, Vol. 62, No. 3, July-Sept. 2007.

Arora, S.S. and Leach, J. (2005): "Towards building an Inclusive Financial Sector: Lessons from South Africa", *Economics and Political Weekly*, April 23, 2005, pp. 1726-30

Chaudhari, P.C. (2007): Total Financial Inclusion—Various Approaches", *Indian Journal of Agricultural Economics*, Vol. 62, No. 3, July-Sept. 2007.

Delvin, F. (2009): "An Analysis of Influence in Total Financial Inclusion", *The Services of Industries Journal*, 29.8; 1021-36.

Garg, A.K. and Pandey, N. (2009): Making Money Work for the Poor in India: Inclusive Finance through Bank-moneylender-linkages, www.afcindia,org

GOI (2003): Household Borrowing and Repayments in India as during 1-7-2002 to 30-6-2003, All India Debt and Investment Survey, NSS Fifty-ninth Round, January-December 2003, Report No. 502 (59/18.2/2), www.mospi.nic.in

GOI (2008): Annual Report, Credit Delivery, www.rbi.org.in

Kamath, Rajalaxmi (2007): "Financial Inclusion *vis-a-vis* Social Banking", *Economic and Political Weekly*, April, Vol. XLII (15), pp. 1334-35.

The Economic Times: Financial Inclusion: Game Changer for Urban Renewal, http://www.peerpower.com

National Rural Financial Inclusion Plan (NRFIP), http://www.nabard.org

Development of Micro-Insurance through Intermediary Institutions

SURESH KUMAR, K.S.

ABSTRACT

Insurance is a part of risk mitigation strategy. Access to insurance is a key issue to facilitate economic well-being, especially for those with limited resources to protect themselves from adversity. At the same time, it may be very serious to note that such people shall be more exposed to risks as they do not have the cushion of savings, formal credit or social security system. It is fast emerging as an important strategy even for the low-income people engaged in wide variety of income generation activities, and who remain exposed to variety of risks mainly because of absence of cost-effective risk hedging instruments. Although the type of risks faced by the poor such as that of death, illness, injury and accident, are not different from those faced by others, they are more vulnerable to such risks because of their economic circumstance. To facilitate micro-credit in its mission of income generation and entrepreneurial initiatives of creating wealth and security for the poor, micro-insurance plays a vital role in making the process sustainable and more effective.

INTRODUCTION

Individuals, households and economic organizations are vulnerable to various types of risks and unforeseen economic shocks.

One of the ways to protect themselves is through the pooling and transfer of risks offered by insurance service. Insurance is a kind of specialized financial service whereby the clients/beneficiaries are required to pay a certain premium on a regular basis in return for indemnifying the risks/perils at a fair rate when they occur. In principle, it is one of the risk management tools to counter the losses suffered from crisis. It works with a pool of resources accumulated from many people and benefit will go to those who are at risk. Depending on an individual response to dealing with risks, the literature classifies all risk management practices into three broad groups: risk reduction, risk mitigation and risk coping strategies. The first two are ex-ante risk management strategies (that is, used before a risky event takes place) whereas the third is an ex post strategy (that is after the event takes place). Insurance, similar to savings and borrowings, is a part of risk mitigation strategy. Access to insurance is a key issue to facilitate economic well-being, especially for those with limited resources to protect themselves from adversity. At the same time, it may be very serious to note that such people shall be more exposed to risks as they do not have the cushion of savings, formal credit or social security system.

Micro-insurance is defined as the protection of low income households against specific perils in exchange of premium payment proportionate to the likelihood and cost of the risk involved. Thus, it is different from insurance in general as it is a low value product (involving modest premium and benefit package) which requires different design and distribution strategies such as premium based on community risk-rating (as opposed to individual risk-rating), active involvement of an intermediate agency representing the target community and so forth. Insurance is fast emerging as an important strategy even for the low-income people engaged in wide variety of income generation activities, and who remain exposed to variety of risks mainly because of absence of cost-effective risk hedging instruments. Although the type of risks faced by the poor such as that of death, illness, injury and accident, are not different from those faced by others, they are more vulnerable to such risks because of their economic circumstance.

NEED AND SIGNIFICANCE OF MICRO-INSURANCE

Micro-insurance is a key element in the financial services package for people at the bottom of the social pyramid. The poor face more risks than the well-off, but more importantly they are more vulnerable to the same risk. Usually, the poor face two types of risks—idiosyncratic (specific to the household) and covariate (common, e.g., drought, epidemic, etc.). To combat these risks, the poor do pro-active risk management—grain storage, savings, asset accumulation, loans from friends and relatives, etc. However, the prevalent forms of risk management (in kind savings, self-insurance, mutual insurance) which were appropriate earlier are no longer adequate.

In the past, insurance as a prepaid risk managing instrument was never considered as an option for the poor. The poor were considered too underprivileged to afford insurance premiums. Often they were considered uninsurable, given the wide variety of risks they face. However, recent developments in India, as elsewhere, have shown that not only the poor can make small periodic contributions that will go towards insuring them against risks but also that the risks they face (such as those of illness, accident and injury, life, loss of property, etc.) are eminently insurable as these risks are mostly independent or idiosyncratic. Moreover, there are cost-effective ways of extending insurance to them. Thus, insurance is fast emerging as a prepaid financing option for the risks facing people, especially the weaker section of the society.

BASIC MICRO-INSURANCE PRINCIPLES

To serve poor people, micro-insurance must respond to their priority needs for risk protection, be easy to understand, and affordable. Depending on the market, they may seek health care, crop, property or life insurance provisions. Basic principles that should be observed by micro-insurance providers are akin to that of insurance and risk management. These principles include:

1. Similar Unit's Exposition to Risk

Insurers require that risks in a particular class or group of policies be similar. Insurers also require that the group insured (or the "risk pool") include a large number of these similar risks, relative to the total population. Large number of policyholders reduce the potential for adverse selection (a situation where claims are higher than expected because only high-risk households purchase the insurance) and increase the likelihood that the variance of actual claims will be closer to the expected mean used in calculating premiums.

2. Limited Policyholder Control over the Insured Event

Insurance protection cannot be offered if policyholders can control whether an insured event will occur, e.g., selling an insured truck and claiming it as stolen; setting fire to an old, insured home to build a new one with the insurance settlement; failing to properly care for an insured goat thereby increasing the chance it will die of disease, etc.

3. Insurable Interest of Policyholders

Insurance cannot be provided to policyholders who have a vested interest in a loss occurring. A property insurance policy, for example, on a home cannot be sold to anyone other than the residents of the home.

4. Losses Determination and Measurability

Insurance providers must have a mechanism for verifying the occurrence of a loss and identifying its cause and value.

5. No Catastrophe

The risk-pooling mechanism of insurance breaks down against risks that cause large losses for a substantial portion of the risk pool at the same time.

6. Chance of Loss Calculation

Setting insurance premiums require estimating the size of expected losses and the chance of loss.

7. Economically Affordable Premiums

As the micro-insurance schemes have been designed for the downtrodden its widespread distribution can be made possible only through the fixing of an economically affordable premium. In short, the cost of premiums must be substantially meager when compared to the benefit offered by the policy.

ACCESSIBILITY OF MICRO-INSURANCE

Micro-insurance is a low-price, high-volume business and its success and market dependent on keeping the transaction costs down. No satisfactory state-run programme of insurance service is now available for the benefit of the weaker section of the population, especially for those working in the informal and unorganized sector of the economy. A number of constraints such as lack of political will, scarcity of public funds and absence of a viable business model make micro-insurance look unattractive. The costs of marketing and processing appear to be too high and, in view of the extremely low purchasing power of the consumer base; it cannot be easily apportioned to the target group. Further, the importance of micro-finance must be looked against the fact that even with wide network of banks in India, the low-income people especially in rural areas, have been largely bypassed by the formal banking system. The government of India has been involved in its promotion in a variety of ways. This movement needs further guidance and direction not only from government but also from semi-government and non-government organisation. Market analysis suggests that progress can be made particularly when public and private sector work together in generating demand-based and innovative products.

In India, it is often assumed that a micro-insurance policy is not simply a low-premium insurance policy, rather it is meant for people who live in rural areas, often illiterate and unfamiliar with the concept of insurance, requiring new approaches to both marketing and contracting; tend to face more risks than the wealthier people do. For example, on average they are more prone to illness because they suffer from malnutrition, forced to work under hazardous conditions and do not get proper medical care and have little experience of dealing with formal financial institutions.

Access to insurance, especially to the above mentioned vulnerable segments of the population is the burning problem faced by the policy-makers in the country in spite of the strong insurance sector prevailing in the country. For the effective accessibility of insurance to all, customers and insurance providers should be able to come together to understand risks and security needs, provide product information, undertake propaganda measures, make payment of premiums, advice, assess and settle the claims, and deal with other required administrative services in a cost effective manner. Economically viable schemes according to the requirements of the weaker sections are the need of the hour. A number of multi-dimensional issues are confronted by the Indian insurance sector which hinders accessibility of insurance service and social security to the bulk of Indian population. Such issues and challenges include:

- The socio-economic circumstances of the people play a crucial role in denying the benefits of the conventional insurance services to those in the informal work force, those with highly variable and unreliable incomes and those with particularly low income.
- The geographical features of Indian subcontinent is really a barrier to those who wish to get benefited from insurance and schemes social security as the formal insurers concentrate in urban and semi-urban areas.
- The business processes and models practiced by the insurance providers to market their products stand as yet another challenge in the accessibility of insurance service to the weaker sections. These marketing models are not viable when applied to a lion share of the market, especially the market segment involving smaller amount of premium per policy. Insurers who attempt to serve the lower premium markets with already established marketing models could not achieve their targets.

- Market-oriented services and product design of the formal insurers, focusing on the well to do sections of the society, also pose a serious limitation causing inaccessibility of insurance to the poor.

MFIs AND MICRO-INSURANCE

Traditional micro-finance schemes do not address the necessity of risk reduction for the ultra poor. The informal coping mechanisms offer limited protection and are less available to poorer households. Formal financial services can offer greater benefits at a lower cost than informal mechanisms but the vulnerability to risk will reduce the effectiveness and financial performance of micro-credit. Insurance or risk protection is one mechanism that ties both the borrower and the institution. Mostly the MFIs only cover lenders part of risk by securing the credit whereas borrowers' part of risk is always overlooked. Any improvement in this area will help the MFIs not only to bring better customer satisfaction through protection of risks faced by the borrowers but also contribute to the poverty alleviation role of micro-finance. Undoubtedly, risk coverage of borrower's part of micro-credit is an important and interesting area to work with.

Micro-finance activity in the country has led to the spread of micro-insurance among its members/clients of the Micro-Finance Institutions (MFIs). MFIs have made integrating insurance with their credit and savings activities possible, making a logical sense of approach as it helps them to reap economies of large scale operation in financial management. It helped them to get equipped with a captive market, and enabled them to use their existing network and distribution channels to sell insurance products. Besides, linking micro-insurance with micro-credit made it cheaper for the borrower to have access both of these financial services. The natural linkage between micro-insurance and micro-finance is already recommended and the significance of such a business combination has been established by national as well as international organizations including International Labour Organization (ILO).

Insurance also helps in reducing the rate of interest charged on credit. Further, it is worth noting that with the help of insurance, interest rate together with the premium may also come down, as compared with the interest rate charged in the absence of insurance. Higher loan recovery is an important determinant of interest rate charged by a lending agency. The higher the loan recovery, the lower is the interest rate charged by a lender. Thus, insurance, by reducing the risk of loan default due to the contingency against which insurance is bought, reduces interest rate charged by the lender. For this reason it makes better sense for micro-credit organizations to introduce micro-insurance. Important here is to stress that when insurance is integrated with credit the total amount charged (i.e., interest plus premium) may be lower than the interest charged in the absence of insurance.

Keeping in view the advantages that will arise from credit-insurance linkage, MFIs should develop some appropriate business models according to their requirements for the smooth marketing process. Studies found that there are several avenues where government can work helping the commercial insurers and micro-finance institutions (MFIs) to go for agent partner model and design schemes for the clients based on respective strengths. All these will ensure the sustainability and the financial feasibility of both the business. Thus, micro-insurance, a market product, along with business development service concept can help to explore possibilities beyond horizon and alternative.

COOPERATIVES AND MICRO-INSURANCE

Majority of the micro-insurance providers in the world are some sort of mutual organizations. Mutual institutions are owned by their member users and usually hold the principle of "One Man One Vote." Under this system, an insurance company is affiliated to a network of cooperatives (usually savings and credit cooperatives) and provides insurance service to the members of the network. Thus, in the cooperative network model, there are two basic components such as: (a) a risk carrier (an insurance company) which creates and underwrites the insurance products, and (b) a network of cooperatives that serves as the distribution channel.

There are many reasons why cooperative insurers can reduce the total cost and hence premium rates can be kept below those of private insurers. A cooperative insurer can also make use of a special sales force with a definite commission. It can also conduct a sales campaign for the entire area of operation through the network of branches or through direct marketing. With the help of local society or network of branches, premium collection and claim settlement become simple and cost effective. Further, co-operative insurance facilitates savings and accumulation of capital in the hands of lower income groups and channelizes a portion of these resources in to the local trade and industry, leading to enhanced living standards of the targeted communities.

CONCLUSION

Micro-insurance is recognized as a useful tool in the economic development in terms of ensuring the social security and economic well being of weaker and marginalized segment of any society or nation. To facilitate micro-credit in its mission of income generation and entrepreneurial initiatives of creating wealth and security for the poor, micro-insurance plays a vital role in making the process sustainable and more effective. Furthermore, micro-insurance makes it possible for people to take more risks. When farmers are insured against a bad harvest (resulting from drought), they are a in a better position to grow crops which give high yields in good years, and bad yields in year of drought. Without the insurance however, they will be inclined to do the opposite; since they have to safeguard a minimal level of income for themselves and their families, crops will be grown which are more drought resistant, but which have a much lower yield in good weather conditions. However, the real problem arises in the distribution of micro-insurance products to the targeted communities. In this direction, active participation of MFIs, Cooperatives, and NGOs in the formal insurance system will certainly give fruitful results.

References

Brown, Warren and Churchill, Craig F. (2000), *Insurance Provision in Low-Income Communities*, Part II, *Initial Lessons from Micro-Insurance Experiments for the Poor,* Bethesda, Md., USA: DAI, 2000.

Brown, Warren and Churchill, Craig F. (1999), *Insurance Provision in Low-Income Communities*, Part I, *Primer on Insurance Principles and Products,* Toronto: Calmeadow, 1999.

CGAP (2003a), Consultative Group to Assist the Poor, Working Group Study on Micro-Insurance, Preliminary Donor Guidelines for Supporting Micro-insurance, 8 October 2003.

MRF (2006), Munich Re-Foundation Into Action. Micro-insurance making insurance work for the poor, Munich Re-Foundation, January 2006.

Roth, J. McCord M., Liber D., The landscape of micro-insurance in the world's 100 poorest countries, 2007, p. 107. Appleton, WI: Micro-Insurance Centre, Limited Liability Company.

Kudumbasree Model of Micro-Finance

ALJO C. CHERIYAN AND BIJU, S.K.

ABSTRACT

It is commonly understood that poverty can be reduced through micro-finance. Kerala introduced a novel scheme of poverty alleviation based on micro-credit and self-help grouping. It seeks to bring the poor women folk together to help enhance their economic security. Kudumbasree plays a vital role in enhancing the financial status of the less privileged women in the state through its thrift and credit societies. These societies facilitate them to save and provide them with cost-effective and easy credit. The poor women should be able to approach the informal banks whenever necessity occurs. The doors of the banks should be open for 24 hours a day. It doesn't need an office building, furniture and other paraphernalia we normally relate with a formal bank. The strength of an informal bank is the intimate relationship between the members of the Self-Help Group. The members know each other's potentials, weaknesses and problems.

1. INTRODUCTION

Poverty alleviation schemes based on micro-credit system have been implemented in many of the developing countries in recent years. The Government of India changed in vision, strategies and programmes, from viewing women as beneficiaries of welfare to involving women in their own empowerment. Several factors have contributed to this, including international commitments, pressure from women's groups and movements and also the factor of 'efficiency' that has contributed to hastening the development process. The Government of Kerala State in India has introduced a novel scheme of poverty alleviation based on micro-credit and self-help grouping. Paraphrased as Kudumbasree ('Prosperity of the Family'), the scheme aims at improving the living levels of the poor women in rural and urban areas. It seeks to bring the poor women folk together to form the grassroot organisations to help enhance their economic security. The project aims at removing poverty among rural women households through setting up of micro-credit and productive enterprises.

The mission of Kudumbasree is "To eradicate absolute poverty through concerted community action under the leadership of Local Self-Governments, by facilitating organization of the poor for combining self-help with demand-led convergence of available services and resources to tackle the multiple dimensions and manifestations of poverty holistically". It was conceived as a joint programme of the Government of Kerala and NABARD implemented through Community Development Societies (CDSs) of Poor Women, serving as the community wing of Local Governments. It was established on 17th May, 1998 in Malappuram District and registered under the Societies Act.

2. STRUCTURE OF KUDUMBASREE

The Kudumbasree community organisation is a three-tiered structure with its apex tier anchored in the local self-governments. The three tiers are:

Neighbourhood Groups (NHGs)

The lowest tier constitutes the Neighbourhood Group with 10 to 20 women members selected from economically backward families. Meetings are convened on a weekly basis in the houses of NHG members. In the weekly meeting all members bring their thrift, which will be collected and recycled to the system by way of sanctioning loans.

Area Development Society (ADS)

The second tier is the Area Development Society, which is formed at ward-level by federating all the NHGs in the ward. The activities and the decision in the ADS are decided by the representatives of the women elected from various NHGs. Ward member of panchayat/ ward councilor of urban local body is fixed as the patron/chairperson to maintain linkage with the local self-governments.

Community Development Society (CDS)

At the Panchayat/Municipal level a Community Development Society (CDS), a registered body under the Travancore-Cochin Literacy Scientific and Charitable Societies Act is formed by federating all ADSs in the local bodies. In order to maintain linkage with the LSGIs, the president of village panchayat as patron, welfare standing committee chairman of panchayat, all women members of the Panchayat, Block Panchayat member of respective division and secretary of Panchayat are ex-officio members of CDS.

Self-sufficient, self-reliant, sustainable Panchayat, these are the three 'S' that Kudumbasree is trying to achieve through CDS. But through special rules for Kudumbasree the Government of Kerala converted the LSGIs only as a watch dog by creation a monitoring committee of nearly 40 members consisting of members of panchayat.

The paradigm shift in the approach is that any woman who is residing in the Grama Panchayat can become a member of the Kudumbasree Ayalkoottam irrespective of the fact that she belongs to a below poverty line (BPL) family. Since this aspect gives an opening for the APL families to enter into the community structures envisaged by Kudumbasree. It is further ensured that majority of the office bearers should belong to BPL families. These structures give added importance to women empowerment both social and economic.

3. PARTICIPATION IN NHGS

Kudumbasree promotes Neighbourhood Groups (NHGs) of 10-20 poor women members as an interface between poor women, banks and government agencies. NHGs are instrumental in thrift mobilization, encouraging the poor to save and to avail low cost formal credit. They facilitate easy and timely credit to the un-reached. The amount of loan to members and the purpose for which the loan should be utilized are decided by the NHG. The repayment is collected weekly during the NHG meetings. It is estimated that the thrift mobilized is on an average Rs. 40 per month per member. It is also estimated that during the year 2009-10, the total thrift collected by all NHGs is Rs. 198.56 crores and the internal loan disbursed is Rs. 892.76 crores.

The Table 1 depicts the Block Panchayat-wise participation of families in the NHGs in Kannur District. A total of 11,400 NHGs are formed in the rural area that covers 2,12,859 families with thrift and credit activities.

TABLE I

Participation in NHG

Sl. No.	*Name of the Block Panchayat*	*No. of NHGs formed*	*No. of Families Covered*	*No. of Families Started Thrift*
1	Edakkad	1094	17455	17455
2	Payyannur	1716	33728	33728
3	Thalipparamba	2009	41532	41532
4	Irikkur	1616	30512	30512
5	Kannur	800	13855	13855
6	Thalassery	894	16237	16237
7	Koothuparamba	957	17351	17351
8	Iritty	1414	26687	26687
9	Peravoor	900	15502	15502
	Total (Rural)	**11400**	**212859**	**212859**

Source: District Human Development Report of Kannur.

4. MICRO-FINANCE

Micro-finance is a short form of micro-financial services and involves the opportunity for small savings, take loan, remit money, and convert assets in to cash through pledging, mortgaging, pawning, as well access to hire-purchase facility, leasing, insurance, etc. The aims and objectives of this programme included formation of a strong network of informal banking for the un-reached and under- served poor women in Kerala. Promotion of Micro-finance is one of the best strategies for poverty reduction. And third specific objective of Kudumbasree is 'encouraging thrift and investment through credit by developing CDS to work as informal bank of the poor'.

4.1. Thrift and Loan by NHGs

Now, 10,687 Thrift and Credit Societies are in operation in the 58 urban areas enveloping the major 58 towns. In the rural segment, 1,45,674 Thrift and Credit societies are in operation covering all the 978 Village Panchayats in the State. Most of the Thrift and Credit Societies are capable of providing financial assistance to income generating activities. Through micro-finance operations, Rs. 651.42 lakh of thrift are raised and internal lending to the extent of Rs. 1473.12 lakh are provided. The NHGs, which are able to avail of loans, are linked with banks under linkage banking programme of NABARD. 99,356 NHGs were upgraded and 71,702 of NHGs were linked with banks. Rs. 258.78 crore is distributed as loan to NHGs for internal lending and credit of Rs. 32281/lakh flow through linkage banking. Linkage banking programme becomes an effective tool to augment resources of NHGs.

The Table 2 shows the details of thrift and loan in Kannur District as an example. Participation of women in the NHGs shows that almost all the families have started thrift and the total amount of thrift stood at Rs. 8,29,266,045, while the amount of loan was Rs. 28,80,341,954. On an average, loan amount of Rs. 2,52,662 was provided per NHG.

TABLE 2

Thrift and Loan by NHGs

Sl. No.	*Name of the Block Panchayat*	*No. of NHG formed*	*Amount of Thrift (Rs.)*	*Amount of Loan (Rs.)*	*Ave. Thrift Per NHG (Rs.)*	*Ave. Loan Per NHG (Rs.)*
1.	Edakkad	1094	65575323	129172231	59941	118073
2.	Payyannur	1716	127785905	557634041	74467	324962
3.	Thalipparamba	2009	164582715	718527496	81923	357654
4.	Irikkur	1616	144470221	510233769	89400	315739
5.	Kannur	800	41136768	117890903	51421	147364
6.	Thalassery	894	49933815	125278592	55854	140133
7.	Koothuparamba	957	58376430	185333769	60999	193661
8.	Iritty	1414	117770704	332406877	83289	235083
9.	Peravoor	900	59634164	203864276	66260	226516
	Total (Rural)	**11400**	**829266045**	**2880341954**	**72743**	**252662**

Source: District Human Development Report of Kannur.

4.2. Linkage Banking

NHG-Bank linkage scheme is one of the flagship programmes of Kudumbasree. NABARD SHG-Bank linkage grading procedures are applied while selecting eligible NHGs for availing loan. CDS assists NHG in getting graded by the bank. Bank will provide loans to those NHGs who pass 80% of marks in the grading. Loan amount to an NHG is linked to thrift amount mobilized and retained within the group as internal loans. Maximum loan amount possible for a NHG is four times of its thrift.

In some cases, CDS borrowd from the bank as bulk loan for lending to eligible NHGs. In Bulk linkage, CDS charges 1 or 2 percentage points more than the bank's interest rate. A certain date is fixed by the bank within which NHGs are required to repay the amount to CDS. CDS in turn pay the collected amount to bank.

The Bank Linkage programme has helped the NHGs to augment their existing resources mobilized through thrift. The total loan amount disbursed under linkage banking in the state from the beginning and upto March 2010 is Rs. 993.65 crores. Cumulative number of NHGs availed bank linkage is 1,18,711 NHGs. For the year 2009-10, the total amount of loan disbursed through linkage banking is Rs. 284.11 crores to 17,605 NHGs.

Kerala State Backward Classes Development Corporation Limited (KSBCDC) has provided loans for backward communities through Kudumbasree Community Development Societies. Kudumbasree in association with KSBCDC has implemented this scheme in five CDSs in Trissur and three CDSs in Palakkad districts. KSBCDC provides loan at 3 percent to CDSs and eligible NHGs avail loan at 5 percent from CDSs. Loan amount of Rs. 2.2 crores were provided to the above mentioned CDSs.

4.3. Matching Grant to Thrift and Credit Societies

Matching grant is an incentive provided to NHGs. This grant linked to amount of thrift mobilized, performance of NHG in the Grading and loan availed from banks. An amount of 10% of the savings of the NHG subject to a maximum of Rs. 5000 is provided as matching grant to each NHG. The grant is released based on their assessment rated using a 15-point grading criteria developed by NABARD. In order to avail Matching, an NHG must have passed the grading and availed loan from bank. In case of SC/ST NHGs, matching grant will be provided if the NHG has passed grading. Availing bank loan for an SC/ ST, NHG is not compulsory in order to be eligible for matching grant.

TABLE 3

Matching Grant

Year	*No. of NHGs (Approx.)*	*Cumulative No. of NHGs*	*Matching Grant for the year (Rs. in Lakhs)*	*Cumulative Matching Grant (Rs. in Lakhs)*
2005-06	413	413	16.50	16.50
2006-07	1800	2213	72.00	88.50
2007-08	10000	12213	400.00	488.50
2008–09	7900	21113	316.00	804.50
2009-10	43693	64806	1559.00	2363.50

Source: Kudumbasree Annual Administration Report, 2009-10.

For the year 2009-10, Rs.1559 lakhs has been disbursed to 43,693 NHGs as matching grant. Achievement in 2009-10 under matching grant is about five times compared to the previous year. It was possible because of the enormous effort put in by Kudumbasree mission.

District Mission Teams devised different strategies which have obviously resulted in manifold increase in matching grant. Some of the strategies adopted for disbursing the matching grant is highlighted as under.

4.4. Credit Sources

(a) From Financial Institutions

Credit sources such as Primary Agricultural Cooperative Societies, Nationalised Banks and other private banks are important supporting agencies for the collective farming groups. PACS provide interest-free loans for selected crops and play an important role in the farming by these women groups. Nationalised banks and some private banks provide crop loan for the group at 7 percent. Out of this 7 percent 5 percent is provided as interest subsidy from Kudumbasree and hence the group gets the loan at a low interest rate. If the group is able to leverage the 2 percent interest subsidy available from GOI for prompt repayment, it would in effect become an interest free loan.

(b) From Local Self-Governments

At the initial stages of Kudumbasree, the LSGIs provided seed capital (revolving fund), special assistance, etc. to the NHGs from their plan fund. Above this many LSGIs are providing infrastructure to NHGs for doing activities and help to link with banks. The LSGIs use Women Component Plan (WCP) for helping the NHGs.

5. WHY KUDUMBASREE MODEL IS RELEVANT?

Kudumbasree plays a vital role in enhancing the financial status of the less privileged women in the state through its thrift and credit societies. These societies facilitate them to save and provide them with cost-effective and easy credit. The savings of the women are pooled together and given out as loans to the most deserving. These loans have been used for purposes ranging from covering hospital expenses to meeting working capital needs for micro-enterprises. The Community Development Societies facilitate bank linkages for farming, micro-housing and micro-insurance. They also serve as the delivery point for skill up-gradation and market development support to micro-enterprises. The activities such as micro-credit and micro-enterprises under the scheme were undertaken by the locally formed Community Development Societies comprising poor women. It is through creating livelihood opportunities for the women that they can be empowered, and the micro-credit and self-help groups are a better means through which their living conditions can be improved. Poverty alleviation schemes based on micro-credit system have been implemented in many of the developing countries in recent years. The project aims at removing poverty among rural women households through setting up of micro-credit and productive enterprises. The activities such as microcredit and micro-enterprises under the scheme were undertaken by the locally formed Community Development Societies consisting of rural households.

The poor women should be able to approach the informal banks whenever necessity occurs. The doors of the banks should be open for 24 hours a day, 7 days a week and 365 days a year. The informal banks are formed with the active involvement of every member belonging to the Self-Help Group. An Informal Bank doesn't need an office building, furniture and other paraphernalia, we normally relate with a formal bank. The strength of an informal bank is the intimate relationship between the members of the Self-Help Group. The members know each others' potentials weaknesses and problems. The members can deposit even trifle amount in the thrift scheme of the banks. Informal bank always tried to encourage saving habit among poor women. An informal bank can provide collateral free loans with the terms and conditions decided by the group. The Self-Help Group behind the informal bank is free to fix market driven rates of interest for advances. Every operation of an informal bank takes place in the group level, including depositing of thrift amounts and sanctioning of thrift loans. The groups itself decide the eligibility of a member to get assistance from the bank after discussions and assessment of the need and repayment capacity.

The very existence of an Informal Bank brings about the homogeneity and affinity among members of the poor. Thrift savings of the members serve as the main bondage among members. The bank promotes regularity in savings and assures sufficient frequency for group meetings. The informal banks will instill collective decision-making capability among the poor women. This sublime quality will be of great assistance to them for their fight against poverty and their participation in planning process and economic development activities. Informal banks will slowly do away with the subsidy syndrome prevailing in the lowest stratum of the society. The poor women will begin to enjoy the unique pleasure of doing things with their own money. The financial empowerment of women achieved through thrift and bank accessibility will improve their status in their own families and society. Naturally, their confidence will increase. Above all Informal Banks provide loans to the poor women at their own doorsteps without any hassle.

Once the informal banks of the NHGs, ADSs and CDS reach a certain level of maturity; they can grant loans to the members for genuine needs. Poor needs financial assistance for several purposes, falling under four major categories.

The Thrift and Credit Societies are formed with the objective of encouraging the poor women to save their meager means to widen the resource base of the NHGs. Women bring their little bit of savings when they come to attend the group meetings. This money is entrusted to the Community Volunteer, who in turn deposits it in the nearest bank. Each member is given an individual passbook. The Thrift and Credit Societies are considered as poor women's bank. The poor women, who were hitherto dependent on their men folk for every need and did not know the meaning of economic independence, have managed the impossible under Kudumbasree.

Members can avail of loans to meet their urgent needs like medical treatment, purchase of school books and uniforms for children, to pay-off their old debts, etc. It is interesting to note that more than 90 per cent of the savings in the thrift societies are given away as loans. The selection of beneficiaries, the rate of interest, the quantum of loans and the period of repayment, etc. are all decided and implemented by the women themselves. Since the decisions regarding the repayment of loans with the rate of interest are taken by the NHGs, the monitoring mechanisms are inbuilt and defaulting is rare. For the same reason the NHGs are also very considerate to genuine reasons of non-repayment and extensions are given. It is observed that 100 per cent repayments are ensured which are rare in banking history. The Thrift and Credit Societies become the largest **informal bank** in Asia.

6. CONCLUSION

Kudumbasree-massive anti-poverty programme of the Government of Kerala aiming at eradicating poverty and salvage the destitute from the wretches of extreme deprivation. The formation of 1,65,840 NHGs of the women from 33,45,509 risk families, covering urban, rural and tribal areas of the State helps develop 2,42,489 poor women into vibrant micro-entrepreneurs with the micro-credit and assistance from various agencies. As a result, the poor women of the State have become active participants in the planning and implementation process of various anti-poverty programmes. By participating in various income generating-*cum*-developmental activities, the morale and confidence of women became very high. Capacity of the poor women of the State in several areas has gone up considerably. Status of women in families and community has also improved. The State Poverty Eradication Mission—Kudumbasree—launched by the Government of Kerala State in India is a massive poverty eradication programme in contemporary history. Kudumbasree became the lifeline to many of the poor women in the State of Kerala. It assumed the status of helpline to many. The Kudumbasree has gained national and international acclaim as an ideal and workable model of participatory development for eradicating poverty. This fame and gain achieved by the Kudumbasree was from the micro-credit arrangements that helped as a base for doing income generating activities to women and saved many from the clutches of moneylenders. That income and public status improved the standard of living and role of women in family and society.

REFERENCES

Annual Administration Report of Kudumbasree, 2009-10.

Government of Kerala (2009), 'Kudumbasree', KILA.

Journal of Local Governance, KILA (2006) 'Evolution is always experimental: Micro-finance Model', Vol. 2, No. 2, pp. 35-40.

Journal of Rural Development, NIRD (2009), 'Micro-credit and empowerment: A study of Kudumbasree projects in Kerala', Vol. 28, No. 4, pp. 469-84.

KILA (2010), 'District Human Development Report—Kannur'.

www.Kudumbasree.org

Banking and Financial Exclusion: The Indian Scenario

DR. MANOJ PILLAI

ABSTRACT

The post-independence economic planning in India revolved around the expansion of financial institutions to rural and un-banked areas with the basic objective of expanding access to formal credit in rural under-developed regions. The Government of India initiated a revolutionary concept of social control of banking for operational flexibility and effectiveness. In July 1969, 14 commercial banks were nationalized through newly formulated Bank Company Acquisition Act. Branch Expansion and Priority Sector Lending became the main engines of the social banking concept. The policy of branch expansion led to an increase in number of bank branches throughout the length and breadth of the country. Similarly, Priority Sector Lending envisaged 40 percent of net credit of all scheduled commercial banks to priority sectors of the Indian economy. Ironically even after six decades of independence, 45.9 million (51.4 percent) farm households in the country do not have access to credit, either from institutional or non-institutional sources. Further, despite the vast network of bank branches, only 27 percent of the farm households are indebted to institutional sources. The concept of financial exclusion is of complex nature and it also varies widely across regions, social groups and assets holdings. This article makes an attempt to analyze the various constructs of Social Banking in India with specific assessment on financial exclusion in India.

INTRODUCTION

Access and availability of finance is an important component of bolstering the socio-economic development of a country and its people. A developed financial set-up will always result in financial stability with favourable implications for economic performance. Access to finance and financial stability is thus the key to economic growth. The post-Independence economic planning in India revolved around the expansion of financial institutions to rural and un-banked areas with the basic objective of expanding access to formal credit in rural under developed regions. Indian planning experts used social banking as the main tool for expanding the flow of formal credit with the twin objectives of displacing private moneylenders and to provide cheap credit to rural households which will help in reducing poverty and indebtedness.

BANK NATIONALIZATION, BRANCH EXPANSION AND PRIORITY SECTOR LENDING: ENGINES OF SOCIAL BANKING

The Government of India initiated the revolutionary concept of social control of banking for operational flexibility and effectiveness. In July 1969, 14 commercial banks were nationalized through newly formulated Bank Company Acquisition Act. The preamble to this act stated:

> "The Banking system touches the lives of millions and has to be inspired by larger social purpose and has sub-verse national priorities and objectives such as rapid growth of agriculture, small industries and exports, raising of employment levels, encouragement of new entrepreneurs and development of backward areas. For this purpose it is necessary for the Government to take responsibility for the extension and diversification of banking services and for the working of a substantial part of the banking system".

Thus, the nationalization of banks in India initiated the process of speedy socio-economic development and rural penetration of credit through the dynamic concept of Social Banking. The period from 1970-92 witnessed a rapid increase in the bank branches in India. During this period the number of bank branches in India increased to roughly 65,000. Similarly, the banking locations in India rose from around 5000 to over 25,000. At the time of nationalization, the rural bank constituted only 22 percent but it increased to almost 60 percent of total bank branches by 1992.

Priority Sector Lending is another notable initiative of the Government of India to strengthen the Social Banking concept. It envisaged the involvement of scheduled commercial banks in the financing of priority sectors like agriculture and small scale industries. Initially, there was no specific target fixed in respect of priority sector lending. In November 1974 the banks were advised to raise the share of these sectors in their aggregate advances to the level of $33^1/_3$ percent by March 1979. In March 1980, it was agreed that banks should aim at raising the proportion of their advances to priority sector to 40 percent by March 1985. At present, the total priority sector advances consist of 40 percent of Adjusted Net Bank Credit (ANBC) or credit equivalent amount of Off-Balance Sheet exposure, whichever is higher. Foreign banks target for priority sector is fixed at 32 percent.

TABLE I

Priority Sector Advances

(Amt. in crores)

As on last reporting Friday of March	*Public Sector Banks*	*Private Sector Banks*	*Foreign Banks*
2004	2,44,456 (43.6)	48,920 (47.3)	17,960(34.1)
2005	3,07,046 (42.8)	69,886(43.6)	23,843 (35.3)
2006	4,09,748 (40.3)	1,06,586 (42.8)	30,439 (34.4)
2007	5,21,376 (39.7)	1,44,549 (42.9)	37,831 (33.4)
2008	6.10.450 (44.7)	1,64,068 (47.8)	50,254 (39.5)
2009*	7,20,083 (42.5)	1,90,207 (46.8)	55,453 (34.3)

* Data are provisional.

Notes: Figures in brackets are percentages to the net bank credit up to 2007; thereafter they are percentages to Adjusted Net Bank Credit (ANBC) or credit equivalent of Off-Balance Sheet Exposure (OBT) which is higher in the respective groups.

Source: RBI Annual Report, 2008-09.

Table 1 highlights the monetary advances made by the public sector banks, private sector banks and the foreign banks towards priority sector lending along with the percentage to the net bank credit and the adjusted net bank credit. It can be seen from the table that all the banks have made advances to priority sector as per the stipulated norms laid by the Reserve Bank of India and Government of India. Table 2 shows the monetary assistance to agricultural sector under special agricultural credit plan.

The most striking aspect of Table 2 is that the target achieved in all the three years is exceptional with some targets achieving more than 100%. Similarly, the year on year growth has always increased in all these years. Another notable development is that even in the case of private

TABLE 2

Disbursements under Special Agricultural Credit Plan

Year	*Target*	*Disbursement*	*Target Achieved*	*Year on Year growth*
1	*2*	*3*	*4*	*5*
Public Sector Banks				
2006-07	1,18,160	1,22,443	130.6	29.9
2007-08	1,52,133	1,33,226	87.6	8.8
2008-09*	1,59,470	1,44,302	90.5	8.3
Private Sector Banks				
2006-07	40,656	44,093	108.5	41.3
2007-08	41,427	47,862	115.5	8.5
2008-09*	57,353	59,805	104.3	25.0

*Provisional.

Source: RBI Annual Report, 2008-09.

sector banks target achievement levels were more than 100% in the three financial years starting from 2006-07.

TABLE 3

Targets and Actual Disbursement of Agricultural Loans by Banks

(Amt. in crores)

Agency	*2005-06*		*2006-07*		*2007-08*		*2008-09*	
	Target	*Disbursement*	*Target*	*Disbursement*	*Target*	*Disbursement*	*Target*	*Disbursement*
Commercial Banks	87,200	1,25,477	1,19,000	1,66,486	1,50,000	1,81,088	1,95,000	2,23,663
Cooperative Banks	38,600	39,786	41,000	42,480	52,000	48,258	5,50,00	3,67,62
Regional Rural Banks	15,200	15,223	15,000	20,435	23,000	25,312	30,000	26,724
Other Agencies*	-	-	-	-	-	-	-	-
Total	1,41,000	1,80,486	1,75,000	2,29,401	2,25,000	2,54,658	2,80,00 0	2,87,149

* Co-operative Societies, State Financial Corporations, Agricultural Development Finance Corporation.

Table 3 focuses on the disbursements made by banks in the form of agricultural loans. The Commercial Banks led in the total disbursement followed by the Cooperative Banks and the Regional Rural Banks. In all the above shown financial years the total disbursement made is more than the targets set. Similarly, there has been an increase in the disbursement in each of these years when compared to the previous year. Table 4 gives an account of the financial assistance made to micro-and small enterprises by banks.

TABLE 4

Outstanding Credit to Micro-and Small Enterprises

(Amt. in crores)

Year	*Public Sector Bank*	*Private Banks*	*Foreign Banks*	*All Schedulded Comm. Banks*	*Percentage Credit to Net Bank Credit*
2007	1,02,550	13,136	11,637	1,27,323	7.2
2008	1,51,137	46,912	15,489	2,13,538	11.6
2009	1,90,968	47,916	18,188	2,57,072	11.4

Source: RBI Annual Report, 2008-09.

Along with the agricultural advances, the priority sector lending was directed towards the small and medium enterprises which is another important sector of Indian economy particularly in the rural and semi urban areas. The above table points out that there is a constant increase in the disbursement of funds from all the scheduled commercial banks to the small and medium enterprises.

Thus from the above facts and figures it can be averred that bank nationalization in India and the priority sector lending are two important components of Social Banking designed specifically for the socio economic development of rural India. The disbursements of loan are sector oriented and the banks were successful to a large extent in meeting the targets and standards established by the Government of India right from the inception.

ACCESS TO FINANCE: THE MYTH

Almost 40 years have passed since the introduction of the concept of Social Banking in India. Even in the contemporary reforms era, priority sector lending is an integral part of the Indian banking system. Concrete efforts have been made by the Government of India to evenly increase the flow of credit particularly in the direction of agriculture and small and medium enterprises operating in the rural areas. Ironically, despite all the integrated efforts of the Indian Government, financial inclusion and an even and uniform financial access is a distant dream. National Sample Survey Organization (NSSO) portrays a dismal picture relating to the overall financial inclusion in India. Even after six decades of independence, 45.9 million (51.4 percent) farm households in the country do not have access to credit, either from institutional or non-institutional sources. Further, despite the vast network of bank branches, only 27 percent of the farm households are indebted to institutional sources. The concept of financial exclusion is of complex nature and it also varies widely across regions, social groups and assets holdings. Social Banking, Priority Sector Lending and Rural Penetration of Bank Branches were designed to spread financial activities and services through the country but even after special targeted approach and financial schemes the concept of Financial Inclusion and broader access to finance is still a myth in India.

FINANCIAL EXCLUSION: A SAD REALITY

Financial exclusion is a prominent factor which has crippled the rural economy of India. It is related with the inability to access necessary financial services in an appropriate form due to problems associated with access, conditions, prices, marketing and self-exclusion. C. Rangarajan Committee on Financial Inclusion has defined it as "the process of ensuring access to financial services and adequate credit needed by vulnerable groups such as weaker sections and low income groups at an affordable cost." Thorat, Usha (2008) opines that the working or operational definitions of financial exclusion generally focus on the ownership or access to particular financial products and services. The financial service is a broad concept and it includes savings, loans, insurance, credit, payments, etc. The financial system has to provide its function of transferring resources from surplus to deficit units but both deficit and surplus units are those with low incomes and poor background. By providing these services, the basic aim is to help them come out of poverty. Sharma, Purti (2009) relates financial inclusion with easy, safe and affordable credit and other financial services to socially and economically weaker sections of the society. Dasgupta (2009) points out the following fundamental factors as the potent reasons for the financial exclusion in India.

(i) Geographical, i.e. non-existence of branches in the area,
(ii) Access exclusion, i.e. restricted access because of bank risk assessment process,
(iii) Condition exclusion, i.e. the condition relating to the products failing to meet the needs,
(iv) Price exclusion, i.e. charges associated with the products or services are very high,
(v) Marketing exclusion, i.e. strategic exclusion of certain markets, and
(vi) Self-exclusion, i.e. some section of the population refuse to approach banks believing that any request would be turned down.

MAGNITUDE OF FINANCIAL EXCLUSION

M. Mahedeva (2008) characterizes financial exclusion by limited service providers, limited goals and limited lending besides a huge area of operations and missing linkages between financial institutions and local organizations. The overall financial exclusion scenario is extremely grim in India. NSSO data reveal that 45.9 million farmer households in the country (51.4%), out of a total of 89.3 million households do have access to credit, either from institutional or non-institutional sources. Further, despite the vast network of bank branches, only 27% of total farm households are indebted to formal sources (of which one-third also borrow from informal sources). The findings of Invest India Incomes and Savings Survey (2007) highlight that 32.8 per cent of the households had borrowed from institutional sources and 67.2 had borrowed from non institutional sources. The Survey also found that 70 per cent of the of earners in the annual income bracket of more than Rs. 400,000 borrowed from institutional sources as compared to only 27.5 per cent in the case of earners in the income bracket of less than Rs. 50,000.

Farm households' not accessing credit from formal sources as a proportion to total farm households is especially high at 95.91%, 81.26% and 77.59% in the North-Eastern, Eastern and Central regions respectively. The findings of All India Debt and Investment Survey (AIDIS), 2002 too revealed ominous results relating to financial exclusion. As per the survey, the share of non-institutional sources of credit for cultivator households declined sharply from 91 percent in 1951 to 30 percent in the year 1991 with the share of moneylenders declining from 69.7 percent to 17.5 percent. However, in 2002, AIDIS revealed that the share of moneylenders again increased to 27 percent and that of non institutional sources overall rose to 99 percent.

Thus it is clear that even though there has been widespread increase in bank branches and banking services the formal banking system has not been able to penetrate the informal financial markets. Thus, apart from the fact that exclusion in general is large, it also varies widely across regions, social groups and asset holdings. The poorer the group, the greater is the exclusion. Renewed interest in Financial Inclusion has emanated from the concern that in spite of all the progress made by banks the position of Financial Inclusion in the country is far from satisfactory. There is a large chunk of the population that remains financially excluded. Financial Exclusion can be thought of in two different ways. One is exclusion from the payments system in the absence of a bank account. The second type of exclusion is from formal credit markets, which drives the excluded towards informal and exploitative markets.

The excluded population has to rely on informal sector (moneylenders) for availing finance at a comparatively higher rate. This leads to a vicious cycle. First high cost of finance implies that the poor person has to earn much more than someone who has access to lower cost finance. Second, a major portion of the earnings is paid to the moneylender thereby the person can never come out of poverty.

MEASURE OF FINANCIAL EXCLUSION

According to C. Rangarajan Committee on Financial Inclusion, 73 percent of Indian households are not indebted to formal financial institutions. The small and marginal farmers, agricultural labourers, artisans and the members of scheduled tribes are the worst victims of financial exclusions.

Table 5 highlights the incidence of financial exclusion both from formal and informal sources and the proportion of non-indebted households belonging to various categories.

TABLE 5

Category of Farmer Households	*Size Class of Landhold (Ha)*	*Total Farmer Household (Lakhs)*	*Non-Indebted Farmer Households (Lakhs)*	*Incidence of Exclusion (Formal and Informal Sources In %)*	*Proportion of Non-Indebted Households (%)*
Marginal	< 1	589.06	324.04	55.0	70.6
Small	1.01 – 2.0	160.60	78.68	49.0	17.1
Semi-Medium	2.01 – 4.0	93.50	39.10	41.8	8.5
Medium	4.01- 10	42.58	14.84	34.9	3.2
Large	10.0 +	7.76	2.60	33.6	0.6
All Sizes		893.50	459.26	51.4	100

Source: C. Rangarajan Committee Report on Financial Inclusion.

It can be seen from Table 1 that 87% of all non-indebted farm households belong to the marginal (70.6) and small (17.1) farmer categories. Similarly, the incidence of exclusion by both formal and non-formal sources is higher in marginal and small farmers. The above table also highlight that 51.4 per cent of all categories of households are still financially excluded.

Table 6 shows that the incidence of financial exclusion among non cultivator households was estimated at 78.2 percent out of which 78.8 are agricultural labourer households, 71.4 percent of artisans, and 79.9 belong to other rural households. Out of the 5.96 crore non-cultivator households about 4.66 crores were estimated to be financially excluded.

TABLE 6

Incidence of Financial Exclusion among Non-cultivators

Households	*Agricultural Labourer*	*Artisans*	*Others*	*Total Non-Cultivators*
Number of Households (Crores)	2.12	0.77	3.06	5.96
Number of Households Facing Financial Exclusion (Crores)	1.67	0.55	2.44	4.66
Incidence of Financial Exclusion (%)	78.80	71.40	79.70	78.20

Source: C. Rangarajan Committee Report on Financial Inclusion.

Table 7 highlights the access to credit since 2002. The most striking phenomenon seen in the figures is that there is a considerable drop in the credit account of Primary Agriculture Credit Society and there is notable increase in the credit accounts of Scheduled Commercial Banks. Another notable development during this phase is that there is significant increase in the credit disbursement through the self-help groups.

TABLE 7

Access to Credit Accounts with Institutions

(In millions)

Institutions	*2002*	*2007*
Scheduled Commrcial Banks	43.3	76.6
Regional Rural Banks	12.6	15
Sub-Total	55.9	91.6
Primary Agricultural Credit Societies	55.5	47.9
Urban Cooperative Banks	4.4	7.1
Self-Help Groups	7.4	40.5
Total	123.3	187.1
All Institutions (Accounts Per 100 Adults)	18	25

Source: Report on Currency and Finance, 2006-08.

Table 8 shows the access to savings accounts since 2002. The figures here highlight that the savings accounts has increased in scheduled commercial banks, primary agricultural credit societies, regional rural banks and urban cooperative banks. There is an increase in the number of accounts per 100 adults in 2007 when compared to 2002.

RESERVE BANK OF INDIA'S INITIATIVES FOR FINANCIAL INCLUSION

The Reserve Bank of India is treating financial inclusion as a very important concept and with the objective of bringing the financially

TABLE 8

Access to Savings Accounts

(In millions)

Institutions	*2002*	*2007*
Scheduled Commercial Banks	246.5	320.9
Regional Rural Banks	36.7	52.7
Sub-Total	283.2	373.6
Primary Agricultural Credit Societies	102.1	125.8
Urban Cooperative Banks	41.6	50.0
Post Offices	60.2	60.8
Total	487.1	610.2
All Institutions (Accounts Per 100 Adults)	72	82

Source: Report on Currency and Finance, 2006-08.

excluded into the mainstream financial system it has introduced important measures and schemes. Some of the important schemes introduced for the financial inclusion are as follows:

INTRODUCTION OF "NO FRILLS" ACCOUNT

In November 2005, Reserve Bank of India advised all banks to introduce the "no frills" accounts either with "nil" or very low minimum balance as well as charges that would make such accounts accessible to large sections of the population. All the public sector banks, private sector banks, foreign banks, except those having little retail presence, are reported to have introduced the basic "no frills" account.

TABLE 9

Frill Accounts

(In millions)

Type	*Number (In million)*	*Points of Presence*
Technology provider enabled No-frill Account	10.752	13077
Estimated Direct Account opened by Banks net of 2.5 million Bhamasha Project	18	
Total No-frill Accounts net of MFI, RSBY and Bhamasha	25.15	
Estimated number of operational accounts out of the above (11 percent)	2.77	
Total number of rural households that are financially excluded	111.55	

Source: Report on the Committee on Financial Inclusion, Jan. 2008.

INTRODUCTION OF GENERAL CREDIT CARD

The General Credit Card is another innovative development relating to financial inclusion, with the basic objective of providing easy and hassle-free credit to the vast financially excluded rural and urban population. Under this scheme a general credit card having a credit limit of Rs. 25,000 shall be issued based on the income and cash flows of the households without insistence on any type of collateral security. This credit facility will be revolving in nature entitling the holder to withdraw up to the sanctioned limit.

BANK/SELF-HELF GROUP (SHG)/NGOS LINKAGE

Reserve bank of India permitted banks to utilize the services of self-help groups, non-governmental organizations and other civil society organizations as intermediaries in providing financial and banking services through the use of business facilitator and business correspondent (BC) models. This allows the banks to do 'cash in-cash out' transactions at the location of the business correspondent and allows branch less banking. Banks have also initiated plans to introduce social security schemes to the unreached masses in association with Self-Help Groups and insurance companies. The Janashree Bima Yojna (JBY) in association with Life Insurance Corporation of India and the Universal Health Care Policy (UHCP) in association with United India Insurance Company Limited are leading initiatives aimed at below poverty line families. The Rangarajan Committee on financial inclusion has recommended the introduction of a separate category of micro-finance—non-banking financial companies and such institutions should be defined as Non-Banking Financial Companies that provide credit to borrowers up to a specified amount.

SIMPLIFICATION OF KNOW YOUR CUSTOMER (KYC) PROCEDURE

A simplified Know Your Customer procedure is initiated by the Reserve Bank of India which facilitates the opening of bank accounts through liberal procedure. RBI announced that banks could open accounts of low balance/turnover (where the balance does not exceed Rs. 50,000 in all the accounts taken together and the total credit in all the accounts taken together is not expected to exceed rupees two lakhs in a year) only with self-certification of address and his photograph.

CREDIT COUNSELING AND FINANCIAL EDUCATION TO THE CLIENTS

Credit counseling and financial education of the clients is an important mechanism for the promotion of financial inclusion. Towards this objective the Reserve Bank of India has advised all the banks to make available all printed material used by retail customers in the concerned regional language. The Reserve Bank of India has launched a multilingual website in 13 languages on all matters concerning banking and the common person so that the language does not become a barrier in acquiring financial education by the public at large.

ROLE OF ICT IN FINANCIAL INCLUSION

ICT can be used as an important tool in the in the spread of financial inclusion. ICT solutions can be used to capture customer details, facilitate unique identification, ensure reliable and uninterrupted connectivity to remote areas and across multiple channels of delivery, offer multiple financial products (banking, insurance, capital market) through same delivery channel while ensuring consumer protection, develop comprehensive and reliable credit information system, efficient credit delivery and credit pricing, develop appropriate products tailored to local needs and segments, provide customer education and counseling, enable use of multimedia and multi-language for dissemination of information and advice. An important initiative relating to ICT linked banking is the use of Information Technology solutions while adopting the agency or BC model for financial inclusion. The Reserve Bank of India has devised a scheme for the development of satellite connectivity for remote area branches. Reserve Bank of India is devising schemes on mobile banking in the public domain and the basic guidelines for this are on the anvil. A nationwide network of automated teller machines (ATMs) is being installed for the customers at no additional costs. All these initiatives are aimed at ensuring quicker, safer currency and fund transfer. Realizing the enormous benefits of ICT many state governments have decided to disburse National Rural Employment Guarantee Act payments and other social security benefits electronically through no frills bank account and also through smart cards with bio-metric identification. The use of Information technology enables banks to handle enormous increase of transaction for millions of households for, credit scoring, credit record and follow-up.

CONCLUSION

Social Banking in general and priority sector lending in particular are revolutionary financial management mechanisms designed to speed up the socio economic development of the country and its people. Bank expansion into unbanked areas and priority sector lending to targeted sectors have succeeded in reducing the poverty in India and bringing about a uniform sectoral development particularly in the rural areas to some extent. The arrival of banks to rural areas has led to increase in aggregate economic growth and these increases were driven by agricultural and non-agricultural output. The main weak link of the concept of the Social Banking can be linked with its failure to bring a uniform and broadly covered financial access mechanism for the people of India particularly in the rural areas. When the banks were given the freedom in case of placing branches they seem to by pass the needy and poor people. The Government of India and the Reserve Bank of India has now realized that uniform financial inclusion is an essential component of overall eçonomic growth. The Reserve Bank of India has designed specific schemes for broadening the access of rural credit to the rural poor. The Reserve Bank of India has introduced the innovative concept of "No Frills Account" which is related with opening of a bank account with "nil" or very low balance. All Scheduled Commercial Banks have reported to have introduced the "no frills account" scheme. The Reserve Bank of India has devised plans for the elaborate use Information and Communication Technology (ICT) as a tool for the spread of Financial Inclusion. ICT solutions can be used to capture customer details, facilitate unique identification, ensure reliable and uninterrupted connectivity to remote areas and across multiple channels of delivery, offer multiple financial products (banking, insurance, capital market) through same delivery channel while ensuring consumer protection, develop comprehensive and reliable credit information system, efficient credit delivery and credit pricing, develop appropriate products tailored to local needs and segments, provide customer education and counseling, enable use of multimedia and multi-language for dissemination of information and advice. The Reserve Bank of India has also introduced the simplified "Know Your Customer" procedure for rural branches. Similarly, specific schemes for credit counseling and financial education to the clients have been devised by the Reserve Bank of India to spread financial inclusion in India. Thus, it can be summed up that the social banking concept had mixed results in India as even after strong efforts, the problem of financial exclusion still prevails in India. Government of India along with the Central Bank has come up with number of specific schemes for a balanced financial inclusion and only time will tell its effects and ramifications on the Indian economy.

References

Dasgupta (2009), Two Approaches to Financial Inclusion, *Economic and Political Weekly*, Volume XLIV, Nos. 26 and 27, p. 41.

M. Mahedeva (2008), Financial Growth in India and Whither Financial Inclusion, *Journal of Applied Economic Research*, Volume 2, Number 2, pp. 177-97.

Sharma, Purti (2009), Financial Inclusion by Channelizing Existing Resources in India, *Indian Economic Review*, pp. 76-82.

Thorat, Usha (2008), Financial Inclusion and Information Technology, *Reserve Bank of India Monthly Bulletin*, October 2008, p. 1643.

Financial Inclusion in India: Issues, Achievements and Challenges

Rajasree, P.S. and Biju, S.K.

Abstract

The financial sector in the country has experienced revolutionary changes. The recent developments in banking technology have transformed banking from the traditional brick-and-mortar infrastructure like staffed branches to a system supplemented by other channels like automated teller machines (ATM), credit/debit cards, internet banking, online money transfers, etc. Eventhough technology advancement is for cost reduction and dissemination of the access to such technology and bank finance for the poor, it is restricted only to certain segments of the society. Access to finance by the poor and vulnerable groups is a prerequisite for poverty reduction and social cohesion. This has to become an integral part of our efforts to promote inclusive growth. Providing access to finance is a form of empowerment of the vulnerable groups. The objective of financial inclusion is to extend the scope of activities of the organized financial system to include within its ambit people with low income. Through graduated credit, the attempt must be to lift the poor from one level to another so that they come out of poverty. Access to safe, easy and affordable credit and other financial services by the poor and vulnerable groups, disadvantaged areas and lagging sectors is recognized as a pre-condition for accelerating growth and reducing income disparities and poverty. Access to a well-functioning financial system, by creating equal opportunities, enables economically and socially excluded people to integrate better into the economy and actively contribute to development and protects themselves against economic shocks.

INTRODUCTION

Rapid economic growth in India in the recent years has brought in its wake a number of concerns, which relate to expanding this growth across regions, sectors, and people. Because of this, the central government and RBI took efforts to harmonise the evil effects of inequitable economic growth. The major objective is to ensure inclusive growth by removing the constraints of poor infrastructure, improving economic efficiency and spreading the benefits of growth over a vast population, which has remained outside the purview of this development process. JNNRUM, PURA central fund for infrastructure development, look east policy are some among them. This growth also brought revolutionary changes in our financial sector. The recent developments in banking technology have transformed banking from the traditional brick-and-mortar infrastructure like staffed branches to a system supplemented by other channels like automated teller machines (ATM), credit/debit cards, internet banking, online money transfers, etc. The moot point, however, is that access to such technology is restricted only to certain segments of the society. It triggered discussion among the policy-makers and thrown light on the corners of the trickledown theory that, it is not to be generalized.

Inaccessibility/equal opportunity of mainstream financial products such as bank accounts, credit, remittances and payment services, financial advisory services, insurance facilities, etc. to all is termed as financial exclusion. Our constitution strongly highlight the need for equity, then why did the policy-makers and politicians long years effort miss that constitutional right, what can be done to get the fruits of this growth to all?

One cannot give a blind eye I this direction. So that government declared for increased inclusive growth through the 11th Five Year Plan policy document. As a proactive effort the RBI initiated for financial inclusion, as a basic step for inclusive growth. Inclusive growth can only be treated as the real economic growth because no one can be restricted from enjoying the prospects of current robust growth, especially a country India which is proudly saying that it is a democratic country.

Access to finance by the poor and vulnerable groups is a prerequisite for poverty reduction and social cohesion. This has to become an integral part of our efforts to promote inclusive growth. Providing access to finance is a form of empowerment of the vulnerable groups. Financial inclusion denotes delivery of financial services at an affordable cost to the vast sections of the disadvantaged and low-income groups. The various financial services include credit, savings, insurance and payments and remittance facilities. The objective of financial inclusion is to extend the scope of activities of the organized financial system to include within its ambit people with low income. Through graduated credit, the attempt must be to lift the poor from one level to another so that they come out of poverty. Access to safe, easy and affordable credit and other financial services by the poor and vulnerable groups, disadvantaged areas and lagging sectors is recognized as a pre-condition for accelerating growth and reducing income disparities and poverty. Access to a well-functioning financial system, by creating equal opportunities, enables economically and socially excluded people to integrate better into the economy and actively contribute to development and protects themselves against economic shocks.

Background of Financial Exclusion

By practice, ambience and operation the operators of banks spread a myth that, Banks are for people with the money hence poor are unbankables. Hence, they are outside the banking and financial sector. This stigma forced the downtrodden to stay in a world with lack of opportunities for financial products and services and increasing poverty and lack of awareness and financial illiteracy. This condition creating opportunities for unorganized banking sectors like—indigenous bankers, moneylenders, chit funds and pawn brokers who often use the financial illiterate population to satisfy their own ends of wealth creation, at the economy at large and it creates unequal distribution of wealth and income and other socio-economic imbalances in various parts of the Country. Therefore, there is a need for systematic organized banking system in these rural areas catering to the needs of agriculturists, self-help groups, low income groups and local entrepreneurs. This will open up tremendous potential with wide opportunities for banking business activity and growing into Inclusive economy and promoting the socio-economic development for all the common villagers for achieving balanced regional development of the Country. The agencies in this regard taken many steps and forced the banks to open branches in rural areas, initiatives for regional rural banks, NABARDs activities and policy formulation are appreciable. Here the Co-operative Banking sector because of its special nature of operations have a bigger role than the other banks in providing sustainable financial inclusion in rural and village areas. Over and above the technological advancement which caused a big leap and the banks are now in a position to provide services at negligible cost, unimaginable speed and facilities. But researches show that majority are still out of the bracket of banks.

Why Financial Inclusion?

We cannot easily blame our policy-makers and governments by saying that it is the poor policy making, inability to forecast and absence of coordination and the like. The topography, cultural differences, vast area, heavy population, lack of education, lack of resources, poor infrastructure, bad weather, natural calamities, etc. played a big role in this exclusive growth and financial exclusion. The apparent and solvable problems are—

- High transactions costs of borrowers
- High transactions costs of savers
- High transactions costs of banks
- High risk cost
- In appropriate products
- In accessibility

The Scope of Financial Inclusion

The scope of financial inclusion can be expanded in two ways.

(a) *Statutory efforts*: through state-driven intervention by way of statutory enactments (for instance the US example, the Community Reinvestment Act and making it a statutory right to have bank account in France).

(b) *Voluntary efforts*: through voluntary effort by the banking community itself for evolving various strategies to bring within the ambit of the banking sector the large strata of society.

As the banks are profit driven organization the RBI and Government should give more diligence to give directions for more inclusiveness. Otherwise when bankers do not give the desired attention to certain areas, the regulators have to step in to remedy the situation. This is the reason why the Reserve Bank of India is placing a lot of emphasis on financial inclusion.

Need for Financial Inclusion

The need for financial inclusion arises due to the following factors:

Physical Distance

At present the bank branches are far away and caters only the needs of 16,000 people which is low according to the banking requirement of our Country. That means the bank per people ratio is high shows that more efforts are needed to open rural branches or agents to cater the need for the rural poor. *Swabhiman banking* programme may eliminate the barrier of distance.

Mutual Disbelief

There is a mutual disbelief between banks and poor people. Banks think that poor people are not bankable because of risk and poor people, on the other side have a pessimistic view that banks and other financial institutions are not for them but for the rich.

Lack of Knowledge of Appropriate Products and Services

The product and services offered by the banks and financial institutions are capable of catering the needs of the rich and the poor are unaware of these products. The common people of rural areas are not within the reach of modern financial and banking products and services offered to other parts of the Country. Thus, these people are not only unaware but also away from the ambit of financial services.

Lack of Awareness and Financial Illiteracy

The low income group people and many agriculturalists are not aware of benefits of banking services and facilities provided to them. The organizations are not keen to provide awareness to these poor because the market segment of them did not include these poor. The ambience, documents, application forms, name boards and directions in banks are not in vernacular language also exacerbate the problem. But now the RBI give direction to all institutions in this regard.

Advantages of Financial Inclusion

- Wider reach of banking products and services to rural areas of the Country.
- It provides more opportunities of providing innovative financial products and Services to rural population.
- Ensures Inclusive economic growth and enhanced banking system in the Country.
- It helps to create more awareness of banking products and facilities (Financial Deepening).
- Financial support for primary sector, self-help groups and local entrepreneurs.
- Enhances employment opportunities in rural areas due to more credit facilities.
- Ensures balanced regional development for a long period of time.

Rationale of Financial Inclusion

Financial inclusion is a necessary condition for sustaining equitable growth. Financial inclusion provides the vulnerable section of society opportunities to build savings make investments and avail credit. Importantly, access to financial services also helps the poor insure themselves against income shocks and equips them to meet emergencies such as illness, death in the family or loss of employment. Further financial inclusion protects the poor from the clutches of the usurious moneylenders.

Financial inclusion will make it possible for governments to make payments such as social security transfers, National Rural Employment Guarantee Programme (NREGA) wages into the bank accounts of beneficiaries through the 'Electronic Benefit Transfer' (EBT) method. This will minimize transaction costs including leakages.

Extend of Financial Exclusion

Effort at financial inclusion is not new; both the Government and the Reserve Bank have been pursuing this goal over the last several decades through building the rural cooperative structure in the 1950s, the social contract with banks in the 1960s and the expansion of bank branch networks in the 1970s and 1980s. These initiatives have paid off in terms of a network of branches across the country.

The extent of financial exclusion is staggering. Out of the 600,000 habitations in the country, only about 30,000 have a commercial bank branch. Just about 40 per cent of the populations across the country have bank accounts, and this ratio is much lower in the north-east of the country. The proportion of people having any kind of life insurance cover is as low as 10 per cent and proportion having non-life insurance is terribly low at 0.6 per cent. People having debit cards comprise only 13 per cent and those having credit cards only a marginal 2 per cent. The National Sample Survey data reveals that, in 2003, out of the 89.3 million farmer households in the country, 51 per cent did not seek credit from either institutional or non-institutional sources of any kind.

Kick from the Government for Financial Inclusion

Approach to financial inclusion aims at 'connecting people' with the banking system and not just opening accounts. This includes meeting the small credit needs of the people, giving them access to the payments system and providing remittance facilities.

This has led to some notable developments:

- In November 2005, the Reserve Bank asked banks to offer a basic banking 'no-frills' account with low or zero minimum balances and minimum charges to expand the outreach of such accounts to the low income groups.

- Banks were asked to introduce a General Purpose Credit Card (GCC) facility up to Rs. 25,000. However, total number of GCCs issued by banks as at end-March, 2009 was only 0.15 million. This provided easier credit facility to the citizen.
- In order to ensure that people belonging to the low income groups, both in urban and rural areas, do not encounter difficulties in opening bank accounts, the 'Know Your Customer' (KYC) procedure for opening accounts was simplified for those accounts with balances not exceeding Rs. 50,000 and credits thereto not exceeding Rs. 1,00,000 in a year.
- Banks have been urged to scale up IT initiatives for financial inclusion speedily while ensuring that solutions are highly secure, amenable to audit, and follow widely-accepted open standards to ensure eventual inter-operability among the different systems. Two of the important initiatives are:
  (i) Smart cards for opening bank accounts with biometric identification. These help the customers get banking services near their doorstep.
  (ii) Link to mobile hand held electronic devices for banking transactions. In October 2008, the Reserve Bank advised banks on issues relating to technology, security standards, and customer protection.
- The Reserve Bank is in consultation with state governments to encourage them to adopt Electronic Benefit Transfer (EBT) by banks.
- *100 per cent Financial Inclusion Drive*: The Reserve Bank launched a financial inclusion drive targeting one district in each state for 100 per cent financial inclusion. In the light of the experience gained, coverage has been extended to other areas/districts. We carried out an external evaluation of the quality of 100 per cent financial inclusion reported by banks. On that basis, in January 2009, we advised banks to:
  (i) ensure provision of banking services nearer to the location of the no-frills account-holders through a variety of channels;
  (ii) provide GCC/small overdrafts along with no-frills accounts to encourage the account-holders to actively operate the accounts;

(iii) conduct awareness drives of the facilities offered to the no-frills account-holders;

(iv) review the extent of coverage in districts declared as 100 per cent financially included; and

(v) efficiently leverage on the available technology enabled financial inclusion solutions.

Above this the poor people are not sufficiently well enough to open bank account due to the minimum required balance, KYC norms and the like. In order to get a grouping effect, Self-Help Group Linkage programme, NABARD shouldered the inclusive growth efforts.

Financial Inclusion through Self-Help Group Bank Linkage

Micro-finance programme through Self-Help Group is considered as a powerful tool to ensure financial inclusion NABARD's programme of Linking Banks and Self-Help Groups aims at providing sustainable access to financial services to the rural poor, with a focus on those who had been considered unbankable. By using the existing rural financial infrastructure of commercial banks, regional rural banks and co-operative retail outlets and linking them to savings and credit groups with joint liability. Under the SHG-bank linkage program, NGOs and banks interact with the poor, especially women, to form small homogenous groups. These small groups are encouraged to meet frequently and collect small thrift amounts from their members and are taught simple accounting methods to enable them to maintain their accounts. Although individually these poor could never have enough savings to open a bank account, the pooled savings enable them to open a formal bank account in the name of the group. This is the first step in establishing links with the formal banking system. Groups then, meet often and use the pooled thrift to impart small loans to members for meeting their small emergent needs. This saves them from usurious debt traps and thus begins their empowerment through group dynamics, decision-making, and funds management. Gradually the pooled thrift grows and soon they are ready to receive external funds in multiples of their group savings. Bank loans enable the group members to undertake income generating activities. Through SHG-bank linkage programme the RBI and NABARD have tried to promote relationship banking, i.e., improving the existing relationship between the poor and bankers with the social intermediation of NGOs.

SHG-Banking through SHGs and the existing decentralised formal banking network including several organisations in the formal and non-formal sectors as banking partners allow for large-scale outreach of Micro-finance services to the poor in India. These banking services (depositing savings, taking loans) are made available at low cost, are easily accessible and flexible enough to meet poor people's needs.

Business Correspondent Model

Possibly the most important initiative of the Reserve Bank has been the Business Correspondent (BC) model. The BC model ensures a closer relationship between poor people and the organised financial system. Recognising this, in 2006, RBI permitted banks to use the services of non-governmental organisations, micro-finance institutions, retired bank employees, ex-servicemen, retired government employees, Section 25 companies, and other civil society organisations as Business Correspondents in providing financial and banking services

Bank Branch and ATM Expansion Liberalized

In the year 2008, the Reserve Bank totally freed location of ATMs from prior authorization. In the October 2009 Policy Review, the Reserve Bank took a further big step by freeing branch opening in towns and villages with population below 50,000. Domestic scheduled commercial banks (other than RRBs) are now free to open branches in towns and villages with less than 50,000 population and are enjoined to ensure that at least one-third of such branch expansion happens in the under-banked districts of under-banked states.

Project Financial Literacy

Financial literacy is a stepping-stone towards financial inclusion. Moreover, as financial markets are becoming increasingly complex with serious problems of information asymmetry, the need for financial literacy has become even more acute. The Reserve Bank has initiated a "Project Financial Literacy" with the objective of disseminating information regarding the central bank and general banking concepts to various target groups. RBIs website is also available in 13 languages. 'Financial Education' website link offers basics of banking, finance and central banking for children of all ages. In a comic book format, RBI try to simplify the complexities of banking, finance and central banking, with the goal of making the learning fun and interesting.

Financial Literacy and Credit Counseling

RBI advised the convenor-bank of each State Level Bankers' Committee to set-up a financial literacy-*cum*-counseling centre in any one district on a pilot basis, and based on that experience, to extend the facility to other districts in due course. So far, 154 credit counselling centres have been set-up in various states of the country. These centres are expected to provide free financial education to people in rural and urban areas on the various financial products and services, while maintaining an arm's length relationship with the parent bank.

Financial Curriculum in Schools and Colleges

The Reserve Bank is furthering the financial literacy drive by collaborating with state governments across the country to include financial literacy curriculum in the school syllabus. RBI had launched a pilot in Karnataka.

Financial Inclusion—Challenges and Opportunities

Despite the rural policy push, there are so many bankable people remain unbanked. There are barriers to access financial services emanating from both demand side and supply side factors. From the demand side, the big barriers are the lack of awareness about financial services and products, limited literacy, especially financial literacy of the populace, and social exclusion. Many of the generic financial products are unsuitable for the poor and there is not much of an effort to design products suitable to their needs. The unfriendly and un-empathetic attitude of the banks to the customers also plays an important role in undermining the demand for financial services. On top of that, exorbitant and oftentimes non-transparent fees, combined with burdensome terms and conditions attached to the financial products, also dampens the demand.

From the supply side, the main barrier is the transaction costs that the bankers perceive. Because of current low volumes, banks find that extending financial services to poor is not cost effective. Furthermore, lack of communication, lack of infrastructure, language barriers and low literacy levels all raise the cost of providing services and inhibit bankers from taking initiative from the supply side.

It may not be possible to cover over 500,000 villages in the country can each be covered through a brick and mortar branch. That is clearly not a 'bankable' proposition. We need to go through the low cost Business Correspondent model and leverage technology to deliver financial services.

CONCLUSION

Financial exclusion is a confluence of multiple barriers: lack of access, lack of physical and social infrastructure, lack of understanding and knowledge, lack of technology; lack of support, lack of confidence, among others. Overcoming these barriers is, in a nutshell, the challenge of financial inclusion In fact, there is a need for banks to redesign their business strategies to incorporate specific plans to promote financial inclusion of the low-income groups treating it not only as a corporate social responsibility, but also as a business opportunity. The business opportunity lies in exploiting the low margins-high volumes situation at the 'bottom of the pyramid' and seen in this context, financial inclusion would not only be socially desirable, but also would make a lot of economic sense. It is for the banks to convert what they see as a dead-weight obligation into an exciting opportunity and move on aggressively on financial inclusion. The efforts taken are on the momentum and need more involvement, monitoring and quality improvement through effective and keen watch on the activities of banks and other institutions involved in this efforts. Banks should consider the need of other segment and design product exclusively for satisfying their needs.

REFERENCES

Dash, R.N., 'Financial Inclusion: An Assessment of New Modalities and Alternative Models', Reserve Bank of India, Pune.

N.P. Mohapatra, Pillars of Financial Inclusion.

Rangarajan, C., Report of Committee on Financial Inclusion; GoI, January 2008.

Reserve Bank of India, Financial Inclusion (Reserve Bank of India, 11 November 2005).

Saurabh Tripathi, A Model for Financial Inclusion.

Subbarao, Duvvuri, 'Financial Inclusion: Challenges and Opportunities', RBI, 2010.

31

Beyond Financial Inclusion: The Case of Decentralised Governance in Kerala

DR. J.B. RAJAN

ABSTRACT

In the era of inclusion of excluded, the inclusive governance is utmost important. The plan guideline on Local Self-Government Institutions for 12th Five Year Plan has 'inclusive face' while providing the procedures and suggestions for local planning; in concurrence with the approach of Central and State Governments. The present article look into the plan guideline from an inclusive lens and sheds light on inclusive approach in the document. The article argues to think beyond financial inclusion from decentralisation governance angle, which provides platform for the excluded in the local governance.
Keywords: Decentralised Governance, Plan guideline, social justice, inclusive approach, Local Self-Government Institutions, Grama/Ward Sabha, Oorukoottom, Matsya Sabha.

INTRODUCTION

Inclusive finance is a buzz word now a days, but akin to the tale of blind men seeing the elephant. For some, financial inclusion ends with ensuring that everyone has a bank account. Whether accounts have any money or how it helps account holder is not the concern. Others consider it as EBT (Electronic Benefit Transfer), assuming that the subsidy payments transferred electronically into the beneficiary's account would curtail leakages and transform the lives of the beneficiaries. Some others considers 'no frill' accounts[1] under financial inclusion agenda. There are also initiatives like GCC (General Credit Card), KCC (Kisan Credit Card), BC (Bank Coverage)[2], pure savings product (ideally, a recurring deposit), ICT (Information and Communication Technology), etc. India has, for a long time, recognized the social and economic imperatives for broader financial inclusion and has found innovative ways to empower the poor. Reserve Bank of India (RBI) over the years has taken multiple steps to ensure financial access to the poor viz. nationalization of banks, priority sector lending requirements for banks, lead bank scheme (LBS), establishment of regional rural banks (RRBs), service area approach (SAA), self-help group-bank linkage programme, etc. Despite all these efforts, statistics shows that bankable population in India is meagre. As revealed by Dr. K.C. Chakravarty (Deputy Governor, RBI)[3] that only 55% of the population in India have deposit accounts and 9% have credit accounts with banks; just 18% had debit cards and less than 2% had credit cards. What went wrong?

Like the tale of blind man's elephant, inclusive finance provides only a part of the answer. It is to be noted that financial inclusion will not be complete until the capabilities and entitlements of poor and under-privileged are ensured. It is high time to think beyond financial inclusion and to promote inclusive development. The stepping stone for inclusive development shall be inclusive governance. The decentralised governance introduced with the enactment of 73rd and 74th Constitutional Amendment Act (herein after, CAA) is nothing but a leap towards inclusive governance. Decentralisation provides platform for the common people to intervene in the planning and implementing of developmental programmes at the level of Local Self-Government. (Haribabu, T.P. and Rajan, J.B., 2009: pp. 31-32). Interestingly, the State of Kerala was far ahead of other Indian States in launching a more democratic model of decentralisation with inclusive approach. This paper looks into the inclusive approach of decentralised governance in Kerala with special reference to 12th Five Year Plan. Also, the present paper retrospects on the decentralisation system in India.

DECENTRALISATION: A RETROSPECT

Decentralised governance as a means of accelerating economic growth in small-scale sectors and for increasing the efficiency of services has been a cherished goal ever since the inception of First Five Year Plan, but which materialised with significant Amendments to the

Constitution only in the last decade. (*Ibid.*) Since the enactment of CAA in 1992, thrust was given on inclusive approach in governance and development. It is a fact that the centralised governance system has the inherent limitation of excessive concentration of power. Exclusion of people from reign paved the way for exclusion in development. Democracy acquires credibility only when citizens, including the underprivileged have the right to participate in the governance process. In the system of representative democracy, power concentrates at the State and Union, with representatives making decision for the people. This system most often results in backward regions and weaker sections being unrepresented, leaving absolutely no forum for the common people to express their voice. Decision-making at the top and alienation from the villages makes the governance weak. (Rajan, J.B., 2007: p. 5).

Of the several institutions in India that upholds the rights of common people and democratic interventionist institutions, the Local Self-Government Institutions (LSGIs) could be termed as the youngest. But this institution is in the forefront to impart powers to the common people and the underprivileged by its very founding functional mode of bottom up approach. After several aborted attempts in pre and post-independent India, the Constitutional Amendment for realization of the LSGIs came into existence in 1992 and thus ushered in a small but firm step towards direct democracy into a caste, religion and untouchability-plagued country. It spread among the remote, under-privileged, and illiterate population and the institution it created challenged the male dominated governing systems in operation thus far. As a third tier of self-government, the LSGIs have got more powers but what is remarkable is the creation of Gram Sabha—a platform for direct democracy. (Rajan, J.B. and Haribabu, T.P., 2010).

The twin proclaimed objectives of CAA viz. local economic development and social justice itself was leap towards inclusive approach that had been missing elements in the discourse on governance and development. The local economic development (LED) would benefit the marginalised sections whose voice was earlier not heard and were denied opportunities. Decentralised governance will be a platform for the real stakeholders of the development segment of local economy. Social justice envisages a society who enjoys dignified life, equality, and human rights. The crux of social justice is equity in distribution of resources, equal opportunities, and justice in distribution of assets for all sections of the society. Not less than one-third of seats and positions reserved for women in the CAA and reservation of seats and positions for weaker sections viz. Scheduled Castes (SCs) and Scheduled Tribes (STs) according to proportion of their population is a step towards political inclusion of prolonged marginalised and unrepresented

[Women, SCs, and STs] for ensuring social justice. The role of Panchayat Raj Institutions (PRIs) in inclusive approach was put forth in a report that "In the rapid changes that will take place in India, and indeed the world in the twenty-first century, governance systems will have to be at the cutting edge of being the protectors of the poor, the oppressed, the vulnerable and the underprivileged .... Poor women, the girl child, the minorities, the tribal and the Dalit, the handicapped and the destitute, will need special attention." (IRMA, 2008: p. 3). In continuation of CAA, the Provisions of the Panchayats (Extension to the Scheduled Areas) Act [PESA] was passed in 1996; recognizing tribals' rights to self-rule. "Hailed as a Constitution within the Constitution, PESA is historic because it legally recognises the capability of tribal communities to strengthen their own systems of self-governance or create new legal spaces and institutions that cannot only reverse the cultural and political onslaught on them but can also create the opportunities to control their own destinies." (*Ibid.*, p. 3).

TOWARDS INCLUSIVE GROWTH

The Eleventh Five Year Plan, which has identified Inclusive Growth in the country as the overarching objective, seeks to 'substantially empower and use PRIs as the primary means of delivery of essential services that are critical to inclusive growth'. (Govt. of India, 2008, p. 3). On historic occasion of the fifteenth anniversary of the 73rd Amendment, Ministry of Panchayat Raj [MoPR] has prepared a Charter on Panchayati Raj, setting an agenda on "Inclusive Growth through Inclusive Governance" to rededicate the cause of grassroots development through grassroots democracy. [*Ibid.*, pp. 1-18].

After re-visiting Eleventh Five Year Plan, the Planning Commission re-instated the approach to the Twelfth Five Year Plan (2012-17) as 'Faster, Sustainable and More Inclusive Growth'. It states that "Inclusive growth should result in lower incidence of poverty, broad-based and significant improvement in health outcomes, universal access for children to school, increased access to higher education and improved standards of education, including skill development". (Govt. of India, 2011: p. 2). It also suggests that "Particular attention needs to be paid to the needs of the SC/ST and OBC population. Women and children constitute a group which accounts for 70% of the population and deserves special attention in terms of the reach of relevant schemes in many sectors. Minorities and other excluded groups also need special programmes to bring them into the mainstream. (*Ibid.*, p. 2). State of Kerala also followed the same path on 12th Five Year Plan approach paper, which at the outset states that "At the heart of the Approach paper, for the 12th Five Year Plan of the State is a strategic intent: to lay the foundation for creating an economy which is productive, competitive, sustainable and inclusive. ......". (Govt. of Kerala, 2012a).

THE INCLUSIVE FACE OF 'PLAN GUIDELINE'

The local planning in Kerala, since its inception during 9th Five Year Plan, has been emphasising on inclusive approach. Following the CAA, Kerala launched decentralised governance in the State through a strategy of People's Plan Campaign (PPC). PPC was launched to ensure maximum support and participation of people in the local governance. The novel aspect of the process was creation of large number of democratic institutions at the grassroots for political participation of people and facilitating it. (Rajan, J.B., 2007: p. 17). The PPC provided space to the common people to intervene in the planning and implementation of developmental programmes at the level of local self-government. (Rajan, J.B. and Haribabu, T.P., 2005, p. 28). The vibrant participatory planning and visionary process during the 9th five-year plan was an opportunity for self-expression to the marginalised sections in particular. (*Ibid.*, p. 28).

The plan guideline on Local Self-Government Institutions (LSGIs) for 12th Five Year Plan [herein after 'plan guideline'] furthering inclusive aspect on its approach, priorities, procedures for project formulation, conditions for fund allocation, etc. (Govt. of Kerala, 2012b, pp. 1-88). The following paragraphs provide a vivid account of the same by scanning the plan guideline through the lens of inclusion.

Priorities

One of the priorities, among seven, insisted by plan guideline is inclusion in local planning. Para 3 (6) of the plan guideline states that ensuring social justice by specially considering marginalised and all sections of people who require special attention viz. women, children, aged, differently abled, scheduled castes, scheduled tribes, traditional fish workers, and workers engaged in traditional occupations. (*Ibid.*, p. 8).

Sectoral Suggestions

The plan guideline provides suggestions on formulating projects for Scheduled Castes (SCs), Scheduled Tribes (STs), Below Poverty Line (BPL) category, traditional fisher people, destitute, women, children, aged, and differently abled. In view of this, Appendix 2 of the plan guideline (*Ibid.*, pp. 45-48) provides lists of suggestions under different heads viz. Special Component Plan (SCP), Tribal Sub-Plan (TSP), Anti-Poverty Sub-Plan (APSP), Women Component Plan (WCP), and People deserving special attention (Children, Aged, and Differently Abled). Appendix-13 of the plan guideline (*Ibid.* p. 75-79) deals with package of care services under TSP. It insists that a minimum 50% of TSP fund shall be utilised for package of care services. Appendix-14 of the plan guideline (*Ibid.*, pp. 80-85) spelt with the preparation of ASHRAYA[4] projects for destitutes. One of the components on APSP is formulating clear projects for ASHRAYA; thus ensuring the inclusion of destitutes. The steps for formulating APSP is detailed in appendix-15 of the plan guideline (*Ibid.*, pp. 86-88), which suggests a rigorous participatory process through CDS[5] (Community Development Society) network.

Mandatory Allocation

The plan guideline insists mandatory allocation of funds in the following areas:

- Nutritious food for *Anganwadi* children, THRS [Take Home Ration Strategy], nutritious food for adolescent girls, pregnant women, bread feeding mothers, SABLA[6], etc.
- SSA [*Sarva Siksha Abhayan*]. Also insists for proportionate allocation of funds for SC, ST, and differently abled.
- Projects on aged, differently abled, and palliative care.

Another striking feature of plan guideline is suggestion on providing priority for special schools in the first year. Also suggests in supporting NGOs/CBOs working in rehabilitation of differently abled.

Sectoral Ceiling

The approach of plan guideline on sectoral ceiling is liberal in nature compared to the three preceding Fivr Yrar Plan periods. The Plan guideline removed the hitherto existed minimum ceiling for productive sector, while enhanced the maximum limit for infrastructure sector. However, the mandatory minimum ceiling of 10% for WCP and 5% for people deserving are re-instated in the plan guideline. The plan guideline also envisages household centred approach in SCP and TSP so as to ensure socio-economic development of each household of SCs and STs. In view of upliftment of SCs and STs, the plan guideline allow financial support to the meritorious students from these communities for seeking admission in national/international educational institutions and also to the youth for finding overseas employment.

Working Groups

The Working Groups are the planning committees of LSGIs. Among the minimum 13 working groups mandated by the plan guideline, working group for Development of Women and Children are also considered is nothing but an inclusive approach. Also working for SC Development, ST Development, and Fisheries insisted wherever there such communities of SC, ST, and fisherfolk respectively.

Grama/Ward Sabha (Village Assembly)

Grama Sabha and *Ward Sabha* are assemblies of people respectively of Rural Local Bodies (LBs) and Urban Local Bodies (ULBs). In view of deliberate democracy, plan guideline suggests to organise *Ayal Sabha* (Assembly of Neighbourhoods), *Matsya Sabha* (Assembly of Fisher People) and *Oorukoottoms* (Assembly of Tribal People); in priori to *Grama Sabha.* It also suggests to organise meetings of Children, Youth, Aged, and Differently Abled prior to *Grama Sabha* and present their deliberations in the *Sabha.* This inclusive approach in local planning would enhance the participation of people in general and fisher people and tribal people in particular; both quantitatively and qualitatively.

CONCLUSION

The inclusive growth re-instated by the Central and State Government in the 12th Five Year Plan Approach Paper has been conceived in letter and spirit in the Plan Guideline; furthering the inclusive approach envisaged in the decentralised governance. Plan guideline ensures systems and space for inclusive governance to the excluded. But the destiny of inclusive governance is vested with the vibrancy of *Grama/Ward Sabha* and active participation of *Grama/Ward Sabha* members.

Notes and References

1. A No-Frills Account is one for which no minimum balance is insisted upon and for which there are no service charges for not maintaining the minimum balance.
2. A village is covered by banking service if either a bank branch is present or a BC is physically present or visiting that village.
3. During his talk on Financial Inclusion at St. Xaviers College on 6th September 2011.
4. ASHRAYA is a special scheme for destitute envisaged in the local plans by LSGIs. The destitute families are identified based on nine risk factors.
5. CDS is a apex body of the Kudumbashree network in Kerala; a poverty eradication mission instituted under Social Welfare Department. The word Kudumbashree is formed by coining two words Kudumba, means family and shree, means prosperity.
6. Rajiv Gandhi Scheme for Empowerment of Adolescent Girls [RGSEAG], named as SABLA.

References

Govt. of Kerala, 2012a: 12th Five Year Plan (2012-17)—Approach Paper, State Planning Board, Thiruvananthapuram.

Govt. of Kerala, 2012b: 12th Five Year Plan (2012-17)—Local Self-Government Institutions' Plan Guideline, [G.O. (M.S.) No. 168/12/LSGD, Thiruvananthapuram dated 15/06/2012].

Govt. of India, 2008: Inclusive Growth through Inclusive Governance—Fifteenth Anniversary Charter on Panchayati Raj, Ministry of Panchayati Raj, New Delhi.

Govt. of India, 2011: Faster, Sustainable and More Inclusive Growth—An Approach to the Twelfth Five Year Plan, Planning Commission, New Delhi.

Haribabu, T.P. and Rajan, J.B., 2009: Ebbing Spaces in Decentralisation—10th Five Year Plan and Marine Fisheries Sector in Kerala, in Pradhan, K.C. and Panigrahy, P.C. [Editors], Towards Integrated Rural Development, Sonali Publications, New Delhi.

IRMA, 2008: The State of Panchayats: 2007-08—An Independent Assessment, Vol. One: Thematic Report, Institute of Management, Anand.

Rajan, J.B., 2007: Kerala's Perspective on Decentralised Governance: Need of the Time, The Living World, *Journal of Philosophy and Theology*, Jan-Feb 2007, Vol. 113, No.1, Pontifical Institute, Alwaye.

Rajan.J.B, 2012: Local Planning – While Implementing, (*Malayalam*) *Mathrubhumi* daily dated 11th June 2012.

Rajan.J.B and Haribabu.T.P, 2005: Fading Images of Decentralisation in Kerala-Study with Reference to Marine Fisheries in 10th Five-year Plan, MCITRA, Kozhikode.

Rajan.J.B and Haribabu.T.P, 2010: *Matsya Sabha* for Ensuring Active Participation of People in Grama Sabha, Local Governance Initiative South Asia (LoGiN), Swiss Agency for Development and Cooperation, Embassy of Switzerland, New Delhi.

Index